Pathways to Inclusion

Building a New Story with People and Communities

Second Edition

John Lord
Peggy Hutchison

Captus Press

Pathways to Inclusion:
Building a New Story with People and Communities, Second Edition

© 2011 by John Lord, Peggy Hutchison, and Captus Press Inc.

Captus Press Inc.
Units 14 & 15
1600 Steeles Ave. W.
Concord, Ontario
Canada L4K 4M2
Phone: (416) 736-5537
Fax: (416) 736-5793
Email: info@captus.com
Website: www.captus.com

Library and Archives Canada Cataloguing in Publication
Lord, John, date
    Pathways to inclusion : building a new story with people and
communities / John Lord, Peggy Hutchison. — 2nd ed.

Includes bibliographical references and index.
ISBN 978-1-55322-242-2

    1. People with disabilities — Services for — Canada.
2. Human services — Canada.   3. Discrimination against people
with disabilities — Canada.   4. Social change — Canada.
5. Social integration — Canada.   I. Hutchison, Peggy, date.
II. Title.

HV1559.C3L67 2011   362.40971 C2011-902117-X4

Canada *We acknowledge the financial support of
the Government of Canada through the
Canada Book Fund for our publishing activities.*

0 9 8 7 6 5 4 3 2 1
Printed and bound in Canada

Contents

1
Setting the Stage for Change

Pathways to Inclusion

2
Values and Vision

Pathways to Inclusion

3
Strategies and Pathways

4
Creating an Inclusive Civil Society

Pathways to Inclusion

Pathways to Inclusion

Acknowledgments

The development of this book was a long journey. Along the way, we met some amazing people who are committed to innovation and social inclusion. The initiatives and stories in *Pathways to Inclusion* encompass several provinces in Canada. We owe special gratitude to the leaders and participants in each of the 34 initiatives. We especially appreciate the hospitality and welcoming attitude we experienced when conducting research with each initiative.

Several other colleagues and friends took the time to have regular conversations with us about the elements of the New Story. Others took time to review drafts of parts of the manuscript in its various stages. Thank you to Elizabeth Bloomfield, Gillian Chernets, Wendy Czarny, Charlotte Dingwall, Bart Forman, Michelle Friesen, Theron Kramer, Barb Leavitt, Marg McLean, Krista Lord, Sarah Lord, Alison Pedlar, Michael Prince, Brian Salisbury, Marlyn Shervill, Judith Snow, Marty Thomas, and Fred VanDerbeck for very helpful comments. Thank you also to Kathryn MacKay for detailed and insightful editing.

We wish to dedicate this book to our children, Jesse, Krista, Karen, and Sarah, for their ongoing support and inspira-

Pathways to Inclusion

tion. Our daughter Karen Lord deserves heartfelt thanks for giving us permission to weave parts of her story liberally throughout the book. We have been honoured to experience the New Story as parents, researchers, and innovators working to enhance social inclusion in our communities.

We hope this book will contribute to the ongoing efforts being made to create welcoming, inclusive communities for all citizens.

Introduction

Millions of Canadians have disabilities or other vulnerabilities or are engaged in supporting roles. In recent decades, the rights revolution has exposed North Americans to civil liberties in all areas of life. Despite this increased focus on rights, research and stories indicate that the supports and services provided to many citizens reinforce outdated attitudes that isolate people from their families and communities. Many citizens who are excluded because of disability, chronic condition, or age are further marginalized by less-than-satisfactory social policy. The reality is that people often experience vulnerability simply because they require a fair degree of support in order to participate and live in our communities. While rights have created conditions for improvement, they have clearly not guaranteed that a better quality of life will follow.

There has been very little mainstream dialogue about how best to provide support to our most vulnerable citizens. The exclusion many Canadians experience demands new approaches. Despite the lack of public concern, a quiet, energetic movement across North America has, in fact, been addressing these issues. This movement includes people who have disabilities themselves, their families, and other allies, such as progressive professionals and friends. An important part of this movement has been the development of innovative community initiatives, the focus of which is a strong desire to move from exclusion to social inclusion.

We have been involved with these developments for some time. In 1982, we founded the Centre for Community-Based Research in Kitchener, Ontario, Canada. Since its inception, this non-profit, community-based research centre has studied issues related to vulnerability and social change.[1] We spent several years conducting research via a wide variety of projects, programs, and organizations across the country that provide supports for a range of citizens. Each group we studied embodied one or more non-traditional approaches. We have extrapolated the common elements to create this book, *Pathways to Inclusion: Building a New Story with People and Communities*. Throughout the book we refer to groups and projects we studied as *New Story* initiatives. The narratives of these groups and organizations represent innovative ways of supporting people to be participants in, and contributors to, their communities.

As our research progressed, we discovered that there were many similarities in the innovative approaches used by different groups. We learned that every innovation was powered by strong vision and principles, whether it was an innovative housing development in mental health, a friendship initiative with people with developmental disabilities, or leisure pursuits for people who are frail and elderly. In our discussions with leaders of these initiatives, there was remarkable consistency in their goals, language, and strategies. These common themes provide a framework for creating new approaches and a better quality of life. In this work, we also learned a great deal about social innovation and what it means to build sustaining pathways to inclusion.

Several types of innovative approaches are discussed in the chapters ahead.[2] We studied new community initiatives, each of which began with an innovative mission and has been sustainable over time. Next, we explored traditional service organizations that have moved to embrace new values and approaches, accepting the turbulence that generally accompanies such organizational change. We studied six organizations that transformed themselves in this way. Then we looked at nine grassroots groups, such as self-help organizations that are directed by people themselves or by their families. Finally, we studied social innovations that are not about one group per se, but are broad-based approaches, such as a province-wide individualized funding program. We studied four such initiatives. Some of the groups actually fit into more than one category.

Although we mention specifics about particular initiatives, the main intention of this book is to identify common themes across a variety of these innovations and communities. Each initiative maintains a unique identity that reflects its own geography, history, and culture. At the same time, common themes and lessons can be drawn from the narratives of people directly involved in these new approaches. The richness of people's experiences brings the social innovations alive and makes them understandable. These themes, collectively, create a pathway for change in the future.

Pathway is a word often used as a metaphor for change. We shall begin by introducing *Pathways* as a framework for new action. The initiatives we studied were designed to directly address shame and exclusion by creating conditions for expanding individualized support, community participation, and citizenship. In this way, people are trying to create *Pathways to Inclusion*. Next, we explore the visions and values of the new approaches, including the importance of community, of compassion, and of shifting power to individuals, families, and communities. We then share strategies, from effective leadership to network building, self-help, and community collaboration. Lastly, we explore policies and funding mechanisms that build partnerships and sustainability shift toward an inclusive civil society.

Our research for *Pathways to Inclusion* was drawn from three distinct, but related, sources. First and foremost, it reflects the stories and insights from more than 30 innovative initiatives. In some cases, we participated in formal evaluations or research projects on-site and were able to use this information. In other cases, we spent time with people from specific initiatives, which usually included informal conversations with leaders and participants. In a smaller number of cases, we used only information that had been generated by the site itself or by other researchers. Most of the time, we were able to use real names, since people wanted to be known and have their story told. As well, we included related literature and research to illustrate how the insights from these social innovations are, or are not, supported by current research.

Finally, our own life experiences are part of the analysis throughout. As we reflected on the wisdom from these initiatives, we realized that the ideas were personal and saturated with values. Over the years, whether as educators, researchers, or community activists, our research was never simply theoretical. Our approach mirrored that of Gunnar Myrdal, who wrote more than 50 years ago, that "[a] disinterested social science is pure nonsense."[3] Like community-based research, New Story pathways are embedded in relationships among family, friends, neighbours, fellow citizens, and personal assistants. The collaborative work of these social innovators reflects a New Story about possibilities, participation, and inclusion within a social justice framework.

Note Regarding Second Edition

When *Pathways to Inclusion* was published in 2007, we were very pleased with the response from across Canada. The book has been widely used by people interested in change and by numerous colleges and universities. As a result of the *Pathways* book, we have been invited to do numerous presentations and workshops on what we had called a New Story in the first edition. We have also led many training events with the Facilitation Leadership Group around New Story ideas and practices. In addition, we have been working with several Ontario communities that are working on building more inclusive communities. As a result of this recent work, we have deepened our understanding of how to implement the New Story. This work is teaching us the importance of "seeding and supporting change" as a key theme in building the elements of the New Story. Insights from this recent work are incorporated into this second edition of *Pathways to Inclusion*.

Notes

1. For a detailed summary of the work of the Centre for Community Based Research, see its website at <www.community basedresearch.ca>.
2. For a complete list of the 34 New Story initiatives, see the Appendix.
3. Myrdal (1944).

Part 1

Setting the Stage
for Change

1

Pathways to Inclusion

A Framework for Building a New Story

John Lord — *I was 12 years old when I first became aware of vulnerability. My neighbour and friend, Blair Tress, was different from other kids. He looked rather sickly and pale, and was somewhat cautious on the playground. I liked Blair for several reasons. He was sincere. He was able to help me with science and math. He had a great smile and could laugh at himself. I spent a lot of time with Blair, except for the three to four weeks each year that he spent in hospital. One day my mother said to me, "I know you are going to be very sad when I tell you this news. Blair won't be coming to school anymore." "Why?" I asked. My mother explained that Blair had a serious illness and would soon die. I remember riding my bike for what seemed like hours that day. It did not make sense. But the next day, I went to Blair's mother and said I would like to help. She told me I could not come around anymore. So I didn't. But I never forgot Blair.*

Several months later we heard that Blair had died. My family and I did not even attend the funeral. As a friend, I felt shut out from sharing the pain and struggle of Blair and his family.

The story of Blair Tress is not a unique experience, but reflects the shame that often accompanies disability, aging, and chronic conditions in our culture. Like Blair's family, many people seek private solutions as a way to protect themselves from vulnerability. The isolation that Blair's family experienced no doubt had as much of a numbing effect on them as it did on those who were touched by Blair's life.

According to the 2006 census data, one out of every seven Canadians reports having disabilities.[1] This rate of 14.3% is an increase of almost 2% from five years earlier. In our aging society, this can probably be accounted for by the fact that disability rates increase with age, with more than 43.4% of people over age 65 reporting having a disability. Almost 6.6% of Canadians report having severe or very severe disabilities, and about a million citizens over age 65 say they have activity limitations due to pain. About one-third of older adults report a mobility limitation. More than 7% of Canadians report having suffered at least one major depressive episode in the previous twelve months. It is clear that a significant number of Canadians experience chronic conditions and disabilities. These numbers will rise dramatically as the baby boomers become seniors. In 2006, almost 4.5 million Canadians were 65 years of age and older, two-thirds more than in 1981. With baby boomers now hitting age 65, the proportion of Canadians over age 65 is expected to grow from 14.1% in 2006 to well over 20% in the next 25 years.[2] In fact, Statistics Canada predicts that, by 2015, seniors will outnumber children for the first time.

Like the experience of Blair Tress, many citizens feel vulnerable because of the isolation and stigma they experience on a regular basis. Although some families and communities are beginning to reclaim a role in the lives of vulnerable citizens, this remains only a dream for far too many people. We believe that traditional approaches to services and supports fail to address the isolation and exclusion experienced by many citizens in our communities. The time for new options that focus on social inclusion is now.

Pathways to Inclusion

Time for Change: The Need for Innovation

Many people are worried about vulnerability, social isolation, and lack of community inclusion. Although the helping professions and community services have expanded dramatically since the 1960s, in the past decade there has been a growing sense that community services often fail to address quality-of-life issues. Families raising a child with a disability often feel alone. People who have a friend or family member with a mental health problem may be concerned when hearing about shortages in hospital staff or community follow-up programs. Neighbours of a senior citizen who is isolated may not know where to turn. People with disabilities may have some services in their community, but feel these services are not suitable, appealing, or helping them to lead the life they want.

In all parts of Canada, there are pockets of innovation that challenge the conventional wisdom about how to provide sup-

---

Social Innovation

We explore the nature of social innovation for people and communities struggling with issues of social inclusion. *Innovation* is often defined as the act of introducing a new idea or new approach. Innovation is also about intentionality. Leaders in New Story initiatives think in new ways and then intentionally construct a new approach. In some ways, innovations are radical because they propose a new paradigm or a break from the conventional way of doing things. Innovative change occurs when people act with principles that are aligned with the right circumstances. Social innovators understand that in today's complex world, relationships are central to effective and meaningful change.

Note: For further analysis of the process of social innovation, see F. Westley, B. Zimmerman, and M. Patton, *Getting to Maybe: How the World Is Changed* (Toronto, ON: Random House Canada, 2006).

Pathways to Inclusion

port in the community. Fundamental to the social innovations we have studied is the belief that people who require support should have power and control over those supports as part of their rights as citizens. In contrast to people who are uncomfortable with others who move, feel, or think differently, people with impairments and chronic conditions have been raising their voices. *Disability Studies* has become an important area of research and teaching, and legislation is increasingly recognizing *all* people as full citizens.

We shall see how the desire for change is gaining momentum. As Peter Drucker has said, "Things that were not possible or not needed yesterday suddenly become possible."[3] In recent years, we have seen the emergence of more and more innovations. The social innovations we have studied reflect a new paradigm, or new way of thinking. Leaders and participants show us that it is possible to move away from exclusion and compliance. Insights from these social innovations point to a New Story framework for action that enhances social inclusion as well as the participation of people and their networks.

Our understanding of the need for a New Story began with our studies on innovation in the community-based research centre where this work all began. From numerous initiatives we researched at the Centre for Community-Based Research, we learned that social innovation, by definition, emerges from the lived experiences of *people themselves* and their allies. In this research on innovative approaches, we spent a vast amount of time over the past several years with people in a variety of community settings. People told us over and over that it is time to change. In this respect, people who require support and their allies can be considered the "pioneers" of *Pathways to Inclusion*. They, more than anyone, have been able to envision socially just ways of involving and supporting people to take their rightful place in society.

In human services, there is growing consensus that change is needed, but there is seldom agreement on the concrete directions needed to create a better future for all citizens. Those who believe that conventional approaches are basically sound tend to focus on the need for more money to expand current services. Others emphasize the need for more efficiency, accountability, and technological change.[4] Proponents of this approach to change often stress the need for a business-oriented approach to human services. Certainly, more money for human services would be helpful, and accountability is essential, but unless these kinds of changes are embedded in a New Story framework with different values, they will not lead to the changes being called for by so many people. Exclusion and compliance are difficult to change, as they require transformation in our attitudes, values, practices, and policies. At the heart of this New Story is social innovation.

Pathways to Inclusion are innovations that respond to the demand for transformative change. The problems that continue to plague services and, in turn, the lives of persons are by no means insignificant. Many of the innovative approaches that we will be discussing are based on the assumption that current services and "care" systems are largely inadequate and require fundamental change. The long, bleak history of services and policies that foster exclusion continues to influence how current service systems support people and to create the attitudes we all hold toward difference. For change to occur more broadly, society must develop more positive images of disability and aging and create different opportunities and conditions accordingly. In these innovative approaches, it is understood that the perception of vulnerability is socially constructed. We as a society have created attitudes and approaches that are often negative and patronizing. We must begin by first acknowledging how we have systematically done so and then dismantling our old ways. Only then can we begin to create new, more appropriate images.[5] In other words, if society's negative view of disability or aging has been created by society itself, then it stands to reason that society can also create a new, more positive view. Individuals, families, community associations, governments, and the private sector each have a role to play in dismantling exclusion and constructing social inclusion.

Change must be done in a manner that results in a New Story! David Hingsburger, a disability consultant and author from Quebec, has been scathing in his critique of how change has often been cosmetic, or simply rhetorical.[6] As he points out, so-called progressive changes have sometimes been quite damaging. Hingsburger cites the closing of sheltered workshops for people with disabilities as an example. Across the country, workshops have been closing because they are correctly seen as dehumanizing. In too many communities, however, meaningful alternatives have not been developed, so now hundreds of people with disabilities sit at home, lonely and isolated. Often this kind of change is driven by ideology, which can be dogmatic and inflexible. We shall see how New Story innovations build change specifically with people and the community while using values and principles so that New Story community alternatives become a reality.

One final word here about definitions.[7] For generations, many citizens who are vulnerable have experienced labels. "Retarded," "crazy," "crippled," and "lazy" are just some of the demeaning labels that have been used. In the past 20 years, however, a shift in language has appeared. Current labels and descriptions increasingly recognize that a person's condition or disability is only part of that person. *Person with a disability* or *older adults* are terms that add some degree of humanness and that move away from terms such as *the disabled* or *the aged*. Some social movements also refer to people in their movement as *consumers* (independent living movement), or *survivors* (mental health and brain injury movements), or *self-advocates* (movement for people with developmental disabilities). In this book, we mostly refer to persons who are part of a New Story initiative as *participants*, *persons*, or *citizens*, since all people have a set of circumstances that are not meant to be defining.

Characteristics of Pathways to Inclusion

There are 10 important characteristics of *Pathways to Inclusion* that can serve as a framework for learning about change and action. Each of these characteristics contributes to the New Story and to our understanding of the central need for social innovation.

First, *Pathway approaches are about change toward inclusion as a journey. Pathways* is an ancient archetype for ways to find inner peace.[8] Thomas Mails, a North American native person, reminds us that these pathways are not passive but are filled with power and action. In visiting many places across Canada, we have been struck by the strong community vision, commitment to partnership, and genuine participation in the change process. People tell us of the joy and energy of participating in a social innovation because of the opportunities to grow and change. Many people say you must "learn as you go." The Mondragon Co-operative in Spain[9] has a saying that "we create our path by walking it." While new ways of working take time

Characteristics of Pathways to Inclusion

1. Change toward social inclusion is a journey.

2. The voices of people themselves guide all change.

3. New values and principles are landmarks of social innovations.

4. New ways of leadership are critical for developing and sustaining innovations.

5. All support or involvement is personalized and centered on the gifts of individuals and communities.

6. Collaboration is central to the way the innovations work, both within organizations and with the wider community.

7. Power is intentionally shifted to citizens and their networks.

8. Many of the community innovations are relatively small, but they contribute to building capacity.

9. The creation of new community infrastructure supports is central to system changes that enhance social inclusion.

10. Community, hospitality, and relationships are crucial to social inclusion.

because of the resulting tensions and dilemmas, one citizen remarked, "It is better to have struggles which we own, rather than to assume others are taking care of the problems for us."

Second, *the voices of people themselves guide all change.* We learn from initiatives that people's "voice" plays a key role in creating change. Having people's voices as the foundation of the innovations makes it possible to explore the root of the problem. Listening deeply to people's experiences and perspectives gives a glimpse into heartbreaking stories. In each initiative, people's voices are respected, understood, and nurtured.

The voice and self-determination of each participant are valued and used to guide how developments with assisting people proceed. This commitment to the human dignity of each participant is a founding principle for many of these innovations.

Third, *new values and principles are a landmark of these innovative approaches.* Innovations require a new way of thinking, which begins with clear values about people and community; these values reflect diversity. As Margaret Wheatley says, the world's desire for diversity compels us to change.[10] The human rights and dignity of each person are seen as paramount. Leaders make explicit their commitment to providing support to people in ways that enhance citizenship and community participation. Values and principles provide a new way of thinking and are often the beginning of intentional efforts at change.

Fourth, *a new way of leadership is critical for developing and sustaining innovations.* Leaders express New Story values and principles in the way their initiatives are organized and implemented. Many leaders are passionate about the need for social innovation in order to build inclusive lives. We see inspirational leadership coming from persons who require support, from families, and from their allies, as well as from a variety of organizations. Leadership is important in grassroots innovative initiatives and in traditional organizations that transform themselves toward the New Story.

Fifth, *all support or involvement is personalized and centered on the gifts of individuals and communities.* For citizens to be able to live as full human beings with rights and responsibilities, personalized or individualized supports are required. A personalized approach involves taking the time to understand an individual's gifts and strengths. Initiatives find that a person-centered approach is always based on a gifts or strengths approach. In several initiatives, people are assisted with planning, navigating, negotiating, and connecting with resources and community.

Sixth, *collaboration is central to the way the innovations work, both within their organizations and with the wider community.* Partnerships among various stakeholders enable people to work together to create innovations in the community. Building the "right relationships" at the right time is significant in the development of New Story initiatives. Collaborative partnerships are needed to address issues and policy reform that will advance a social justice agenda. Social innovators know how important it is to engage people in the process of collaborative change. As Peter Senge says, innovation is too daunting for leaders or individual organizations to do it alone.[11] Collaboration is one key to the survival of innovations because "together is better."

Seventh, *power is intentionally shifted to citizens and their networks*. Lack of power and control is common among people with chronic conditions and disabilities. People in these initiatives recognize the benefits to health and well-being when they experience more decision making and empowerment. In some ways, these approaches help to re-shape our understanding of power. It is not about vulnerable people being powerful. It is about building a sense of "power within" that moves people from passive to active citizens. This process of empowerment happens as people gain personal skills, awareness, and confidence as environmental constraints are being removed. "This allowed me to stand up for myself" is a typical comment we often hear when people have experienced such personal transformation. This power shift can be subtle, but people tell us it is vital to their self-determination.

Eighth, *many of the innovations are relatively small, but they contribute to building capacity*. Examining small, promising approaches can really make a difference to understanding social inclusion. Much evidence indicates that large-scale change is often unsuccessful. In fact, the failure of large system change in human services has stimulated people to look at small local approaches as a catalyst for change. As Robert Theobold reminds us, there is evidence that the connections between small-scale shifts in thinking and action are the building blocks for the more fundamental change we need.[12] Other research shows that small-scale community initiatives lend themselves to the building of social capital, which refers to relationships, trust, and cohesion in a community.[13] The reality is that the social innovations we worked with usually started small and grew as they gathered momentum over time. In this second edition, we deepen our understanding of how small projects can contribute to building capacity of a community for New Story work. With our recent work, we are also noting how communities are learning to leverage smaller projects as a base for broader social change.

Ninth, *the creation of new community infrastructure supports is a central part of system changes that enhance inclusion.* Infrastructure refers to the functions and structures that are put in place that help people build a life in community. Most of us understand that communities need roads and bridges as infrastructure for strong communities. Similarly, human services have created infrastructures. Unfortunately, in most communities this infrastructure is dominated by service monopolies and formal systems. Innovators we met were working hard to reverse this kind of trend. The New Story requires that agencies no longer "do it all." Peer- or family-driven self-help is one example of a New Story infrastructure. Finding and nurturing community connections is another.

Tenth, *community, hospitality, and relationships are crucial to social inclusion.* In more traditional approaches, community organizations provide programs and services to people with little involvement of the wider community. We have learned that community and relationships create pathways to inclusion. Another way to look at this is that social innovations can be thought of as a pathway that begins with community and relationships. In this vision, paid support, while vitally important for some citizens, is never the first resort, and it is always provided within a context of community and relationships. As such, some developments are adept at looking for and nurturing hospitality with people they support. Community and hospitality become the essence of citizenship. As John McKnight and Peter Block have written in *Abundant Communities*, community and neighbourhood life is rich with possibilities and relationships.[14]

It is interesting to note that the characteristics of New Story approaches parallel the principles of "new paradigm" thinking in science. Quantum physics, for example, challenges conventional science and the mechanistic paradigm. In the old scientific paradigm everything in the world was considered separate, whereas in the new paradigm everything is connected.[15] Relationships are central to this new science, and hierarchies are seen as limiting our understanding. Whether biology or physics, the new science is ecological, which means that diversity is valued and, in fact, essential for health and well-being. That human beings are now creating human innovations at the very time that science is giving us insights into ourselves and our environment reinforces the timely importance of building a New Story.

New Meanings Attached to *Inclusion*

Inclusion is a concept that emerged in the mid-1980s. Social movements that had been working on "integration" felt that the deeper issue was how social inclusion could become possible for people previously excluded from community life. In one sense, inclusion is a response to the divide between "us" and "them."[16] Some have called inclusion *an agenda about solidarity* that is attempting to reduce social distance. This explanation recognizes that many social groups, including people who are disabled, poor, immigrants, or racial minorities, are often excluded from the fruits of the modern labour market, civil society, and the political system. In this context, social inclusion was a reaction against decades of social and economic exclusion.

At a more practical level, society is now learning the difference between "integration" *and* "inclusion." We are learning that many people are typically "in the community" but not "of the community." In the late 1980s and early 1990s, many advocates and scholars began to see the limitations of "integration" efforts. They recognized that simply being in the community did not guarantee social acceptance and full participation.[17] In a social inclusion picture, communities are welcoming, diversity is respected, full participation or engagement in all aspects of community life is encouraged, and conditions enable everyone to be valued, contributing members of society.[18] The New Story is clearly about inclusion, not integration. People in all initiatives have been working toward social inclusion. Leaders of innovative initiatives note that "inclusion is broader than integration." Inclusion does, however, begin with integration, where people who are marginalized join with other citizens in shared physical settings. For inclusion to occur, people must then experience deeper processes and more meaningful social interactions. Leaders of such initiatives believe that every person needs an inclusive life, which is quite different than just being integrated at school or in the community.

New meanings attached to inclusion include insights into social inclusion as a *goal, outcome*, and *process*. Although this book focuses mostly on the process of inclusion, New Story initiatives often frame their work around larger inclusion goals. As a goal, social inclusion is designed to create opportunities and conditions for citizenship. Several initiatives emphasize the goal of honouring diversity within community. Finally, inclusion as a goal emphasizes full participation, as well as social and economic inclusion in all aspects of community life.

Leaders in New Story initiatives sometimes describe the inclusion outcomes they are working toward, including the following: people would feel valued and accepted in all public places; people would feel that their differences matter much less than their gifts and strengths; communities would value diversity in the ways they embrace and accommodate differences; communities and organizations within the non-profit sector would create various policies and vehicles for enhancing social inclusion.

Inclusion as a process emphasizes the ways that groups, organizations, and communities build pathways to citizenship and full participation. Relationship building is one vehicle for implementing the inclusion process. The importance of relationships comes up time and time again with the social innovators we meet. Relationships matter if social inclusion is to be a reality. Catherine Frazee, former chief commissioner of the Ontario Human Rights Commission and a strong disability activist, emphasizes that relationships matter as much as a rights agenda: "Citizenship means having rights, but it also means belonging.... Belonging in schools and universities, in places of work and places of worship, in politics, art and commerce; belonging in family, community, and nation."[19] Relationships are central to the inclusion process because they are the primary vehicle by which people gain access to other people and settings in their communities and, in turn, have opportunities to belong.

A sense of belonging through relationships can be facilitated in many ways. Relationship building happens when people share a common interest, which, as John McKnight says, is one of the powers of community.[20] People in a photography club or in a political group, for example, feel engaged because of a common interest in photography or politics. Differences can be more easily accommodated when people are together because of a common interest and the potential for relationship building is increased. This strategy is used by several initiatives by gradually building a culture of acceptance within community associations. It is about intentionally building relationships with people in those settings and about those settings becoming inclusive and welcoming. Sandra Nahornoff, co-ordinator of Project Friendship in Prince George, British Columbia, describes the evolutionary nature of the change that has been brought about in her northern community. "Over time, more and more parts of the city have become welcoming," says Nahornoff. Welcoming communities mean that *all* members can acquire a sense of belonging.

Social inclusion as a process builds pathways or bridges to community by promoting positive connections among all sectors in society through creative alliances and new partnerships. These alliances bring people together to talk about citizenship and removing barriers. The outcome of this type of community process can change organizations and community structures in ways that are more welcoming of diversity. The use of New Story values and policies creates frameworks or vehicles for change. Inclusion as a process keeps the broader picture in mind and helps people search for strategies that promote equity, both economically and socially.[21]

New Story approaches, in small but significant ways, are casting social inclusion in a new light. When an inclusion lens is used, cultural norms of vulnerability, disability, or aging are affected. Part of this involves seeing the potential of all kinds of relationships in community and the valuing of difference and diversity. Inclusion thus involves a commitment to citizenship for *all*. We find that this involves the collaboration of neighbourhoods, networks, and welcoming organizations to move an inclusion agenda ahead. Certainly, people collaborating together in community is a tenet of all New Story initiatives.

Walk the Talk

Many social change movements use the phrase "Walk the talk" to support a culture of innovation. If we had to summarize what we, as authors, believe and what we have found in our research, this metaphor is a good one. Our experience is that "Walk the talk" is first and foremost about having a critical perspective. Being critical means being able to see beyond the status quo, looking beyond symptoms and labels, seeing the reality of people's situations, and understanding how they are linked to attitudes, policies, and systems. Being critical is essential for making vulnerability visible and for talking about how we, as a culture, respond to aging, disability, and chronic conditions.[22] Starting with a critical perspective often gives social innovators the rationale and inspiration for their new ideas.

For people who are building the New Story, "Walk the talk" is about change. Being critical of the "old story" is a first step in having a new vision and being open to change. Leaders in initiatives articulate a clear vision by encouraging a critical perspective and by proposing alternative values. They are deeply embroiled in the struggle for social justice and work from the basic assumption that citizens should experience equal opportunities and conditions. We have found that those who are working on these issues recognize the need to address the causes of oppression. Exploring discrimination and naming oppression are useful steps in the process of change. The new vision includes new ideas as well as transformation of the "old story."

"Walk the talk" is not only about vision, it is also about action. If we truly want to build the New Story, we must be prepared to live the basic values and vision we are supposedly promoting. It is a call for us to ensure that we do what we say we are going to do. Sometimes people report that the language of change is used without significant action. So we must be prepared to walk in ways that are congruent with the message contained in our vision. Principles are used in New Story initiatives to link vision with action and to create space for ongoing dialogue and critical reflection on implementation approaches. People constantly "Walk the talk" by trying to be sure that both vision and action are present and consistent. When social innovators do this clearly, their message often becomes a catalyst for mobilizing others. As we shall see, this is sometimes difficult in a culture that uses language, policies, and programs to limit people's capacities rather than nurture them.

In another way, "Walk the talk" is about linking the personal and the social. Having a more critical perspective has helped us realize that the personal and social cannot be separated. John's unforgettable experience with Blair may have contributed to our later decision to adopt our daughter Karen, who has Down syndrome. Karen, third of our four children, was a vibrant three-year-old who created a new family awareness of the gifts and contribution of each person and of the struggle and advocacy that is required in our culture to ensure that all persons can experience valued roles and full inclusion. More recently, we lived nearby our parents who were experiencing Alzheimer's, cancer, mental health issues, and dying. These personal experiences with disability and chronic conditions have reinforced our concerns about becoming too dependent on formal services as the answer. We learned about chronic conditions, but more important, we learned about relationships we were called upon to have with parents who required compassion and creative responses to their situations. Family and other informal support were vital in enhancing quality of life. Formal, paid support was also very important but often could not be organized in ways that were individualized and respectful. We have learned about the importance of friendships and the values of hospitality, courage, forgiveness, compassion, and community. Our journey as authors can best be described as a combination of community research, social justice, and our own personal stories, although it is often difficult to tell which is which, as the three are usually so subconsciously interwoven.

The final way that "Walk the talk" speaks to this work on social innovation is its commitment to egalitarian approaches. In innovative initiatives, stakeholders participate as equal partners. As we learn with these initiatives, participation ebbs and flows, depending on circumstances and the stage of the innovation process. The lives of citizens who are vulnerable and of those around them are enriched by these efforts to create meaningful pathways to inclusion. The message, "We are all in this together," provides energy and a framework for self-reflection, critical thinking, and collaboration which are needed for sustainability and to make a difference.

Notes

1.   Statistics Canada (2007).
2.   Government of Canada (2007).
3.   Drucker (1998), p. 1.
4.   For an analysis and critique of the recent push for efficiency, see Stein (2001). It should be pointed out that technocratic human service systems are in reality an invention of the past 20 to 30 years.
5.   Gadacz (1994).
6.   Hingsburger (1997), p. 4.
7.   Several authors have explored the negative impact of labelling. Erving Goffman was one of the first to understand labelling and its relationship to stigma; see Goffman (1961). More recently, Lise Noel analyzed the basis of intolerance and how

"differences" often lead to labelling and, subsequently, alienation. See Noel (1994).
8. Mails (1988).
9. Mondragon Co-operative is part of the Basque Region in Spain, where a number of economic activities have been developed based on the co-operative system. For an analysis of this model and research information, see its website at <www.mcc.es>.
10. Wheatley and Kellner-Rogers (1996).
11. Senge (1998), p. 2.
12. Theobold (1997).
13. Putman (2000). Also see Putman and Feldstein (2003).
14. McKnight and Block (2010).
15. For a popular review of the nature of paradigm shifts, particularly as seen through the field of quantum physics, see Arntz, Chasse, and Vincente (2005).
16. Bach (2002).
17. Biklen (2000). Also see Northway (1997).
18. See Frazee (2002), p. A15; also see Pedlar et al. (1999).
19. Frazee (2002), p. A15.
20. John McKnight served as an advisor for the Prince George project. See also McKnight (1995).
21. In 2002, the Laidlaw Foundation in Toronto began publishing a Working Paper Series entitled *Perspectives on Social Inclusion*; these papers are available at the Foundation's website at <www.laidlawfdn.org>.
22. Biklen (2000).

Pathways to Inclusion

2

Clienthood and Compliance

The Failure of Traditional Approaches

*The significant problems we face cannot be
solved at the same level of thinking we were
at when we created them.*

Albert Einstein

People are excluded in our culture for many reasons. People
with impairments or chronic conditions or who are aging may
experience vulnerability by virtue of their condition. A person
can be left physically and emotionally excluded if they cannot
get into a house to visit a close friend because of stairs. Other
times, exclusion and vulnerability result from external social
conditions, such as poverty, abuse, or discrimination.[1] People
may also be excluded from community life because of their
dependence on formal services. We know, for example, that

people who live in institutions or other congregated services, such as nursing homes or group homes, are more at risk of physical, emotional, and financial harm than people who live with families in the community. For many people, these environmental issues intensify their impairments, resulting in the person having a significant social handicap. Over time, a wearing down of the spirit and sense of self can also occur.

These issues are not insignificant in the Canadian context. As we have already seen, 14.3% of Canadians report having a disability or related activity limitation. Disability increases with age, leaving many frail seniors dependent on services or isolated from community life. The issues related to aging are bound to increase in importance in the years ahead. In 2006, one Canadian in seven was age 65 or over. By 2026, it is expected that one Canadian in five will have reached age 65.[2] And children are also at risk, particularly children with disabilities such as asthma, attention deficit disorder, and autism. Many children with labels such as "severe disabilities" are segregated at school from their peers, which has been shown to increase exclusion. Children who are most often segregated have developmental disabilities, such as cerebral palsy and Down syndrome, or chronic conditions, such as severe allergies, epilepsy, spina bifida, or obesity.

There is much darkness associated with the stories of citizens who experience exclusion on a daily basis. As part of our research, we inevitably heard people's stories. The experiences are indeed grim, and the statistics underlying these stories are also daunting. We need to explore in depth some of these realities, many of which cause people to be marginalized. People's "realities" are the reason why many social innovators are critical of traditional approaches. In her compelling book about child poverty, *Within Our Reach*, Lisbeth Schorr writes that most conventional programs and services that she researched produced "rotten outcomes."[3] In Canada, we spend millions of dollars every year, federally and provincially, to provide services for people with disabilities and for frail seniors.[4] Do we have rotten outcomes from these expenditures?

To explore this problem, we will first describe some of the ways that people are excluded. We begin by answering the following questions: what is the problem, and what is the nature of the suffering? We then explain some of the reasons and causes that might have led to this problem and suffering. Peo-

Pathways to Inclusion

ple associated with New Story initiatives consistently emphasize that being critical of traditional "old story" approaches is often the first step that people need to take before moving toward an innovation that will enhance their path to empowerment and citizenship.

Rotten Outcomes

Our friend John Nevard was sent to an institution when he was nine years old and remained there until he was twenty. Nevard has described this as a "horrible time" in his life, being disconnected from family and friends and suffering greatly. Nevard's experiences were not unusual, as Canada and many other Western countries have had a long *history of institutionalizing people*. The first institutions were built in Canada in the 1860s, and led to more than a century of segregating citizens because of physical disabilities, intellectual disabilities, mental health problems, and aging.[5] During the 100-year period until 1960, thousands of children were institutionalized and separated from their families. Since the emphasis in all Canadian provinces is now on helping families keep their children with disabilities at home, only a few hundred children with disabilities now live in institutions. However, thousands of adults across Canada continue to live in facilities.

Among citizens over the age of 65, in 2006 approximately 7.6% were residing in institutions, down from 10% in 1971. This figure is still significantly higher than most European countries, however. The Canadian percentages are beginning to rise again, and this is before the baby boomers hit age 65 in North America. Betty Friedan's book *The Fountain of Age* shows research that residents tend to get worse after their admission to a nursing home.[6] Friedan points out that institutionalization profoundly affects people's sense of power. One woman we met talked about this struggle: "When I lived in the institution — that's when I felt the most out of control.... They tell you what to eat; they tell you when to go to bed. You don't have a choice to say, 'Well, I don't want to go to bed now.' So there was this constant struggle between me and the system." Despite this sense of disempowerment among many people living in facilities, in most provinces there is continued growth of long-term care facilities for seniors.[7]

One hundred and fifty years of institutionalization has also influenced the way we go about providing services to people in the community. Although the rate of institutionalization has significantly decreased for most segments of society, community services often mirror institutionalized realities. A few years ago, we conducted a study of people who had returned from institutions and were now living in group homes in the community.[8] Most of the homes we visited were attractive, detached houses in nice neighbourhoods. From the outside, you could not tell these houses were group homes, and they appeared to be an integral part of the community. Each house was usually home to four to five persons who had been living there for a few years. As we got to know the men and women who lived in the homes, we learned they were treated as clients, their daily routines were controlled, and "outings" into the community were always in groups of four or five people. Our conclusion was that, despite being "in the community," these citizens were not "of the community."

In this same study, we found a minority of homes where residents had a high degree of control over their living environment and were supported to be part of community life, encouraged to get to know their neighbours, and given opportunities to build genuine relationships in their community. The term *community institutionalization* has been coined to describe how those who have been institutionalized within their community settings and community services often fail to rise above institutional realities. This institutionalized way of thinking and acting has been hurtful for thousands of people.[9]

Many of these citizens also experience *poverty and high unemployment*. In our society, employment provides one indication of an adult's level of social and economic status. Research shows that people with disabilities are less likely to be employed. For example, Statistics Canada indicates that among persons with disabilities the employment rate is 41% for men and 32% for women, while employment rates for non-disabled peers are 83% for men and 70% for women.[10] As a result, many people live on government disability pensions. In Canada, a disability pension rate is similar to the poverty level. Poverty is thus very common among adults with disabilities.

The strong connection between poverty and employment can best be illustrated by women. The term *feminization of poverty* has been created to describe the situation that so many older women find themselves in as they age.[11] They are often susceptible to poverty because they generally live longer than their spouses and therefore end up living alone for extended periods. For women who may not have achieved a large enough pension from continuous, long-term, high-paid employment, poverty is often a distinct possibility. Add disability to that picture, and the impacts are even more serious. The failure of the government to provide an adequate standard of living for all its citizens can have devastating consequences on people's lives.

Many people living in poverty experience *health-related problems*.[12] The following story about Michael Smith shows how poverty and unemployment for one person with a disability had devastating effects. Smith was involved with People First, a self-help group for people with developmental disabilities. He also worked at a factory as part of a "supported employment" program offered by a large service provider. At one of his People First meetings, he told the group how upset he was that he and a few others had been laid off because the company's production was down. The service provider insisted that he return to the sheltered workshop, a segregated work setting only for people with disabilities, until a new job could be found. In this segregated setting, there were 180 other adults with disabilities who received approximately $20 every two weeks for so-called training. Smith hated working there and was becoming more and more anxious about the situation. At the next meeting of his self-help group, Smith reported that the service provider still couldn't find him a community job. He was even more upset than he was at the last meeting and could talk about nothing else. Six months passed and still no job. He reported he could not stand to stay at the workshop any longer. The self-help group was exploring its role in supporting Smith to make a change when he suddenly died of a heart attack. Not yet 50, Michael Smith had been a kind man. He rented an apartment right next to his mother's nursing home so he could visit her every day. He was the official photographer for his People First group. Whether or not his death was related to his extreme anxiety about losing his "real" job in the community, we will never know. But all of his friends believe this to be so. Since medical research has clearly documented the effects of stress on people's health, this is probably the sad reality.

Pathways to Inclusion

Many citizens now receiving support through New Story approaches had previously *experienced abuse* in their traditional settings. Recent research on the psychological, physical, and sexual abuse of dependent children and adults paints a similar picture, which suggests the need for a closer look by society.[13] People with disabilities, for example, are more at risk for abuse for many reasons: negative stereotypes about disability, lack of family support, social isolation, and reliance on others for support. The levels of violence against citizens who are vulnerable are greater than in the general population; these levels partly depend on location and context. Studies consistently show that people with mental health problems or psychiatric disabilities, for example, have very high rates of abuse, ranging from 60%– 90% of the population surveyed.[14] Many people we have met mention the powerlessness and oppression that results from such violence. Sadly, much of the abuse occurs in institutional and community settings, further increasing fear in those who have to depend on formal services for their support.

In our experience, some administrators of conventional services deny there could be any abuse within their programs. Yet research completed by many groups across Canada, such as Disabled Women's Network, Canadian Association of Independent Living Centres, Council of Canadians with Disabilities, People First Canada, and Canadian Network for Elder Abuse, all challenge this assumption.[15] The work of these groups indicates that people with disabilities and frail elderly persons, particularly women, continue to be exposed to sexual, emotional, financial, and physical abuse in institutions, community services, at home, and in the wider community. The important point here is that abuse contributes to rotten outcomes. The elderly person who is abused may develop a fear of going outside, which in turn increases social isolation. The child with a physical or developmental disability is already at risk in our culture. Abuse makes it very unlikely that the child will develop positive self-esteem and healthy relationships, central ingredients for quality of life.

The final "rotten outcome" of traditional approaches that needs to be mentioned here is *weak social networks*. An extensive body of research shows that people with rich personal networks can call on others for support and that people who have meaningful relationships lead healthier lives.[16] The same research is clear that people who are isolated and have weak networks have far more health issues. People we meet at various projects often mention lack of friends and loneliness as significant issues. The Foundations Project in Kitchener that works with youth with disabilities finds that isolation and the desire for friends are the two most common issues identified by people coming into the project. William Thomas, an innovator of aging services in the United States, says that the true plagues of old age are loneliness, helplessness, and boredom.[17]

There are many reasons why weak social networks have become a disturbing outcome of traditional approaches. First and foremost, many human services pay little attention to this vital dimension of health and well-being. Doug Cartan, past executive director of the Brockville and District Association for Community Involvement in Ontario, says that "people [staff] in human services struggle terribly with their personal ability to ask on behalf of someone they support. Extending skilful invitations to the community seems so foreign to many workers in human services." Second, children with chronic conditions and disabilities often experience limited relationships early in life. Families often feel shame, and combined with the professional advice they receive, there is a tendency to overprotect their children. The problem is worsened by the fact that many children still do not attend local schools with their neighbourhood friends and are not integrated into regular classrooms.[18] These experiences contribute to citizens with disabilities and chronic conditions being viewed as the "other," those who are different and separate from other citizens.

We know there are many other "rotten outcomes" and suffering associated with the "old story." However, before moving on to explore a variety of effective ways that citizens are being supported in the New Story, it is important to understand the process by which these rotten outcomes have been created. If we understand the conditions that cause poor outcomes and suffering, we will be in a better position to be clear how we need to change those conditions to build *Pathways to Inclusion.*

Constructing Vulnerability

Rotten outcomes are caused by attitudes, approaches, and systems that see some people as being of less value because they require support or accommodations. Some years ago, when one

of our parents moved into a nursing home, several professionals noted that "it was the best thing." Our experience is that
when people say this, they usually mean "it is natural that
institutionalization was your response." Yet institutionalization
and any other responses we might have chosen are not natural,
but have been constructed by our society. In earlier centuries,
nursing homes would not have been a choice for people, since
the concept of congregating elderly people together in a large
facility had yet to be created. This example illustrates how a
belief that is constructed by society can take on a "naturalness"
or "certainty" over time.

When we say that vulnerability is constructed, we mean
that it is not the impairment or aging itself that causes vulnerability, but the social conditions of segregation, rejection, isolation, and loneliness that so often accompany our response
to "differences." Sometimes in the world of disability, this is
referred to as a social model, where the problem is located
in the environment, and not in the person.[19] Robert Murphy,
in his biography about "becoming disabled," says that disability contradicts the values of youth, manliness, and beauty
that our culture cherishes.[20] By creating and continuing to reinforce negative meanings about the concepts of disability or
aging, our society unconsciously reinforces vulnerability and
marginalization.

Becoming a "Client"

The process of creating or constructing "clients" may
happen in an abrupt fashion, or it may occur in a more
subtle and gradual way. As an example of an abrupt
change, persons who have been hospitalized due to a
mental health crisis often describe the emotional pain
they experience becoming a client. One of the outcomes of this sudden move to clienthood is what Lise
Noel calls the "stigmatized identity," where people
quickly become the "other" to both family and community. The subtle approach to becoming a client happens

Becoming a "Client" (continued)

more gradually but can be just as damaging. One mother we met whose child had a physical disability told us, "Kids in the neighbourhood would call on our son Ryan. On more than one occasion, I remember saying he could not come out because the physiotherapist was coming or we were going to therapy.... It took me years to realize what was happening, but one day I became aware that the kids no longer came calling for Ryan." This dilemma of competing demands makes it challenging for families to avoid the client role for a person with a chronic condition or disability.

A formal diagnosis is often the beginning of a labelling process, where a person's condition comes to define them. The making of a "client" is further entrenched through a professional assessment process in most areas of disability, chronic conditions, or aging. Many people tell us that professionals who reinforce clienthood emphasize an "us" and "them" approach. If the "other" person is seen as a client to be "fixed," it is easier to feel separate from that person's struggles. Our own daughter's experience in the early school years is testimony to this process of keeping clients separate. Once the school realized that the new grade one student had Down syndrome, the principal and the teacher were clear that Karen had "needs" that could not be addressed in the regular classroom. "Her needs require special education," we were told. When we asked for a clarification of these needs, we were told she needed one-to-one support and special technologies. She needed to be separate from her peers. Deficits were generalized to a "solution," which in professional terms translated into a segregated option. It is not surprising that the scholar Ivan Illich calls the second half of the twentieth century the "age of disabling professions."

References: L. Noel, *Intolerance: A General Survey* (Montreal, PQ: McGill-Queen's University Press, 1994); I. Illich, *Disabling Professions* (London, UK: M. Boyers, 1977).

Pathways to Inclusion

If we have an understanding of "constructing vulnerability," we can begin to explore how these concepts and practices have developed in our society. Many of the social innovators stress that being open to "systems thinking" is an important part of understanding why things are the way they are. "Systems thinking" includes being critical of the way things are and noticing the interdependence and relationships among all events and conditions. Some people call this an ecological approach.[21] One professional recalled, "I remember early in my career visiting a recreation program for people with disabilities and being told that people could only participate in certain activities. This experience was confusing because it didn't fit with my knowledge or my intuition. I wondered if I would be able to work in environments that treated people in ways that I would not want to be treated." Critical questioning as part of systems thinking enables us to look beyond the surface of a program or service and examine the concepts and values that are maintaining the program. By understanding underlying concepts, we can see both the limitations and potential for change. Leaders we interviewed said that conversations about underlying values and concepts form the basis of creating more valuing and positive meanings. We recall one such conversation at an Independent Living Resource Centre. Staff and volunteers were reflecting on the word *client* and on how most community agencies still use the word. After exploring the limitations of such a label, people considered other terms, such as *individual*, *member*, and *citizen* and their meanings and potential as alternative concepts.

Understanding how to change the realities experienced by many citizens requires that we not only examine outcomes but also look closely at conditions that contribute to these outcomes. There are two conditions or processes that explain the rotten outcomes that have emerged from people's stories and experiences. These conditions are clienthood and compliance. Once we have an awareness of these causes, we will be in a better position to create new meanings attached to some concepts, including disability and aging, that often have had negative connotations.

Making Clienthood

Traditional approaches to provide services and supports to people often reinforce clienthood. In clienthood, the person is seen as needing services in order to meet most aspects of life. Professionals are in control of the person's most important life decisions, and a "deficit approach" is most often the framework used. As Tana Dineen has written in *Manufacturing Victims*, the formal human service industry casts a long shadow over the lives of too many citizens and their relationships.[22] When a person is treated as a client, rather than as a citizen, serious limitations in the person's quality of life often result. People are typically surrounded by services. In contrast, when the person is considered a citizen, life takes place mostly in community, the person participates fully in life events, and a "capacities or strengths approach" flourishes. In community, people are surrounded by relationships, not services.

It may come as a surprise to hear that the concept of *needs* is connected to clienthood, particularly within a deficit approach. Michael Ignatieff, in his book *The Needs of Strangers*, argues that a theory of need makes certain assumptions about human nature. To define human nature by needs, says Ignatieff, is "to define what we are in terms of what we lack."[23] Typically in human services, a need is defined and then a program or service is developed to respond to the need. Too often, only basic physical needs are met; the need for relationship, companionship, and community is ignored. Ignatieff puts it bluntly when he writes, "needs are met, but souls are dishonoured."[24] In reviewing dozens of "needs assessment" instruments over the years, we have discovered that needs are generally described within a deficit framework. This further strengthens services and weakens community.

In a deficit approach, the focus is on weaknesses, not on the person and his or her strengths. The process normally begins when a person with an impairment or "difference" is given a label. For example, a parent might be informed that "Your child was born with a disability" or "Your child has diabetes." Getting a diagnosis is important, but in time the child often learns the language of clienthood, such as "I am diabetic" or "I am disabled." Too often, decisions about a person's schooling, housing, recreation, or employment are made based on the assumption that having a disability or chronic condition is the most important aspect of the person's identity. Research has shown that when people become engulfed in the client or patient role, it is difficult for them to see their own capacities and strengths.[25] People are robbed of their power and trapped

Pathways to Inclusion

in their passive role. This focus on needs within a deficit framework is one of the ways our society constructs vulnerability. As we shall see, in all of the New Story initiatives disability or frailty is seen as only part of the person, with the central focus being on each person's strengths and capacities.

We know dozens of families who transferred their children out of schools or school boards that promoted segregated classrooms because they felt their children were labelled and excluded. Similarly, a major complaint of families who take their children regularly to rehabilitation is that the focus is only on "problems." So not only do needs assessments focus on problems and deficits, they also assume that specialized interventions are required. Furthermore, such assessments often confuse needs with responses to needs. One-to-one support, for example, is a response, not a need. What were our daughter Karen's real strengths and capacities? Karen loves to learn, loves to be with people who provide her with a challenge, and imitates extremely well, especially with her peers. If we created a strengths approach, we would begin to ask, "How can we use Karen's strengths as the basis for planning her education and her life?" In this way, there is a conscious shift away from a deficit approach.

Throughout our research we have noted that people who are participants in New Story initiatives usually describe themselves and their peers in quite positive terms. It is as if the diminished self-definition has been replaced by a worthy and capable sense of self. People describe themselves more in terms of "wholeness" and "connections." Understanding how labelling, assessment, and language impact people's status as clients is central to creating new approaches that go beyond clienthood.[26] Through an analysis of deficit approaches, we have discovered that citizenship, community, and hospitality can replace clienthood as the space for experiencing relationships, human capacities, and quality of life.

Creating Compliance

Most conventional service systems demand that a person comply with a series of procedures and regulations, whether they are in a nursing home, group home, day program, or homecare in the community. It has been shown that people who get caught in the "patient" or "client" role are more at risk of becoming passive and seeing themselves as unable to influence their world.[27] Similarly, researchers who have studied frailty note its strong association with lack of hope and negative attitudes.[28] These examples illustrate a most damaging and ever-present feature of most traditional community service systems designed to provide paid support to people — a focus on compliance. Compliance takes different forms, but may include passivity, conformity, submissiveness, or acquiescence to the directions of others. In examining hundreds of these services over the years, we have found that many service system procedures benefit the system more than the persons requiring support.

Many social services operate on the belief that compliance and control are a necessity for ensuring the effectiveness and survival of their organization. This belief, while often subconscious, may have its roots in patriarchy, which tends to prescribe to others how they should live, often to male advantage.[29] While organizations built on compliance may be effective in the short term, in the long run compliance wears down the receivers of the service, not to mention the workers themselves. When workers devote energy to ensuring compliance, they are basically maintaining people as clients in community services, rather than assisting people to achieve roles as valued community members with strengths and voice. There is no mutuality of respect in services where compliance is dominant. We have found that many workers are aware of these dilemmas but feel trapped in systems they have little control over.

Some workers bristle at the idea that they are "promoting compliance." Of course, people may not intentionally support compliance — it is often much more subtle. Many service providers, for example, have preconceived notions of what a good life is for the people they support, or work in a system based on these notions. In many conventional services, we note that a good life is supposed to be happy and without challenges, disappointments, or chaos.[30] Yet when people are trying to empower themselves or trying to explore what really matters to them, there will sometimes be the excitement of chaos. Building a good life with someone is not a passive process and certainly does not happen if others are subtly setting the boundaries of what a person can think, feel, or do.

There are several additional ways that compliance takes place in our culture. *Segregation* of people with differences is

Pathways to Inclusion

one of the most blatant ways of ensuring compliance.[31] Control of people may or may not be a visible goal of segregated services, but assumptions are often made that people with disabilities or frailties need to be segregated, and grouped with others with similar labels, from the "real" community. Once people are segregated and isolated, it is very easy for controls to be applied, away from the watchful eye of family and other community members. For example, many residential services inadvertently cut people off from community life with rules and regulations, leaving residents excluded and vulnerable. Over the years, we have explored whether segregation is *always* problematic. Our own conclusion has been that short-term, intensive rehabilitation with safeguards for successful community reintegration is often positive. Also, citizens choosing to organize themselves for self-help can be a positive experience; people often claim that membership in these groups is, in fact, enabling and empowering.

As well, *Agency-controlled services* that demand compliance were created in the 1960s. During this time when deinstitutionalization began, governments generally assumed that the best way to meet the needs of people was for the state to give money to community agencies to provide necessary programs and services. Agency-controlled services were supposed to foster participants' growth and development. What often happened was that "service systems" reinforced the idea of people as "clients," or, at best, "clients" who must "fit" into residential, vocational, or recreational programs. We have seen hundreds of examples where agencies' good intentions have not been useful. John Ralston Saul, author of *On Equilibrium* and other essays, reminds us that, "What happens to good ideas is that they are often obscured by the structures designed to implement them."[32] Government guidelines that transfer money to community agencies have tended to be inflexible and bureaucratic. In most cases, service providers make the decisions, set the parameters, and require people to comply with agency patterns and procedures. In recent years, a trend to individualized support has challenged many agency services to begin to move away from this kind of program approach. Few agencies, however, have systematically addressed issues of compliance, in part because government funders have not yet embraced alternatives.

The *continuum of services* is another way that compliance is maintained. The concept of a "continuum of services" was developed in the 1970s as community-based service systems began to emerge across North America. It was seen as the latest solution in the new wave of reform. *Continuum of services* was a phrase used to visually depict how a person might move from segregation to integration. Before becoming fully part of community life, people were told they would have to go through several steps along the way. Each step would be less and less restrictive. It was expected that only the "least vulnerable" would, in fact, make it to the fully integrated end of the continuum. We think the most profound way to understand the continuum and its limitations[33] is to describe Anne Morrison's experiences in a small community in southern Ontario for over 20 years of her life.

Anne Morrison lived for 18 years in a large institution in southwestern Ontario. When the first wave of deinstitutionalization hit the province in the early 1980s, Morrison had a chance to be "deinstitutionalized." Returning to her native community, Morrison was moved to a core residence that housed 18 people, located in the countryside outside of town. In reflecting on that experience, Morrison emphasized that "it was so noisy, and they told me I could move on when I had improved my skills and when other places became available." Three years later, Morrison did move on, this time to a six-bed group home in the country. After three years in that setting, Morrison's arthritis was worsening and she needed a walker to get around. So once again she was moved, this time to an eight-bed home in the downtown area, close to a shopping mall. The problem with both of those homes, said Morrison, is that she could not do her own cooking and she had very little privacy. Fortunately for Morrison, a second wave of deinstitutionalization hit Ontario in the early 1990s, forcing agencies in her community to once again open their doors to new people. People from the institution were moved into the 18-bed and the eight-bed facilities, while people like Morrison were "bumped" into even smaller community residences. Only at this stage was Morrison actually given a choice of where she would live and with whom she would live. She chose to live with her friend Jane in a small duplex apartment that was next door to a similar apartment that housed another woman with a disability.

We recently met with Anne Morrison in her spacious kitchen of the duplex apartment, where she was moving freely around in her wheelchair preparing coffee and muf-

Pathways to Inclusion

fins for her visitors. Morrison makes all major decisions in
her life. Now 61 years old, Morrison says she has "moved
so many times that it is tiring." When we asked Morrison
where she would like to be in 10 years when she is
70 years old, she was very quiet and then said cautiously,
"I hope that I can still be here in my kitchen cooking and
being with people."

For now, Morrison's story has a happy ending. Thousands
of other citizens are not so lucky. They often get "stuck"
at various stages in the continuum, or bumped for the wrong
reasons. Although the continuum of services concept is now
often presented as "an array of services," the powerlessness
associated with this approach remains unchanged. It is compliance of the highest order when professionals determine when a
person is ready to move through the continuum. Unfortunately,
many human service systems continue to operate under this
philosophy.

*Limited participation in organizational governance and deci-
sion making* maintains compliance. During the last decade the
language of "citizen and consumer participation" has guided the
thinking about governance of support organizations. In most of
the cases we have observed, this means that individuals and
families are represented on the board or some other advisory
group for the organization. Although this is a positive trend,
far too often the rhetoric of participation in governance results
in little redirection of agencies.[34] In order to achieve the New
Story, the participation of people at all levels of service development, delivery, and evaluation must occur. In our experience,
many community agencies use the language of new ideas
without seriously transforming their values and approach to
community governance.

Using "citizen or consumer participation" as a reform strategy often makes agencies appear as if they are changing. At
the same time, many agencies continue to maintain control over
all aspects of the way support is provided to people. For example, many mental health organizations have added consumer/
survivors to their board of directors. Yet few of these organizations have done the work required to really understand the
power issues that affect psychiatric survivors and how this
understanding might change the way they provide individualized
support. Similarly, there have been many critiques of the mental health system in professional and scientific literature. Until

recently, however, there has rarely been an analysis of the powerlessness of psychiatric survivors in the scientific literature, even though this issue of power has been presented extensively in the psychiatric survivor literature for decades.[35]

Social service cutbacks that occurred throughout the Western world in the 1990s have had a devastating impact. Although some have argued that cutbacks in funding should have made citizens and their allies more self-reliant, the opposite has in fact happened. Compliance has increased because many organizations have not had the funding to develop and execute new ideas. In 1995, the federal government and several provincial governments essentially eliminated their social housing programs. In New Zealand, which had the most sweeping cutbacks of any industrialized country, a recent report shows that these changes increased the susceptibility of children to social and emotional problems and widened the gap between rich and poor.[36]

Social service cutbacks raise critical questions for traditional social services as well as for those critics calling for reform. In our view, there are at least two issues that impact on compliance. First, we must address the fact that people require adequate income to be able to live meaningful lives in the community. Second, resources from the state for community supports must be able to get directly into the hands of people, so that they can manage and direct their own support requirements. Increasingly, advocates in Canada have been addressing these two issues, and a 1998 federal/provincial/territorial government document, *In Unison*, addresses these concerns.[37] We shall explore these policy issues in depth later.

A list of 10 reasons why citizens and their families do not like traditional services, as presented in the focus box on the next page, might be a good way to summarize our discussion thus far. Other research supports these insights.[38] This list represents the diverse range of comments we have heard from people we have met through New Story initiatives, who believe they are poorly served by traditional services and programs.

Who Really Cares?

It is difficult sometimes to know who really cares. Is it families who are called on to provide so much support but often experience burnout? Or is it the human service system, which seems

Reasons Individuals and Families Believe Traditional Services and Programs Fail Them

1. Services and supports are based on *deficits*, so the *true nature* of the person is seldom understood.

2. Many services cannot be *trusted* because they do not listen to users and, in turn, are not open to innovation, experimentation, or training in new values.

3. Individual service planning downplays the dreams, ideas, and *goals of the person* and family because professional knowledge is valued over knowledge learned directly from people themselves.

4. Services *label* and use language that is disempowering and hurtful.

5. Services assume people's needs are best met through *their "programs"* (the "continuum of services" is confused with individualized supports).

6. *Compliance* is valued and people are taught to be passive, sometimes through overt things like rules or policies, other times more subtly as when staff assume that they know what a person's life should be like.

7. Resources for supports are *inadequate*, inappropriate, and seldom under the control of the person.

8. Community services do not understand or utilize *genuine community*, often misinterpreting "community" to mean "services in the community."

9. People are viewed as clients of services and not encouraged to participate in valued *social roles* in the community.

10. Support from staff and volunteers is seen as being more important than *relationships* with friends and family.

Pathways to Inclusion

to be so important in the lives of many citizens? Or is it the wider community of neighbours, friends, and networks? David Schwartz, in his book, *Who Cares? Rediscovering Community*, argues that one of the "certainties" of modern life is the assumption that we need complex, formal human service systems to respond to the needs of people.[39] This "certainty" has been ingrained in our thinking and in our policies for decades. We have described the construction of vulnerability in detail to show how this thinking became prevalent in the second half of the twentieth century. Yet it is also clear that depending entirely on formal services to "care" for a person is problematic and often produces rotten outcomes. Clienthood and compliance severely limit the lives of people being supported and do not contribute to inclusion.

There is also so much shame associated with "being vulnerable7"[40] that it is sometimes difficult to sort out if anyone cares. Several decades ago, we gained a wonderful stepmother. Helen, for all her beauty and warmth, had great fear of growing old. She insisted that her grandchildren call her Helen. As she reached 70 and then 80, Helen refused to tell her actual age, and if anyone else revealed it, she became furious. After her death, we discovered that her birthdate had been scratched off her baby cup. Fear of aging is very real in a society that values youth and beauty. This fear impacts people as they age because society does not value the gifts afforded each stage of development, particularly the latter stages. When older persons are in denial or fear being seen as different due to being old, chronically ill, or even near death, they are less likely to be open to their vulnerabilities. As a result, they may be more challenging to "care for" than those brave few who have embraced aging. Yet the subtleties of "who cares" are often more complicated than simply the attitude of the person. For example, we all know persons who are in need of support but are not getting it because they have the attitude that they don't need it. On the other hand, there are people who avoid support because they associate it with their unhappy experiences with traditional approaches.

Similarly, shame of "being different" influences our ability to relate to and "include" people with disabilities. We well remember our shock when people stared at our newly adopted daughter Karen who, as mentioned, has Down syndrome. At first, we focused on helping her look nice and be like the other kids. This attempt to "normalize" helped relieve our frustration with her difference. Slowly, however, we began to realize that we needed to fully embrace Karen's humanity and her differentness if we expected others to care. How could we expect others to engage Karen and include her fully if we were feeling shame and caution? This experience is repeated thousands of times each day in every community. Consider the following examples. An aging aunt is too ashamed to use a walker out in the community. A neighbour leaves his wife, claiming he couldn't care for her since she was diagnosed with multiple sclerosis. And a family member with a mental health problem is rejected by friends after spending months in a treatment centre. Because of our human tendency to separate ourselves from suffering and differentness, we often create boundaries in our interactions with people that make it difficult to determine who cares.

The question of who really cares about citizens who are vulnerable because of age or disability is not easily answered in a society that experiences differences so negatively. Is it possible that families of persons with disabilities or spouses of frail elderly persons, who have been called on to carry so much of the support for their loved ones, need a totally different approach so they can *really* care? And is it possible that human services need a different approach so that they, too, can contribute to the overall care scenario?

Fortunately, new paradigms and new ways of thinking and acting that point us in a new direction have been emerging in the last 20 years. The 10 reasons why people believe traditional services and programs fail have opposite, positive reactions that are being explored in New Story initiatives. Community and citizenship replace clienthood. Personal support enables people to experience participation and contribution. Communities are creating meaningful initiatives. These social innovations create a touchstone for possibilities of what alternatives could really look like. Dialogue and reflection are central to this work of social change. The experience of social innovations challenges governments, service providers, and communities to change the way fellow citizens are supported. In essence, "helping" is being redefined, and who really cares takes on new meaning. Let us begin the journey to explore the Pathways to Inclusion that are being developed by people and communities.

Notes

1. For several challenging works on exclusion, see Barnes and Mercer (2005). For an exploration of exclusion based on race, gender, sexuality, age, and disability, see Sibley (1995). Also see Crawford (2003); for an examination of exclusion in aging, see Scharf et al. (2001). For examination of abuse, see Roeher Institute (1994).
2. Statistics Canada (2002).
3. Schorr (1988), p. 1.
4. The Roeher Institute in Toronto has done the most comprehensive research related to disability supports in Canada. See Roeher Institute (1995).
5. For ideas on institutionalization, see Rothman (1981). Also see Wolfensberger (1975). For a more recent account of the history of disability in Canada, see Neufeldt (2003).
6. Friedan (1993).
7. For a very interesting Canadian study, see Hebert et al. (2001).
8. Lord and Pedlar (1991).
9. For more about community institutionalization, see the new definition for an institution from the website of People First of Canada at <www.peoplefirstofcanada.ca>: "An institution is any place in which people who have been labelled as having an intellectual disability are isolated, segregated and/or congregated. An institution is any place in which people do not have, or are not allowed to exercise, control over their lives and their day to day decisions. An institution is not defined merely by its size." Also see Metzel and Walker (2001).
10. Statistics Canada (2002).
11. Townson (2003). Also see Dobrowolsky (2004).
12. Avison (1998).
13. Roeher Institute (1994). Also see Harbison and Morrow (1998). They say elder abuse and neglect are not just symptomatic of individual behaviour, but are influenced by the culture and by service systems.
14. Roeher Institute (1994).
15. For research on abuse, see Calderbank (2000); Canadian Association of Independent Living Centres (1995).
16. Lyons, Sullivan, and Ritvo (1995). Also see a multitude of articles by Ben Gottlieb from the University of Guelph, Ontario, on many diverse aspects of social support. A new book summarizes the way networks influence our lives. See Christakis and Fowler (2009).
17. Hsu (2006).
18. Crawford (2005).
19. Berger and Luckmann (1966); Oliver (1990); Tregaskis (2004).
20. Murphy (1990).
21. Prilleltensky, Nelson, and Peirson (2001).

Pathways to Inclusion

22. Dineen (1996). Also see Hall, Juhila, and Parton (2003).
23. Ignatieff (1984), p. 14.
24. Ignatieff (1984), p. 50.
25. Beanlands (2001).
26. Hall (2003).
27. Beanlands (2001).
28. Brown, Renwick, Raphael (1996).
29. Henning (1993).
30. Sanders (2006). Also see Cimarolli, Reinhardt, and Horowitz (2006).
31. For an analysis of segregation, see Oliver (1996).
32. Saul (2003), p. 4.
33. For a history of the concept of the continuum as well as its limitations, see Wieck and Strully (1991).
34. For an extended discussion of tokenism in human services, particularly the mental health system in Canada, see Nelson, Lord, and Ochocka (2001). Also see Newberry (2004).
35. McCubbin, Spindel, and Cohen (2002).
36. Blaiklock (2002).
37. Federal/Provincial/Territorial Ministers Responsible for Social Services (1998).
38. Recent research with families that have a son or daughter with a disability identifies several areas of family quality of life. Families generally rate support from disability-related services quite low. See Brown et al. (2003). Also see Pedlar and Hutchison (2000).
39. Schwartz (1997).
40. For a discussion of shame, consider Swain and French (2000). For discussion of shame in aging in the context of a range of identities such as widow, native American, nursing home resident, gay or lesbian, etc., see Gubrium and Holstein (2003).

Part 2

Values and Vision

3

Values and Principles

The Foundation for Change

The void in our society has been produced by the absence of values. And values are not established by asserting issues.... The constant base needed to supply values is the result of methodical participation. The individual gains his [her] powers and responsibilities by being there.... Participation produces, and is also the product of, practical values and common sense ... not expertise and reason.

John Ralston Saul[1]

In the last half of the twentieth century, many reports were written about changes needed in various human service systems that serve citizens who are vulnerable.[2] Typically, these reports were written by professionals. They usually emphasized how services can be better co-ordinated, how citizens can receive services when they need them, and how assessment procedures can be simplified. Few of these reports were guided by explicit or clear human values, and until the past 10 years, almost none focused on the role of genuine community in people's lives. As a result, many of these potentially useful ideas often ended up emphasizing efficiency and technological solutions, rather than human values and quality of life. Ed Pomeroy, a retired professor from Brock University, Ontario, and long-time volunteer in the mental health movement, describes the twentieth century era as "modernist" because of the dominant assumptions about professional control and authority, and "bigger is better."[3]

In the 1990s we were working with a group interested in creating change for people with complex support needs. The group consisted of people with disabilities, family members, community activists, and service providers. For several meetings the group explored how the current service system could be changed to support persons more effectively. The group was somewhat stuck, until the question was asked, "What values and principles would we like to guide us in developing our project?" This critical question freed the group to be creative, and a number of value statements were generated. The result was an innovative project called Support Clusters, which brought together values and principles grounded in the need for natural support and citizenship opportunities.

The compelling idea here is that values drive innovation. Too often groups do not begin intentionally with values and principles but focus immediately on problem-solving solutions. We have already seen that clienthood and compliance result when traditional approaches lack strong values. Working without explicit values and principles often means that service providers ignore the possibility that their well-intentioned decisions cause harm. Most New Story innovations we have been studying began in a similar way to the Support Clusters Project. Unlike system changes in the middle part of the twentieth century, the establishment of values and principles are central in the very early stages to the development of New Story initiatives.

We have learned much about how values and principles serve as a foundation for change. While the terms "values" and "principles" are often used interchangeably, it is helpful to uncover their differences. Values reflect a kind of universal set of beliefs. As Janice Gross Stein says in her book, *The Cult of Efficiency*, "Values are the bedrock of political and social life; they are our conception of the good, of what is desirable."[4] On the other hand, principles serve as guidelines or markers for making the values concrete. They are not a recipe, but a way to organize and act in our daily lives. Values must be explicit to be a foundation for New Story innovations that are guided by principles. In turn, the principles provide a base for action. Together, values and principles provide the foundation for new paradigm approaches that lead to meaningful change. Several leaders describe their principles as a reflection of their values and as a link between theory and practice. Paulo Freire talks about "praxis" as the link between theory and practice and the reflection that we need in the world to create change.[5] It is in this sense that many innovations use the word *principles*.

Values Are Central to the New Story

When we say that values are central to the New Story, we simply mean that certain values help ensure that clienthood and compliance are avoided. One way to understand how the New Story reflects the "new paradigm" with people is to think of examples from our daily experience. Most of us would think it unusual today to have cars without pollution devices, to promote the idea that women not have a voice, or to refuse to live next door to a person from a visible minority. As we can tell from these examples, a paradigm shift refers to change from an "old story" way of thinking to a new way of seeing or understanding. A new paradigm normally has a different set of assumptions, language, and processes for implementation.[6]

Fortunately, in the past 20 years, there have been significant challenges to the old paradigm. Old story services and programs tend to be separate and charity-based, and demand compliance and clienthood by the users. Kenneth Gergen points out that paradigm shifts are usually preceded by tension among competing concepts.[7] Some leaders in New Story initiatives note that there is currently tension between people who favour agency-controlled supports and those innovators who believe in person- and family-directed supports. As Gergen suggests, this is not an unhealthy situation but a natural tension in the process of change. Many older people experience this tension in a very personal way. In the field of aging, the paradigm shift toward community and individualized alternatives is just beginning. Presently, nursing homes are the main option in most provinces for frail seniors who require medical support. Despite the lack of alternatives, there is a strong desire among many family members for more humane alternatives. This tension was experienced quite dramatically for us when one of our fathers moved to a nursing home. We wanted a more family-friendly alternative. As a positive contrast, our other parent was able to stay in his own home, receive palliative care supports, and die at home with family at his side. The shift to individualized homecare that is based on new paradigm values is slowly emerging across Canada.[8]

Peter Drucker has helped us understand that innovation and new ways of thinking emerge from multiple sources.[9] For example, some new paradigm ideas have come from thinkers in the field and have tended to be more conceptual. Another source of ideas comes from on-the-ground participation in local initiatives, which tend to highlight more practical application of values and new ideas. Research also provides a source of ideas for innovation. Most important, people themselves have, for some time now, been the most articulate spokespersons about the need for a shift to a new paradigm in North America. Raymond Kilroy, as early as 1987, addressed the United States Senate about his vision for people with disabilities:

> We are moving away from emphasizing my needs toward building upon my capacities. We are moving away from providing services to me in some facility toward building bridges with me to communities and neighbourhood associations. We are moving away from programming me and other people with disabilities toward empowering us and our families to acquire the support we want. We are moving away from focusing on my deficits to focusing on my competence. We are moving away from specialized disability organizations so that we can develop and sustain relationships with people who will depend upon people like me and upon whom people like me can depend.[10]

The values and principles of the New Story provide the foundation for people to have an enhanced quality of life. People in several initiatives we studied identified core dimensions of quality of life, including self-determination, physical well-

Key Values of the New Story

- Human rights and social justice
- Diversity and person-centeredness
- Participation and empowerment
- Hospitality and community

being, participation, relationships, and inclusion. Recent studies show that when individualized supports are provided with these kinds of principles, quality of life is improved. Other studies stress that quality of life is related to determinants of health.[11] As a result, we can say that people with a good quality of life enjoy better health and well-being. In one study on four innovative initiatives in Ontario, quality of life was enhanced over four years. Approximately 85% of people's goals were met, 50% of participants had many relationships, and 70% had strong community participation.[12]

Innovative approaches we have studied all have a similar set of values that together represent the new paradigm or New Story. For each set of values, it is possible to see why the values were paired, how the values were critical to the new paradigm, and why they were such an important foundation for *Pathways to Inclusion*. Although there may be others, the values we have witnessed that are most common in the new paradigm include human rights and social justice, diversity and person-centeredness, participation and empowerment, and hospitality and community.

Human Rights and Social Justice

Human rights and social justice as fundamental values in New Story approaches grow from a strong belief that all people should have the same rights and conditions. It is quite remarkable that, in all initiatives, the rights of people being supported is a given. It is assumed in language, in the vision and mission

Pathways to Inclusion

statements, and in working principles that people of all abilities and differences should have equal rights. Marsha Forest, a strong advocate for inclusion, had a wonderful motto, "all means all." There has been an attitude in many human services, sometimes conscious, sometimes subconscious, that people with certain characteristics or differences, such as people with frailties, deserve fewer rights. As Michael Ignatieff says, "to believe in rights is to believe in defending difference."[13]

Human rights can be seen as a lens through which one can address issues such as access, accommodation, and equality. A human rights lens allows us to see injustice as well as possibilities that should exist for citizens who are marginalized. Experience from the initiatives we studied shows the power of the human rights lens to reveal an incredible range of issues that need to be addressed. Catherine Frazee writes from the perspective of a person with a disability: "Seen through the lens of human rights, segregation and stigmatization of people with disabilities is a deep wound, not only to people with disabilities themselves, but to society as a whole. This wound can only heal through policy accomplishments, public education and community development."[14]

While some people see rights as the only framework for change, Mark Kingwell notes that individual rights are not enough by themselves.[15] He emphasizes that rights need to be embedded in a broader social justice framework. People we have worked with in most initiatives are very aware of a broader social justice framework and see their work as part of a systematic struggle for change. There is recognition that the complexity of change requires rights to be one of the ingredients, but not the only one. A small number of innovations seem preoccupied with the day-to-day work of implementing support arrangements, and do not connect their work to a social justice framework. This is perhaps understandable, given the on-the-ground work required for innovations to take hold.

In 2008, Canada was one of 147 countries that signed the United Nations (UN) Convention on the Rights of Persons with Disabilities. This important document now provides an international standard on human rights. The UN Convention is unique for two reasons: first, it provides a framework and 52 articles that guide how rights can be enhanced for persons with disabilities. Second, the document itself was conceived and developed by persons with disabilities.[16]

In one sense, the UN Convention reflects the rights that are legitimate for all people. In another sense, the Convention provides a way to value diversity by providing guidelines for specific areas of living, such as housing and transportation. The UN Convention is a powerful document that expresses a New Story for people who are vulnerable. It also provides a way for community groups to monitor policies and services. Disability Rights Promotion International is providing training and support to groups that want to monitor communities and services in light of the UN Convention.[17]

A commitment to rights and social justice reflects the desire to enhance people's citizenship. Although citizenship is a value we often take for granted, people are often denied the rights and responsibilities of being full citizens. Citizenship includes access, rights, valued status, and full participation.[18]

Diversity and Person-Centeredness

Diversity and person-centeredness are strong values crossing all innovations. Diversity is often equated with tolerance. Experience suggests, however, that diversity is a much deeper, more profound concept related to human beings accepting and embracing one another in their differences and similarities. William Chase has expressed the meaning of diversity most aptly: "Diversity, generally understood and embraced, is not casual liberal tolerance of anything and everything not yourself. It is not polite accommodation. Instead, diversity is, in action, the sometimes painful awareness that other people, other races, other voices, other habits of mind, have as much integrity of being, as much claim on the world as you do."[19] By their genuine acceptance of differences, diversity is honoured in New Story initiatives.

People involved in the innovations understand that acceptance of diversity also means honouring each unique person. As a result, there is a strong commitment to the values of person-centeredness. To be person-centered is often a technique or approach that people use, but person-centeredness is much more than a technique. It is about how we relate to each other as full human beings. John Ralston Saul says the basis for justice is being able to imagine the "other" person as a full human being.[20] As the term implies, person-centeredness values the uniqueness of the person and respects the right of

---

Declaration on the Right to Live and Be Different

- Nothing about us without us.
- We recognize that the only way to ensure universal support for and positive recognition of our particular qualities is through stating our right to diversity clearly, with good arguments, in open and democratic discussion. We must form alliances with scientists, the medical professions, ethicists, policy makers, human rights advocates, the media, and the general public.
- We believe that a society without disabled people would be a lesser society. Our unique individual and collective experiences are an important contribution to a rich, human society.
- We demand an end to the bio-medical elimination of diversity, to gene selection based on market forces and to the setting of norms and standards by non-disabled people.
- All human beings are born free and equal in dignity and rights.

Source: Disabled Peoples' International Europe, Declaration on the Right to Live and Be Different, Conference on Bioethics and Human Rights (Solihull, UK: DPIE, 2000).

---

the person to self-determination. This contrasts with traditional approaches that often emphasize benevolence or compliance over self-determination. In February 2000, 130 people with disabilities and their families from 27 countries met in London, England. This group created an important declaration that speaks to person-centeredness and diversity.

People's commitment to self-determination reflects a desire to move person-centeredness to action. Self-determination is a process whereby people determine their own needs and interests. It means people choose and decide their life choices and the type and quality of support they want. These concepts are important in several initiatives, such as mental health reform

Self-Determination and Community

In recent years, the values of self-determination and community have been seen by social innovators as central to the new paradigm of community supports for inclusion. These two values, while seemingly opposites, in fact complement each other and are quite interdependent.

Self-determination as a value is the belief that *all* citizens desire to have choice and control in their lives, especially over the supports they require. Self-determination is about being intentional and taking responsibility for our actions. Self-determination challenges compliance and clienthood.

Community as a value is the belief that all human beings desire to belong and participate with others in families, neighbourhoods, networks, and groups. In community, people collaborate and work and play in interdependent ways. Community thinking challenges the predominance of "service" thinking in the "old story."

Self-determination and community are central in the new paradigm because they capture the essence of what a good life can look and feel like.

Based on these values, the participation and contribution of individuals, families, friends, and others become central to the New Story — participation in deciding how to build a good life, participation in deciding what kinds of supports make sense, and participation and contribution as citizens in the wider community.

projects that stress self-determination in the context of recovery.[21] Some advocates and researchers in aging are concerned that as our population ages, we are failing to pay enough attention to seniors' quality of life. In one study for which elderly persons were interviewed, older people were clear about their rights to personal control and self-determination to pursue a chosen lifestyle.[22]

Participation and Empowerment

Participation and empowerment are strongly held values in New Story approaches. The previous declaration of *right to live and be different*, where people with disabilities say "Nothing about us without us," provides a strong hint about these values. The value of participation is expressed in terms of people participating in all aspects of their lives, including civic life. Participation is a strong value because, in many ways, it pushes against years of passivity that society and services have come to expect. In traditional approaches to disability, aging, and chronic conditions, professionals tend to have power *over* people, while in New Story approaches, there is more mutuality and power *with* people. In fact, we found that staff members are deeply respectful of the value of participation and their role in supporting principles of participation. As we shall see, this commitment to participation includes principles related to community connecting as a way of supporting people to build valued social roles in ways in which they can contribute to their community.[23]

Empowerment as a value includes intentionally shifting power and decision making toward individuals and families. Participation has been shown to be central to empowerment and to the development of personal control and confidence. As well, becoming more informed and aware is an important part of the empowerment process, and learning and education opportunities for participants are built into many initiatives. As research has shown, shifting power and control to citizens does not just happen. It must be intentional, with attention paid to the values and principles and support for decision-making strategies that will make this a reality. The values of participation and empowerment are reflected most clearly in New Story initiatives, with the focus on supports that are determined and directed by the person and/or the family.

Hospitality and Community

The final set of values critical to the New Story consists of hospitality and community. Time and time again, we meet people who are actively looking in the community for places that offer hospitality. When hospitality is valued, citizens feel they are respected and welcomed. Imagine a public library that was not hospitable. It would be barren, devoid of places for reflection and gathering, with no offer of guides or helpers to assist people in accessing resources. Hospitality is stressed by people in initiatives by making their settings welcoming and by connecting people to community life.

As well, in the past 20 years, community has emerged as a strong value among advocates working for change. Community is something we all know from experience. Yet we have found that community as a value in the lives of many citizens is often new. It is not possible to truly understand the value of hospitality without being aware of the power of community and civic society. When a community is working well, it can be a place where people think creatively, dream their dreams, and join with others to celebrate their common humanity.

We must understand community in order to nurture social inclusion. Yet our society often overlooks the idea that neighbourhoods and communities are genuine places of caring. Too often, systems and services are seen as safeguards for vulnerable citizens. In the New Story, community and relationships are two of the fundamental values for building inclusive lives.

Reflection on Values

We learn from the experience of New Story initiatives that values are needed as the foundation for nurturing positive conditions, enhancing participation, and building pathways to full inclusion in community life. No community, of course, would have full consensus on these values. New Story leaders, however, have been able to inspire and mobilize enough people around the values in a community to make a difference. These values are so fundamental to these initiatives that we explore them in depth in the next three chapters. While each of these values has some impact in its own right, we have learned the obvious — that the values have greatest potential when working in unison.

Despite the clear presence of these diverse but connected values, it must also be noted that some people struggle with a seeming paradox between some of the values. While this is understandable, some people working from the New Story interpret this as an issue of complexity and paradox. This "paradox of principles," so aptly named by Charles Handy in his book *Managing Paradoxes*, is played out in everyday language and action.[24] One of the most common paradoxes relates to self-determination and community. In the dualities that often mark our era, self-determination and community may be thought of as opposites. "If I stress my autonomy, don't I run the danger of ignoring what others think and feel?" Similarly, "If I stress community and collaboration, might I not possibly ignore individual needs and desires?" As John Friedmann, a philosopher of planning, has pointed out, these two principles only appear to be opposites. They actually inform each other and together give us an understanding of the whole.[25] This is living with paradox. Similarly, Rene Gadacz writes in *Rethinking Disability* that participation in community life in many ways satisfies the desire for self-determination.[26] With this understanding, it is not surprising that the New Story affirms seeming opposites.

Making Values and Principles Explicit

We have found that people who feel passionate about full inclusion for all citizens can usually articulate their values and principles clearly. Leaders in New Story initiatives stress the importance of having explicit or intentional values and principles that promote innovation. Peter Clutterbuck, former executive Director of the Toronto Social Planning Council, and a leader in NABORS (Neighbors Allied for Better Opportunities in Residential Support), emphasizes that clear values and principles enable the person and project "to be able to think in new ways." And, as people learn to think in new ways, new language often emerges before values and principles actually become explicit. This has been particularly true with the values of hospitality and community. In the 1970s, as people struggled against segregation and stigma, community participation and integration began to emerge in everyday language, before we really understood how central this value was to social justice and liberation.

Another reason for making values and principles explicit is the tendency for people to think they are doing a better job than they are. We all know of situations where inappropriate interventions have been made with the best intentions. Because of this human tendency, making values explicit and useful is often an urgent task for progressive initiatives. When values are neither explicit nor comprehensive, it is easy to pervert their intention. We have met many people, for example, who claim they are utilizing person-centered approaches. However, in exploring the value of diversity and principles of self-determination with them, it is often evident that they are only focusing on the individual or addressing individual needs. These are hardly substantive claims for new paradigm thinking or acting, since these two ideas can readily be implemented in the traditional paradigm. Keeping values and principles explicit helps ensure that people continually refer to them and that the approach has a strong, clear foundation.

Values and principles are made explicit in several ways. The process of clarifying new ideas is important and often occurs during the development of innovations. In 1990, the Flying on Our Own Conference was an historic event in the history of people with physical disabilities in Ontario.[27] "The three day retreat was really about refining the concept of attendant service and ensuring that we had a strong, shared value base to move forward," said one community leader. What was significant about this leadership group, the Attendant Care Action Coalition, was how their concept development and clarification was always intricately tied to a set of clear values. The Ontario Direct Funding Project, one of the outcomes of the Coalition's work, is a New Story initiative that continues to illustrate the importance of continually reflecting on values and principles.

Some groups make values and principles explicit by ensuring that they are incorporated into their mission statements, goals, and objectives. In terms of rights and social justice, several Ontario Peer Development Initiative groups have similar statements of values and principles: "We believe in the individual's right to exercise freedom of choice and self-determination" and "We believe in social justice for all."[28] Relative to participation and empowerment, Independent Living Resource Centres across Canada reflect this value with their focus on the principles of self-determination and member control.[29] For diversity and person-centeredness, several individualized support initiatives reflect this value with their focus on respect for differences and the worth of each participant. In terms of community and hospitality, various local and provincial family support networks reflect this value with principles such as, "All children have the right to acquire the daily social and coping skills that develop through life in the community."

Pathways to Inclusion

These examples illustrate the importance of writing values and principles and using them to guide actions.

Finally, explicit principles provide a base for day-to-day work. Principles guide staff in their daily work, provide a framework for people to access and use the innovation, and are utilized by leaders for decision making. Principles consciously act as a lens for problem solving and goal setting. A principle-centered approach helps people to think about conditions and to work collaboratively for change. With explicit principles guiding day-to-day work, problems are not fixed but are engaged, reflected on, and mindfully considered in light of the values and principles.

The values and principles we use to guide our work with the Facilitation Leadership Group[30] are summarized in the focus box on the following page. Organized around three themes that have emerged from our New Story research, they reflect the central directions that we believe communities must move toward if they are to embrace the New Story. These themes reflect key values of self-determination, community, and capacity building of individuals, families, communities, and systems.

Some years ago, we were asked to talk about community values to a large organization that was attempting to be innovative. The administrator admitted that "We think mostly in terms of buildings and units of service." Making the shift to thinking about New Story values can be very difficult and time consuming. Many mainstream organizations have difficulty moving from understanding the "superficial" nature of the alternative values, to actually using explicit values and principles to provide a base for daily decision making.

Beyond Ideology: Values and Principles Are a Viable Alternative

The emergence of New Story initiatives reflects the beginning of a cultural shift in the way we provide support to citizens. What we are witnessing are small groups feeling confident enough to begin a journey that involves new language, new concepts, new values, and new practices. Although the initiators of these innovations do not always realize it, they are engaged in significant social change. Most of these social innovators are

Pathways to Inclusion

New Story Principles

Self-Determination

1. The power of *decision making* about the person's life (including supports) rests primarily with the person and who he/she chooses.

2. *Dreams* (intention) and *strengths* (identity) guide how we build a life and what supports we require.

Community

3. Community is seen as a *first resort* in building a good life.

4. Relationships and networks of people are *intentionally created* so that they are supportive, connected, and empowering.

Capacity Building

5. *Autonomous peer groups and family networks* educate, empower, and advocate.

6. *Independent facilitation* deepens personal growth and community connections.

7. *Funding* is individualized and portable.

8. *Collaboration* builds capacity and enhances problem solving.

9. *Social innovation* inspires creativity, learning, and broad change.

Source: J. Lord and C. Dingwall, Facilitation Leadership Group, <www.facilitationleadership.com>.

clear, however, that their work is embedded less in a particular ideology and more in the spirit of collective values and principles that guide community processes. In other words, social innovators are not tied to a strict ideology but recognize the need to be open to "learning as they go" and knowing that they cannot control the development of their innovation. We find this insight quite compelling, which in itself may be part of the cultural shift.

This past century has been dominated by diverse ideologies, with Marxism, capitalism, and science being the most predominant. In the social sciences and human services, ideologies such as "normalization" or "community-based services" have also been dominant. Ideologies usually assume certain givens or inevitabilities, regardless of the ideology. John Ralston Saul says ideology is akin to the gods and destiny.[31] These metaphors remind us of times when citizens thought life was inevitable and determined by forces outside themselves. Saul argues that the current belief in the marketplace as the salvation of many problems is an example of an ideology. It is not unusual today for many people to believe that the private sector can resolve issues more effectively than the non-profit sector.

Several years ago we attended an international conference on community-based health services. Most speakers addressed the ideology of "community-based services" from the perspective of an improved health system. Speaker after speaker outlined how this new system would produce all kinds of benefits, including "restructured health services," "improved coordination," and the "capacity for health-promotion interventions." This experience reiterated for us that ideologies are usually high in rhetoric and low on values and principles. A non-professional attending that conference would have been bewildered by the specialized language and ideological rhetoric. It was a rare speaker who talked about human beings and citizens. It was even rarer to hear a discussion of the experiences of people who were vulnerable or excluded from community life. This is a clear example of how ideologies create hope without necessarily doing the right or wise thing. Searching for the right values and principles establishes a base that grounds an innovation in doing the right thing for the right reasons.

Occasionally, there are ideologies that help unmask the dominant assumptions of the day. Such was the case with normalization, a very attractive set of principles for "devalued" citizens within North America adopted from Sweden in the 1970s throughout human services. Essentially, normalization, and its more recent version, social role valorization, proposed that many ideologies operating in human services were "unconscious."[32] People trained in normalization became very aware of how subtle ideologies can be. Why was it, they asked, that devalued citizens were often housed in the poorest housing in the poorest part of town? Why were people who were devalued often segregated in large groups? More subtly, why was it that people with very different vulnerabilities were often placed together? Normalization challenged these devaluing approaches. Like most ideologies, however, normalization supporters often presented these ideas in dogmatic and technical terms. Sometimes citizens and professionals with genuine concerns and sensitivities were left confused. Others felt excluded because of the tone of "certainty" that pervaded many of the presentations about normalization.

Most proponents of the New Story seem very cautious about embracing a single ideology. Rather, people speak in terms of values and principles. Some talk about working on a new "paradigm," a viewpoint that contrasts with traditional services and paradigms. People seem open to learning, to having difficult questions raised, and to re-examining their assumptions. Like all human beings, these people exhibit a degree of defensiveness about their own work, but in a protective manner. We were continually impressed with people's commitment to values and to the ongoing quest for improvement. In many initiatives, space is created for reflection on principles, what is possible, and how goals can be achieved.

We need values and principles to guide the New Story and to respond to the oppression experienced by many citizens. We conclude with a warning from Susan Griffin, who writes that ideology "begins to destroy the self and self-knowledge. Originally born of feeling, it pretends to float above and around feeling.... It organizes experience according to itself, without touching experience."[33] This is a challenge to social innovations to remain grounded in values and principles, and to not make them into an ideology. The values and principles we have experienced are far from a fixed position; rather, they are a template for reflection, learning, and action. As we shall see, the participation and stories of individuals, families, and communities further ground the principles in people's lives.

Notes

1. Saul (1992), p. 584.
2. For a more detailed analysis, see Simmons (1990). Also see Nelson, Lord, and Ochocka (2001).

3. For a critique of modernist assumptions, see Illich (1977); Saul (1995); McKnight (1996).
4. Stein (2001), p. 58.
5. Freire (1970).
6. Carling (1995). An example of a paradigm shift from aging stresses the concept of "aging in place" and provides an example where co-housing options that are new paradigms are proposed: Scott-Hanson and Scott-Hanson (2005).
7. Gergen (1995).
8. MacAdam (2000); also Keating et al. (2003).
9. Drucker (1985).
10. Kilroy (1987).
11. For more information on quality of life, see Brown and Brown (2002); Schalock et al. (2002).
12. Lord (2006).
13. Ignatieff (1984), p. 53.
14. Frazee (1999), p. 6.
15. Kingwell (2000).
16. The United Nations Enable: Rights and Dignity of Persons with Disabilities is a UN website that details the Convention on the Rights of Persons with Disabilities. <www.un.org/disabilities/>
17. Disability Rights Promotion International Canada is a community–university alliance that works to build capacity and systems for monitoring the human rights of people with disabilities: <www.yorku.ca/drpi/files/DRPICAN_Ovr0708.pdf>
18. Kingwell (2000); Ralston Saul (1995).
19. Chase (1994).
20. Saul (2001).
21. For more thoughts on self-determination projects, see Lord, Zupko, and Hutchison (2000); Bach (1998).
22. Disabled Peoples' International Europe (2000).
23. Holburn and Vietze (1992).
24. Handy (1994).
25. Friedmann (1987).
26. Gadacz (1994).
27. Attendant Care Action Coalition (1990).
28. Waterloo Region Self-Help (1998), p. 12.
29. Hutchison et al. (1996); Valentine (1994).
30. Lord and Dingwall, *Facilitation Leadership Group.* <www.facilitationleadership.com>
31. Saul (1995).
32. Wolfensberger (1972).
33. Griffin (1982), p. 648.

4

Community and Hospitality

Rediscovering Where We Belong

Community. Somewhere, there are people to whom we can speak with passion without having the words catch in our throats. Somewhere a circle of hands will open to receive us, eyes will light up as we enter, voices will celebrate with us whenever we come into our own power. Community means strength that joins our strength to do the work that needs to be done. Arms to hold us when we falter. A circle of healing. A circle of friends. Somewhere where we can be free.

Starhawk[1]

We raised our four children in a housing co-operative. We lived in a three-bedroom townhouse, surrounded by many different types of families. In that setting, we experienced community with all of its wonders, ambiguities, and imperfections. We knew our kids were safe as they played with other children hour after hour. We worked with others to make our communal garden productive and our community centre hospitable. As several persons with disabilities, people of different ages, and persons of different ethnic and cultural backgrounds became part of the fabric of the co-op, we saw co-op members gradually embrace diversity. Our memories of those co-op days focus mostly on the trust that was built among co-op members. Trust, as we have come to understand, is a key part of hospitality and community.

Whether community is seen as a place, a network of caring people, or a community association where people gather around areas of common interest, hospitality is the ingredient that creates true community.[2] We have learned from New Story approaches and from our own family and friends that community and hospitality are essential ingredients to quality of life.

Hearing the very word *community* conjures up positive images because of its inherent nature or meaning. Sometimes when people speak of community, they are expressing a romantic ideal, a desire for a return to earlier times when towns and villages experienced genuine hospitality. People in the initiatives have moved beyond romanticism and instill community in the everyday life of neighbourhoods, families, and welcoming organizations. Community and hospitality enable people to experience belonging and participation. However, the reality is that the hospitality and trust we experienced in those co-op days have not often been the community experience of many citizens. Dating back to the 1700s, people who were vulnerable due to age, frailty, or poverty were isolated from the community. Industrialization and the growth of cities in the late 1800s decreased the importance of community in the lives of all citizens. In the first half of the 1900s, thousands of Canadians lived in facilities away from their communities or families. As the century unfolded, patterns of helping became professionalized, and formal human services took hold. Community and hospitality had clearly become submerged as a response to vulnerability.

Since the 1960s, "community-based services" has been the mantra of governments and service providers. A wide array of community services was developed to serve people already living in the community, as well as those returning to the community from institutions. Many services added *community* to their name, such as community living associations, community care access centres, and community mental health organizations. David Schwartz, in his book *Who Cares: Rediscovering Community*, shows how the history of hospitality has gradually been taken over by formal systems. Schwartz argues that in North American culture, a "certainty" pervades our thinking in terms of how we respond to vulnerable people.[3] When people think of someone's need for support, there is often a deeply embedded belief that formal helping systems should be the response. We personally often experience this certainty with our own daughter. People ask if she will be moving to a group home, rather than asking a more open-ended question about her hopes and dreams around moving away from home.

The Emergence of Community

In the 1960s and 1970s, three events unfolded that would eventually introduce community into dialogue about how best to organize supports for people. First, the American Civil Rights movement was creating an awareness of the human rights of not only black Americans, but also other groups that had long been marginalized. This emphasis on rights helped create conditions for people to live together in community. A focus on rights necessarily forces people to clarify the meaning of *community* and how all people must have access to valued community settings and resources. The Independent Living movement in Canada was strongly influenced by the American Civil Rights movement. The American Independent Living movement grew out of the disability rights movement and in the 1970s formed the basis of a new paradigm for people with disabilities.[4] The approximately 30 Independent Living Centres across Canada reflect a strong commitment to rights, self-determination, and community participation.

The second catalyst in the emergence of community was a strong parent movement in North America. In the 1970s, this movement of families demanded services in the community for their sons and daughters with disabilities. More recently, family leaders have been quite outspoken about the need for community and inclusion to be available for their vulnerable children.

As well, the school inclusion movement has been mostly led by parents of children with disabilities.[5]

The third catalyst for community in the late 1970s was that researchers and thinkers were beginning to critique traditional approaches to supporting people. Less congregation and more community living were seen as positive alternatives. Although relatively few intellectuals had shown an interest in community, those who did explore this issue made a significant contribution.[6]

It was not until the 1980s that pioneers and social innovations began to emerge in response to criticisms about formal service systems and their lack of genuine community focus. The underlying assumption of these criticisms was that, despite some limited changes, the use of *community* to describe human services belied the fact that the nature of these formal services was in sharp contrast to genuine community. Formal systems were actually seen as a barrier to hospitality and community because of their bureaucratic and professionalized nature. Definitions of *community* grounded in the concepts of citizenship and hospitality began to be explored. Simultaneously, by the 1990s, social innovations that were springing up in resistance to the professional "certainty" began to embrace the language and values of community and hospitality. Projects began to emerge in ways that reflect the importance of neighbourhoods and relationships in enhancing social inclusion and personal well-being.

Pioneers to Learn From

The first true pioneer who influenced the community movement was active long before the 1980s, but her work resonates well beyond that decade. Jane Addams was a progressive thinker and founder of the Settlement Houses in Chicago in the early 1900s. A Nobel Peace Prize winner, Addams worked tirelessly as an educator, activist, and writer. She believed that industrialization tended to segregate the classes and separate the generations. As a community developer, she worked in solidarity with poor people and realized that democracy would thrive only if everyone was included. Education and participation in decision making were central features in the unique community centres that Addams developed. To this day, Addams' essays provide insight and clarity about inclusion, citizenship, and participation.

Fortunately, scholars recently re-discovered her work and have made her writings more widely available.[7]

Jean Vanier, a Canadian best known as the founder of L'Arche, an international network of communities for people with developmental disabilities was another pioneer in the community movement. Vanier's work with L'Arche started in the mid-1960s and has been inspirational for many people who are trying to find alternatives to barren institutional life. After Vanier established the first L'Arche community in France, he began to support the development of L'Arche homes in other countries, including Canada. L'Arche homes, as reflected in Vanier's writing and speaking, have been framed in terms of a spiritual community and the need we all have for belonging. In a typical L'Arche home, a few adults with disabilities live together with assistants who agree to be there for a minimum of a year. The spirit of community can be quite evident, with people typically cooking, singing, and praying together. It might be evident why a L'Arche home is often referred to as a community rather than just a home. Vanier has argued passionately that we are better off when we live with people who are vulnerable in our midst; it connects us with our hearts and makes us aware of our own vulnerability. Although Vanier's ideas are only indirectly used in New Story initiatives, his influence has been significant, especially with ordinary citizens who attend his lectures and buy his books.[8] It is possible to be critical of some L'Arche homes for being too segregated. Nevertheless, their approach to building community and hospitality has much to teach us about the importance of context and home. This contrasts sharply with many human service systems that focus more on housing than on home and hospitality.

John McKnight first came to our attention when he was writing with Ivan Illich in the 1970s about the limits of professional intervention. A professor from Northwestern University in Evanston, Illinois, he came to Canada in 1985 to address a group of mental health leaders consisting of individuals, family members, and professionals. McKnight emphasized that formal human service systems had essentially separated people from community life. As a way of illustrating his point, he showed how a young man named Charlie experienced hospitality, became accepted, built relationships, and regained citizenship by participating in a community association. The most important information McKnight imparted to the audience was the limits of professional helping. In fact, like Jean Vanier, his stories of community building were on the opposite side of the professional paradigm. McKnight's writing and lectures have been a powerful catalyst for people thinking about community.[9] What we personally remember most about that day more than 20 years ago was the audience's reaction to John's talk. Many of us felt that we were being told what we already sensed but did not yet have the language, awareness, or knowledge to articulate. Today, innovative initiatives have community as an intentional part of their planning and perspective.

Judith Snow is a leader who has played a very strong role educating about and promoting the community vision. A member of NABORS, Snow's story is well known across Canada.[10] When Snow was 25 years old, she was living in a chronic care hospital. While working on her master's degree, she met Marsha Forest at York University. Marsha heard the plight of her new-found friend — the inappropriateness of a young woman having to live her life in a hospital, seemingly because of the severity of her physical disability. Together, Snow, Forest, Jack Pearpoint, Peter Dill, and a few other friends formed the first support circle in Canada. Snow named her support circle the Joshua Committee because of its tenacity and effective advocacy in "breaking down walls." Within weeks of this circle gathering, Snow obtained an Order-in-Council from the Ontario government in 1981 to receive the first individualized funding in Canada. This funding enabled Snow to move into her own apartment, hire her own attendants, and see employment as a possibility for the future. From the first time we met Judith Snow in the mid-1980s, we realized she had a unique vision about community. Her message stressed the giftedness that we all possess, regardless of the labels others may try to put on us. Over the years, she has been inspiring countless people to follow their dreams by re-framing issues of vulnerability around community, relationships, and citizenship. In her own life, Judith Snow personifies the values of hospitality and community.

As illustrated in Judith Snow's story, we believe that the real pioneers for community have been people themselves, whose calls for change have been getting louder. Disillusioned with community service systems that held so much promise but in fact did little to connect people with community life, many groups of senior citizens and people with disabilities have increased their advocacy efforts. While the pioneers got us started in thinking about the power of community, many national, provincial, and local groups are now taking up the cause.

Capacities of Caring Communities

Many New Story initiatives have the stated goal of contributing to or building caring communities. Exploring the capacities of these communities is revealing. In our studies on innovative initiatives, it became apparent that community can be interpreted in multiple ways: most stress hospitality in informal life; some emphasize community as neighbourhood; others focus primarily on personal networks and relationships; and many work on community engagement and connecting people with associations of common interest. In reality, most of these approaches to community building overlap to some degree, and regardless of the approach, several shared characteristics seem to be evident.

We are learning that *hospitality* gives community true meaning. Hospitality contributes to welcoming community places, whether they are in neighbourhoods or community settings. Hospitality has a long history related to people inviting others to share of themselves and what they have to offer. When Jamie Fredericks became involved with NABORS as part of a large housing co-op in downtown Toronto, it was the first time he had lived on his own. He had spent the previous 12 years in an institution located one hour north of Toronto. There were significant differences between his life in his new apartment and life in the institution. He has experienced hospitality since the day he moved into the co-op. Neighbours came over with some refreshments during the move. In the first week, Fredericks discovered the community room, where he met more welcoming people. While he now has privacy and can make choices about what to eat and when to go out, Fredericks never misses the potluck gatherings, an important part of co-op life. At one of these gatherings he met Jane Addams, who works with a local neighbourhood organization. Fredericks has since started doing volunteer work with Addams's organization. Although Jamie Fredericks does not express himself verbally, his family and friends make it clear that he is finally experiencing rights and citizenship at age 32.

Pathways to Inclusion

As at NABORS, other people in the initiatives work hard to create welcoming, hospitable organizations. This might mean creating a welcoming office, or having a philosophy that reflects welcoming goals. Even the most innovative settings can be easily distracted by funding worries. A clear vision and set of values that constantly reinforce the principles of community and hospitality reduce the effects of bureaucracy and the demands of the service system.

For community to be truly grounded in everyday life, the possibilities of *informal life* need to be understood and respected. David Schwartz reminds us that "the remnants of hospitality are not always easy to find, but they "can often be found in the fragmented informal life beneath our feet."[11] Many initiatives are learning that in informal life, there tends to be more focus on "hanging out" in community settings such as malls, coffee shops, churches, and bars. Conversations and just being together are central to these settings. When we are aware of the potential of informal life, we begin to discover hospitality in unexpected places. In traditional approaches, informal life tends not to be noticed, and regular citizens are seen as uninterested or incapable of providing support or having relationships with many persons who seem different. A focus on informal life makes it possible to pay attention to relationships rather than services.

Citizenship can be one of the bridges between community and hospitality. Mark Kingwell describes citizenship as "a way of meeting one's deepest needs, the need to belong; it gives voice and structure to the yearning to be part of something larger than ourselves. By the same token, citizenship is a way of making concrete the ethical commitments of care and respect, of realizing in action an obligation to aid fellow travellers."[12]

Civic engagement is one way citizens participate in the political, social, and economic life of their communities. Civic engagement means being involved in community life in regular roles, such as neighbours, volunteers, family members, participants, and decision makers. Civic engagement is important to vulnerable citizens because it represents the opposite of the traditional belief that their difference makes it impossible to function as a valued member of society. Innovators find that involvement in civic life leads to more people and places being part of the vulnerable person's life. A recent study of four New

Story initiatives showed that participants were involved in more than three community settings or citizenship experiences on a regular basis.[13] By participating in these valued roles within community associations, people experience the rights and responsibilities of citizenship. In several initiatives, for example, people are employed in meaningful work where fellow workers see these persons as valued co-workers and friends. Many of these persons also volunteer on community committees and boards.

Another characteristic of community relates to the belief that *fellow citizens are willing and able* to get involved. This concept embraces elements of what community and belonging has always meant to people and sees community as part of a new vision.[14] Leaders in New Story approaches have a strong belief that fellow citizens can and will welcome people who are vulnerable into their communities and into their lives. Leaders assume that the informal world of hospitality and community provides the vehicle for finding citizens who will become involved with their fellow citizens. Catherine Duchesne, long-time executive director of the Personal Support Community Association of Alberta says, "The difference in the lives of people is shown by relationships given freely by members in the community and the family." Al Etmanski from PLAN (Planned Lifetime Advocacy Networks) in British Columbia believes that "most ordinary people are caring, hospitable, and willing to assist." One important role of innovations is to support citizenship by identifying places and people that are hospitable and to nurture these connections.

Finally, when citizenship and hospitality guide an initiative, a community lens becomes the focus. No longer do innovative groups and organizations ask: What services or programs do you need? Instead, they engage people in thinking about questions such as, What dreams or goals do you have? What might assist you in improving your quality of life and connections with your community? or Who in your network could we invite to assist? By focusing first on dreams, goals, and relationships, people are moving away from formal services as the first response to "community as first resort." Catherine Duchesne reflects on this intentional re-focusing, "We believe that people have the right to participate in full community life through membership, friendship, citizenship, sharing common places, and accessibility to all community resources."

Pathways to Inclusion

Caring Communities

A number of recent studies have explored the question: What is a caring community? In summarizing this work, Julie White from the Ontario Trillium Foundation notes that caring communities share a number of characteristics:

- An abundance of social capital, such as opportunities for engagement and belonging; a wide range of informal community associations; and formal supports

- Strong connections and networks within the community and with other communities, which create opportunities for dialogue and co-operative learning

- A willingness and capacity to welcome and integrate newcomers, which includes volunteer efforts and community initiatives that support inclusion

- The ability to adapt and be innovative, including citizens having confidence in their capacity to address local issues.

- The capacity to promote collaborative relationships and community partnerships, reflecting a new value that social issues are the concern of the entire community, not just government or agencies

Few communities, of course, will have all of these characteristics in full bloom. Yet, communities that are involved in the New Story are working on various aspects of these characteristics.

Source: J. White, *Building Caring Communities* (Toronto, ON: Ontario Trillium Foundation, 1991).

Pathways to Inclusion

Finally, we can think of caring communities as people and places that welcome diversity and fallibility. Caring neighbourhoods do not try to fix people, as many service systems do. As John McKnight and Peter Block emphasize, communities are abundant. Community abundance means we value the strengths and gifts and diversity of all citizens and recognize we all have a common interest in caring for each other. Caring is not the purview of service systems, but rather is central to the community.[15]

Social Movements That Are Rediscovering Community

In the past decade, several movements for change have begun to focus on the importance of building strong communities. These social movements have been rediscovering the value of community, particularly as it relates to citizenship, civic engagement, and democracy. The anti-globalization and poverty-reduction movements, as well as the healthy communities, senior citizens, and disability movements are all noteworthy.

All around the world, we see citizens, many of them youth, challenging the corporate establishment through *anti-globalization* advocacy. Most people have heard about the World Trade Organization protests in Seattle and Quebec City. On first look, these protests appear to be only about an economic agenda and how wealth is distributed in society. A closer examination of the people and the issues involved reveals a deep concern for building more democratic structures and strong communities.[16] Many social activists argue that the major decisions for our planet need to be made in a more democratic fashion and that our local communities are among the best arenas for these decisions. What we do locally affects what we do globally, and vice versa. Two of our adult children and many of their friends reflect this new understanding. These young adults can be seen at anti-globalization protests. Many have worked, studied, or travelled overseas and know first-hand the inequalities that exist in the world. They are also very committed to their local communities. Many of them are involved with food co-ops, community gardens, and volunteer placements in a variety of community initiatives. They tend to be less interested in voting, one traditional indicator of citizenship, but can be counted on to participate in issues that relate to building strong communities or nations.[17] Although this group of young adults may well be the minority, they reflect a growing movement of citizens in many parts of the world who are yearning for more democracy and participation. As this movement expands its influence, it will hopefully benefit from the efforts of those working toward inclusion and community for marginalized groups.

The *Canadian Healthy Communities movement* has been a significant force in educating and mobilizing citizens in many cities across Canada to build healthy communities.[18] Healthy Communities projects tend to stress citizenship and community participation as central to building a healthy community. Healthy Communities projects work with city councils and citizens' groups to clean up parks, make transportation more accessible, and promote prevention through family resource centres. Launched in 1984 in Canada, the concept was adopted by the World Health Organization in 1986. There are now more than 3,000 municipalities around the world committed to working on healthy communities issues.

When most people think of health, they think of health care. Some significant research in the past 20 years has forced us to re-think our understanding of health. We have learned that health has more to do with the control people have over their own lives. As well, we have learned that "determinates of health" have almost nothing to do with health care.[19] On the other hand, income, poverty, social support, and the environment all significantly affect our health. This profound insight lends further credence to the idea of inclusion, since citizens who are vulnerable experience greater health-related problems than does the general public. Unfortunately, few Healthy Communities projects see this as part of their mandate. There is tremendous potential here for new partnerships with an expanded social movement.

The *poverty-reduction movement* has been growing across Canada. Led primarily by the Vital Communities initiative, this movement has engaged a diverse group of stakeholders. Vital Communities understood in 2000 that poverty reduction is not possible when governments are the only player. Using a multi-sector approach, Vital Communities demonstrate the power of community collaborations to begin to address and resolve complex social issues. Tamarack: An Institute of Community Engagement, has played a major role in leading the Vital Communities initiative. Not surprisingly, Tamarack emphasizes "community" as the conduit for meaningful action on poverty reduction. This community emphasis does not reduce the importance of policy and government support, but stresses that policy should be the servant of community.[20]

A few months ago, we experienced a night to remember as we watched the *senior citizens movement* in full swing. The Raging Grannies, activist women in their 60s, 70s, and 80s, were the after-dinner entertainment at a seminar we were attending. The Raging Grannies are great representatives for the seniors' movement. They challenge the myth that older people are passive or docile. At the heart of their humour and sarcasm is their belief in people and community. They are direct, irreverent, and provocative.[21] The movement representing senior citizens has been gaining momentum in Canada and elsewhere.[22] Many senior citizens are realizing that most formal supports being offered run the risk of removing them from community. Although issues such as pensions and drug plans have dominated their concerns, the role of community and hospitality is increasingly seen as vital to their futures. "Aging in place" is a concept and slogan that is gaining momentum. Our work with the York Region Alternative Community Living program in Ontario shows that many older people want to stay in their chosen homes. This means that supports should be available wherever people live.

As the baby boomers reach retirement age, it is expected that the demands for genuine community options and individualized support will grow. As we know from demographics, the boomers make up a significant and growing percentage of the population and therefore will be able to wield considerable influence and demand more appropriate services.[23] Many boomers see themselves as active, healthy citizens with many years remaining to contribute to their communities. Seniors' movements are working to create more humane services before they find themselves too old and fragile to be able to solve these problems. Older adults are raising many questions about feeling unproductive and how to maintain community in the face of many media and more subtle messages that it is time to withdraw from community life. The seniors' movement has the potential to re-establish elderly people into our communities in

Pathways to Inclusion

ways that the wisdom of aging can be honoured, supported, and welcomed.

The *disability movement* has identified community presence and participation as central values.[24] In particular, three sub-movements within the disability movement have contributed significantly to rediscovering community. First, the Community Living movement for persons with developmental disabilities was influenced by normalization in the 1970s and became a leader in training and education related to citizenship and community. A few New Story initiatives came from innovative community living associations. Second, the Independent Living movement, represented by the Canadian Association for Independent Living Centres and its 30 local centres, has focused primarily on helping persons to increase their rights and personal control. Although citizenship and community participation have been core movement values for some time, in recent years community development has played a more central role in the goals and activities of the Independent Living Resource Centres, some of which we studied. Third, the mental health movement has also begun to address issues related to community building. This movement has long been challenging hospitalization and the "revolving door," but only recently has the problem of community institutionalization come to light. The Canadian Mental Health Association Framework for Support project and its slogan, "Community is the answer," reflect the slow but steady progress toward understanding and implementing a community vision in the mental health field. The recovery movement in community mental health sees "community" as an essential part of participation and recovery.

The anti-globalization, healthy communities, seniors, and disability movements may be considered new social movements. Old, traditional social movements focused only on social and economic issues, whereas new social movements also focus on community, citizenship, quality of life, and participation. Some scholars say that new social movements create the foundation for social change in contemporary society.[25] However, despite progress within each of these powerful social movements, our experience is that they seldom work together for change. All of these separate movements are recognizing community as a symbol for interdependence, connections, relationships, and democracy. We can only speculate that the potential for social change would be much greater if the different movements

Pathways to Inclusion

found ways to increase their collaboration. While each move-ment certainly has its own unique set of priorities, it is also clear that there are some common values and principles across all the movements.[26] It is in this context that we call for soli-darity within and across movements in terms of rediscovering that the essence of our humanity lies in community and hospi-tality. In community and civic engagement we will ensure that all citizens experience true citizenship.

Thinking and Acting Like a Social Movement

The leaders of several New Story organizations and initiatives speak eloquently about being part of a social movement. These leaders' commitment to change is anchored in community and social movements, not in human service systems. This in itself is a significant paradigm shift.

Al Etmanski and Vicki Cammack from PLAN (Planned Lifetime Advocacy Networks) in British Columbia describe their work in social movement terms. PLAN is a family-driven orga-nization that builds relationships with people with disabilities and supports families to build a good life in the commu-nity. Etmanski and Cammack have a larger vision, which they describe as the need to embed a community and citizenship perspective into all structures and institutions in our society. They also believe this vision needs to include changing cultural consciousness from "needs and ability" to "contribution and participation." This "big picture thinking" combined with on-the-ground work has made it possible for PLAN to become widely influential across Canada.[27]

Thinking and acting like a social movement means having a vision about how change occurs, working across traditional boundaries with other organizations and groups, and having a mechanism to identify and involve constituents in meaningful ways. Perhaps most important, it means doing genuine commu-nity work that involves collaboration among key stakeholders in a community.[28] Many of the New Story initiatives are about people thinking like a social movement and collaborating with others for maximum community impact.

Notes

1. Starhawk (1996), p. 471.
2. For an excellent book on community and hospitality, see Gilchrist (2004). Also see Lord (2000).
3. Schwartz (1997). Also see Schwartz (1992).
4. Valentine (1994).
5. See Valentine (2001); Heath et al. (2004). See also Porter (2004); and Biklen (2000).
6. McKnight (1995); Saul (1995); Schwartz (1997); Kingwell (2000); Condeluci (1991).
7. For the most comprehensive summary of Jane Addams' writings, see Elshtain (2002).
8. Although Jean Vanier has written several significant books, his 1998 book is probably the one that speaks most clearly to the issues raised in this book; see Vanier (1998).
9. John McKnight is well known as a speaker and has written a number of short papers about community; many of these are compiled in McKnight (1995). Also see O'Connoll (1990); and Kretzmann and Green (1998).
10. Pearpoint (1991).
11. Schwartz (1997), p. 68.
12. Kingwell (2000), p. 5.
13. Lord (2006).
14. To understand the diverse ways that Canadians are experiencing community, see Berlin (1997).
15. McKnight and Block (2010).
16. Carroll and Little (2001).
17. For ideas on youth and activism, see Pancer and Pratt (1999).
18. Higgins (1992).
19. National Forum on Health (1998).
20. Gamble (2010).
21. Narushim (2004).
22. Cheal (2003). Also see Cusak and Thompson (1998).
23. Foot with Staffman (2000).
24. Stienstra and Wight-Felske (2003).
25. Habermas (1981). Also see Rifkin (2000).
26. For ideas on cross movements, see Carroll and Ratner (2001).
27. Cammack and Etmanski (2006).
28. For further analysis, Building Movement Project <www.buildingmovement.org>

5

Shifting Power

To Individuals, Families, and Communities

Nothing about me without me.
South African proverb[1]

The sadness was pervasive. A small group of men and women with physical and mental disabilities were sharing their stories. One by one, truth was revealed. All the participants had experienced abuse, segregation, or sterilization. Citizens who have had this "power-over" experience in human services often live with anger or fear. Finally, one woman in her early forties expressed what everybody knew: "You feel powerless, but you never give up hope," she said quietly. It is testimony to the power of the human spirit that more people have not given up hope.

Exploring the concept of power is important because lack of power and control is so pervasive among many citizens. Although we all know what it means to be powerless in certain situations, we have found that many people who have power over others have little understanding of power. When we are involved in training sessions with managers and others who work in community support services, one of the questions we ask is, "Do you feel that you effectively use your power?" It is not uncommon for people to resist answering this question by saying something like, "Power is not the right word" or "It's not really about power." We believe that leaders in service systems often resist discussing power, in part because they are comfortable with the status quo that gives professionals power over people. James Hillman reminds us that "power stands behind our fear of loss and desire for control."[2] Equally concerning is the reality that many people at the receiving end of "power over" have had few opportunities to learn about the meaning of power and how to access power.

Re-shaping Power into a Usable Resource

In our culture, power is usually equated with domination by some kind of authority. Kenneth Boulding expresses it most clearly when he writes, "There is a certain tendency among humans to identify power with the capacity for victory, that is, overcoming some other person, will, or institution."[3] When power is described in this "power-over" way, certain assumptions often follow. For example, service systems generally assume they have power and control, and citizens and their allies assume they have little. Such a "power-over" mindset keeps everyone from changing, since in practice it creates an atmosphere of hegemony — domination by one group over language, policy, and practice.

We concur with Michel Foucault, who says that power is always there and no one is ever outside it.[4] Although "power over" is the most common interpretation of power, "power from within" and "power with" are other interpretations.[5] The experience of New Story initiatives shows that the concept of power can be re-shaped into a valuable resource. A power-from-within definition recognizes that everyone has power inside themselves that can be nurtured. Experience with several initiatives shows that as people become aware of their own strengths and power, this insight can be used as a valuable resource. In projects such as Spark of Brilliance in Guelph, Ontario, the focus on personal development and personal choice provides the context for people to gain knowledge, insight, and self-awareness. This kind of process helps people develop internal power that is one part of personal empowerment.

In this sense, a shift in power begins to happen as more awareness is acquired by people themselves. The challenge faced by many initiatives, however, is how best to shift power and resources to the person and significant others in their lives. When people in initiatives talk about shifting power, they are not just talking about giving the same kind of unsettling power previously given to professionals and transferring it to individuals. Shifting power more accurately reflects a commitment to self-determination and the belief that individuals and families can best define their own needs. The voice and choice of the people they work with is honoured at all initiatives. Shifting power and control away from professionals also recognizes that the New Story goal of community support is citizenship and participation. People and their personal networks must have the power to dream, to set goals, and to choose what is of value to them.

One recent framework defines power as having the opportunity to access resources that satisfy basic human needs, participate according to one's interests, and experience competence.[6] This interpretation of power reinforces the concept that those who shift power to citizens must also create positive circumstances for participation and the expression of power from within. This also implies that communities need to work on changing external conditions that will give people access to a wide range of valued community resources, not simply access to services designed specifically for people who are devalued.

This process of exploring power makes New Story approaches different from traditional approaches. The new assumption is that others in the community must learn to share power. The role of professionals and others shifts away from being experts to facilitators and resource persons. Part of being facilitators and shifting power is helping people learn to access valued resources.[7] Valued resources are regular community resources that are typically accessed by all citizens. Restaurants,

Pathways to Inclusion

the library, public transportation, sports leagues, parks, and hairdressers are called "valued resources" because they are open to the general public. And there are a multitude of them. Non-profit service organizations that offer sheltered employment, recreation, or housing for a particular group of people with disabilities are closed to the public. Government departments such as Community and Social Services that serve people with disabilities or people on welfare are also limited in terms of who they serve. Services are not considered to be as valued if they are closed to the public, tend to be controlled by professionals, have narrow criteria for attendance, or often have waiting lists.

Several New Story initiatives help people to access valued community resources. They begin by creating community options based on a person's strength and by intentionally linking people with citizens with similar interests. For example, people with an interest in art are connected with other artists. Participation itself becomes part of the process of shifting power.

The Powers of the Weak

In 1980, an important but little-known book called *Powers of the Weak* was published.[8] Written by Elizabeth Janeway, this social history explores power from the perspective of women and relationships. In her analysis, Janeway contributes much to our understanding of power and vulnerability. She describes several ways that oppressed groups can exercise power. Perhaps the most important power held by "the weak" is the refusal to accept the definition of oneself put forward by the powerful. The power of people "to disbelieve," as Janeway calls it, is common among New Story initiatives.

An early experience with one of our daughters gave us insight into this phenomenon. When we adopted our daughter Karen, she was three and a half years old. She was not yet walking or talking, the result, in part, of her Down syndrome but also of the lack of stimulation in early life. Her favourite place in those early days was the couch, curled up, with her head tilted and her tongue hanging out. As cute as she was in that position, we encouraged our other two children to "not let her blob," but to involve her in their play. At first Karen resisted any attempts to engage her or to get her off the couch. We sometimes labelled her "stubborn," but became aware that her resistance was a way of exerting her power. As we got to know her and strengthened our relationship with her, Karen began to welcome invitations to move off the couch and play. She had needed to trust us, to believe that we were acting on her behalf, before she would participate. She then began to use her power to influence the kind of play that took place.

We learned from Karen and many other people that power is not always what it seems. In the initiatives, we saw that people assert personal power in a variety of ways, sometimes in ways that society considers inappropriate. For example, staff in some initiatives note how power is sometimes expressed by challenging behaviours, particularly by people with dementia and significant disabilities. Rather than simply developing strategies to discourage bad behaviour, the question is asked, "What is this person trying to communicate with this behaviour?" Approaches such as gentle teaching and positive communication are widely used because they respect the person, see his or her strengths as a resource, and recognize that people have different ways of expressing "power from within."[9]

Perhaps the most dramatic illustration of "powers of the weak" comes from studies that have supported the idea of people leaving institutions. In the 1980s, we were involved in documenting the closure of the Tranquille Institution in British Columbia. As each person was being supported to leave the institution, a person-centered plan with goals and expectations was developed with the individual, the family, and significant others, such as care providers from the institution and community. As people settled in the community, an astonishing insight emerged. People's capacities had been consistently under-estimated. Almost immediately upon entry into the community, their abilities, initiative, and skills were evident. Similarly, a Manitoba deinstitutionalization project, In the Company of Friends, found dramatic changes for participants. These included improved material well-being, self-determination, participation in the community, friendships, and social interactions.[10] Studies of New Story initiatives extend Janeway's notion that people can express power by their refusal to accept the definition of themselves put forward by the powerful. These studies show that latent "power from within" exists in many people and that we have much to learn about how to nurture

Vulnerability and Personal Power

We meet people within New Story initiatives that are very thoughtful about personal power and control. The first time we met Matt Percy, we were struck by the calm and deliberate focus of this disability advocate. Now a user of the Ontario Direct Funding Project in Toronto, Percy describes how he used power, "I felt powerless for years after becoming paralyzed due to a diving accident, but in retrospect, I realized that I was learning to use my power even when bedridden for months." Percy explains that he would tell nurses and others what he wanted, whether it was the way he wished to be fed or how he wanted his letters to be written. As he moved from the rehabilitation hospital to the community, Percy utilized his power by hiring personal assistants of his choice, teaching art lessons to children in his neighbourhood, and working with other people with disabilities to create a much needed peer support group. More recently, he has married and had a child. Recent biographies written by people with disabilities or chronic conditions reinforce Percy's experience that citizens have powers, and part of facing vulnerability is being aware of those powers and how to use them. Although "being vulnerable" can be frightening, especially for people who have an acquired injury or chronic condition, Percy's story illustrates that starting in small ways can build confidence and enhance "power-within."

Note: There are several biographies that give insight into this process of gaining or regaining personal power. See, as examples, B. Sherr Klein, *Slow Dance: A Story of Stroke, Love and Disability* (Toronto, ON: Knopf Canada, 1997); R. Murphy, *The Body Silent* (New York, NY: W.W. Norton, 1990); D. Williams, *Nobody Nowhere: The Extraordinary Autobiography of an Autistic* (New York, NY: Random House, 1992); K. Church, *Forbidden Narratives: Critical Autobiography as Social Science* (Luxembourg: Gorden and Breach Publishers, 1997).

this human capacity. Furthermore, we can add that when conditions are right, the capacity of people to redefine themselves is far greater than we thought possible.

No Quick Fixes: The Challenging Journey of Personal Empowerment

The process by which families and organizations shift power and control to people they are supporting is a slow one with no easy answers. There are six lessons from New Story initiatives and from persons who have experienced the journey of empowerment.

First, *it is important that powerlessness be understood and that people realize they have more power than they think they do.* We have found that too often in traditional approaches the word *empowerment* is a catch-all phrase for anything that is done to make the "client" feel better. At the same time, it is not unusual for people's powerlessness to be denied, labelled, or dismissed. "Powerlessness is real and must be faced," says one facilitator who spends a lot of time with people who are recovering from mental health problems, such as severe depression or schizophrenia. People in the initiatives have learned that people may experience what Michael Lerner calls "surplus powerlessness."[11] This refers to the set of feelings that make people think of themselves as being even more powerless than they actually are. This in turn leads people to act in ways that reinforce their powerlessness and makes it difficult for them to use their internal power in effective ways.

It is important to create a safe place for people to express their feelings, doubts, fears, and hopes, despite their feelings of powerlessness. At both the Ontario Peer Development Initiative and the Independent Living Resource Centres, peers engage each other in dialogue. It is there that people begin to have an awareness and understanding of surplus powerlessness. What helps them at this point is deep listening and respect, as well as a sense that there is very little power imbalance with the people who are assisting them. It is not another expert telling them what to do. This process can impact both sides. As Kathryn Church so aptly puts it, when citizens "enter into empowerment relationships or learning dialogues with vulnera-

Pathways to Inclusion

Elements of the Personal Empowerment Process

Experiencing Powerlessness	Gaining Awareness	Learning New Roles	Initiating/ Participating	Contributing
Social isolation	Acting on anger	Connecting with others	Joining groups	Being a role model
Service dependency	Responding to information	Linking with resources	Speaking out	Having influence
Limited choice	Responding to new contexts	Expanding choices/ opportunities	Expanding participatory competence	Increasing self-efficacy

Source: J. Lord and P. Hutchison, "The Process of Empowerment: Implications for Theory and Practice," *Canadian Journal of Community Mental Health*, 12, 1 (1993). Reprinted with permission of CJCMH/ RCSMC.

ble people ... we will be confronted with our own surplus powerlessness as well as theirs."[12]

Second, *empowerment is a process.* Our research over many years reiterates that empowerment is indeed a process, as illustrated in the headings of the "Elements of the Personal Empowerment Process" table, which indicates how people gradually increase their participation and contribution. But often we hear the phrase "she's empowered," referring to empowerment as an outcome. While it could be argued that empowerment is also an outcome, we have not found this to be the most useful focus. The experience of the initiatives is that these stages of empowerment are not linear. Participation, for example, may come earlier or much later in the process. For some people, it is engagement that creates awareness.

The third lesson is that *empowerment is deeply embedded in relationships.* As we explore power in different contexts, we find that relationships are the thread holding the process of empowerment together.[13] People usually gain awareness because other people who have had similar experiences reflect with them or challenge them. Learning new roles is also embedded in relationships. People connect with others, link with resources, and try out different ways of being. Participation means being engaged in the little things in our lives, but also being involved in the wider community. A facilitator with the Options Project in Toronto describes the relationship paradox: "As people gain more power and control, they usually have more people in their lives." It is in relationships that people can test their sense of internal power, build social networks, and expand their personal capacity.

Fourth, *participation, choice, and control are intricately linked.* We hear many stories in the initiatives about participation. Martha Klassel's story reflects the way in which participation encompasses many levels of involvement. After living at home for 33 years, Klassel moved out into a small home for people with disabilities. She suddenly found herself in a situation with expanded opportunity for participation. "My control over even minor things felt like a breathtaking freedom," explained Klassel, "especially in comparison to the social isolation and lack of independence I had been experiencing at home." After years of assuming she could not do anything, Klassel began to discover otherwise. "Suddenly I had control over lots of little things, like getting my own bank account. When I got my electric wheelchair, I finally got to go off to the shopping mall. It's when you are brought up to think you can't do it, it's hard to convince yourself you can and then to take the time." Klassel began to take advantage of the options in front of her, including doing the payroll for the agency that ran her house. "For the first time, I was doing things that my family didn't know about," Klassel said proudly. "All of these involvements around my living setting expanded my feelings of confidence and control."

Although these experiences in this small group setting were important along her journey, within two years Klassel's life changed again when she applied for and was accepted into the Ontario Direct Funding Project. The individualized funding she received each month allowed her to move into her own apartment, hire her own attendants, and direct the attendants to address her disability support needs. She now does volunteer work with two community groups and has a part-time job doing payroll for a local agency. Klassel's story reminds us that self-determination, which many people take for granted, is only possible when opportunities and conditions allow for genuine choice and participation. These opportunities and conditions need to exist in the community as well as in the organizations that provide support.

The fifth lesson is that *facilitating empowerment requires a coupling of internal motivation of the person with the provision of resources and supports.* This implies that people can increase their power and control when the proper supports are available and when they are personally motivated to utilize those resources. This insight has been evident in many studies on empowerment.[14] On the surface, this finding makes sense: internal power and external resources coming together in some coherent fashion. Yet there is a shadow to this finding that is disturbing. When we first started presenting this theme from empowerment studies in the early 1990s, we noticed that some used this knowledge about the role of internal motivation as an excuse or justification for why certain people they worked with were unmotivated or "stuck." Saying someone is not motivated can easily become victim blaming. We found almost no victim blaming within New Story initiatives but rather sustained attempts to find the right support, at the right time, designed by and for a particular person. As one parent with the Foundations Project in Kitchener said, "We were amazed that the staff were so patient and kept trying and trying to find things that would work with our son." Furthermore, when people are "stuck," we need to recognize that there may be a variety of reasons, including their personal history, systemic barriers, and stigma. Addressing different barriers to self-determination is very different than blaming the victim.

And finally, the sixth personal empowerment lesson is *shifting power demands a transformation in the way professionals, staff, and volunteers relate to people.* In research on the empowerment process, participants identify effective supports as those that are highly individualized and interactive, and that nurture personal control. Similarly, staff in New Story initiatives note they are primarily facilitative and collaborative. For staff coming from more traditional settings, this new way of working can cause a "role strain." The Framework for Support Project, sponsored by the Canadian Mental Health Association, identifies knowledge of individuals and families based on real life experience as a principle for collaboration. We saw this in many situations: staff listening to people and following their directions; staff working with a person's support network and helping the person build relationships; staff spending a lot of time with a person and gently reminding the person that his or her voice and choices matter. This lesson, as well as the others, is not easily understood or attained. Leaders in the initiatives agree it is a long, slow process but, in the end, worthy of sustained effort.

Empowerment: A Personal, Community, and Political Affair

We learned from New Story initiatives that using a "power-with" framework that focuses on individual empowerment is not enough. Understanding the way out of powerlessness requires a commitment to the person, as well as an understanding of the wider community and socio-economic conditions. Empowerment is a complex process that must consider the broad context of people's lives and their communities. This reminds us of Annie Proulx's enchanting novel, *The Shipping News*, where quotations about knots are used as a metaphor throughout the story.[15] Tying and untying knots is a complex process that requires practical skill and knowledge. To nurture personal and community power, there are many knots to understand.

As we have seen, most initiatives focus quite effectively on personal empowerment. This means that goals and resources emphasize creating a framework for people to gradually gain more power and participation in their lives. However, facilitators in initiatives have found that as they work on a person's plan and goals, the involvement of family, community organizations, and the wider community is also needed to make personal empowerment possible. This discovery is supported by other research that shows that the concept of personal empowerment has no meaning without reference to others and the environment.[16] Community is also the context for participation and empowerment. Some initiatives, therefore, intentionally work on empowering their communities to become more engaged and willing to embrace *all* people. As explored earlier, Project Friendship in Prince George has worked with the wider community for the past 10 years. With a steering committee made up of community leaders, Project Friendship connects with a wide range of community associations, supporting them to be welcoming of people with disabilities.

Pathways to Inclusion

It is challenging to facilitate and assess community empowerment because communities are made up of many different stakeholders, including municipal government, industry, education, and human services. Also, communities themselves are made up of diverse members who all have different goals and aspirations. Can we say that Project Friendship contributed to community empowerment in Prince George because more programs are now welcoming *all* people to their organizations? We suspect that this might be one measure of community empowerment, because organizations can be seen as the mediating structure between personal and community empowerment. However, other elements, such as community partnerships and citizen participation, also need to be considered when looking at community empowerment.[17] More recently, *community capacity* is another phrase that has been used to describe how communities can grow and increase the involvement of citizens and resources for the common good.

Regardless, people feel their communities are responsive when they provide resources for small innovative initiatives,

---

Research and Empowerment

Research on empowerment and related community issues has been influenced by new paradigm thinking. Julian Rappaport, one of the early empowerment researchers, wrote in the mid-1990s about the importance of narrative theory to better attend to the voices of people who are often ignored in research. Rappaport argues that a definition of *empowerment* that asserts personal stories and communal narratives can benefit research and practice.

Participatory Action Research (PAR) was used as the main methodology in some of the New Story initiatives. PAR is an empowerment-oriented approach because it invites research participants to be stakeholders in all aspects of the research process. Research participants are seen as significant contributors rather

Research and Empowerment (continued)

than subjects. Researchers who work with PAR are committed to increasing the power and voice of marginalized groups in research and evaluation.

The principles guiding PAR are a good fit with shifting power in the New Story. Some of the principles include the following:

- Nothing about us without us
- Researchers share power with participants
- Collaboration among all stakeholders
- Clear and frequent communication
- Strong relationships ensure that trust is built
- Sharing meaningful information contributes to project improvements
- Leaders stay focused on effective research methodologies
- Effective partnerships help the process build capacity

Sources: J. Rappaport, Empowerment Meets Narrative: Listening to Stories and Creating Settings, *American Journal of Community Psychology*, 23, 5 (1995): pp. 795–807. Also see J. Rappaport and E. Seidman, *Handbook of Community Psychology* (New York, NY: Springer, 2000). For a detailed description of PAR, see P. Park, M. Brydon-Miller, B. Hall, and T. Jackson, *Voices of Change: Participatory Research in the United States and Canada* (Westport, CT: Greenwood Publishing Group, 1993). See also Nelson, Lord, and Ochocka (2001); and G. Nelson, J. Ochocka, K. Griffin, and J. Lord, "Nothing About Me Without Me": Participatory Action Research With Self Help/Mutual Aid, *American Journal of Community Psychology*, 26, 6 (1998): pp. 881–912.

demonstrate leadership, and intentionally support political and cultural activities that enhance cohesion. Recent research is showing that significant problems in communities are more likely to be solved when there is broad collaboration across various sectors in the community.[18] Several initiatives expanded their impact through such collaboration. It is clear that the New Story must include both personal and community empowerment.

In this regard, leaders find that the support of political structures and civil society are critical to the empowerment of individuals and communities. If public buildings are not made more fully accessible to citizens in wheelchairs, people will continue to be disempowered and denied access to civil society functions. If municipalities continue to support urban sprawl, more and more citizens will depend on the automobile for transportation, and those who can't drive will be isolated. If senior citizens have limited access to homecare when they need it most, the institutionalization of elderly Canadians will continue to rise. If most employers believe citizens with disabilities cannot contribute to the workplace, despite evidence to the contrary, more than 70% of Canadians with disabilities will continue to be unemployed.

While few groups we studied are working directly on changing socio-economic conditions, many are involved with others in coalitions to empower and build the capacity of their communities. These on-the-ground efforts of the initiatives often lead to insights that are useful for broader coalitions. For example, many Independent Living Resource Centres across Canada have been engaged in Navigating the Waters, a national employment project where facilitators work directly with people who are interested in finding stable and gratifying employment. Training, mentoring, and subsidies to employers have been used to promote empowerment. Despite these efforts, a low percentage of people have found permanent employment. Centres recognize this dilemma, and in collaboration with other groups, are calling for a national labour strategy for people with disabilities.

Putting the "Power Shift" into Personal Action

In some areas of professional and social life, there is great resistance to shifting decision making to citizens who are vulnerable due to age, disability, or chronic conditions. Sometimes this resistance involves fear of giving up control.[19] But at times, the resistance is a kind of hesitation about how to experience the "other" person. We had some of these same hesitations ourselves many years ago when we were engaged in a project designed to facilitate citizen participation in community mental health. As we listened to stories about how to involve users of services in the governance of those services, we ran headlong into a huge amount of anger and frustration on the part of mental health consumers/survivors. Even though we felt that we were allies of these people, this experience challenged some of our assumptions and exposed our hesitation. In retrospect, we realized that it challenged us to become vulnerable, and to expose more of who we were and what we felt. From that experience and others, we have tried to become what Ruth Behar calls "vulnerable observers."[20] We have learned that putting the "power shift" into action begins with awareness of our own power and powerlessness.

Exploring one's personal vulnerability is not an easy process. When staff and volunteers in New Story initiatives fully engage with the empowerment process and become open to learning about vulnerability, they often initially experience some disconnection from their own training and experience. Boundaries may seem blurred and questions may surface. How do I have encounters with people without appearing too professional or controlling? How do I deal with my own feelings and emotions related to the suffering I see? How do I ensure that my power relationship with the other person stays true to "power with"? Answers to these questions are seldom definitive, but tend to form an ongoing tapestry of understanding. However, one thing is clear: people who have faced their own wounds and vulnerabilities are more able to see and be comfortable with the wounds in another person.

Engaging with their own personal vulnerability is one way people in the initiatives get to know people they are supporting. This engagement reduces the polarization that exists between people who have power and those who do not. People tell us they come to realize that these relationships should never be about "us" and "them." We like to think of those who are committed to the liberation of all citizens as allies in the journey of empowerment. Once people acknowledge and become concerned about their own potential to be in positions of power or to use power inappropriately, they can become compassionate and vulnerable co-participants. This struggle to be aware of one's own vulnerability, while supporting others in their empowerment journey, is an important feature of the New Story.

Another way of putting power into action relates to language. We find that leaders are comfortable using the language

Pathways to Inclusion

of power. In fact, *empowerment* has been such a buzz word in human services that some initiatives no longer use it. But all initiatives have principles related to "shifting power," "taking direction from the person," or "nurturing people's choices and capacities." Some initiatives put their principles on the wall during their meetings and spend a lot of time negotiating the meaning of their words. There can be dilemmas associated with these negotiated meanings, such as being unclear about how to describe power relationships. This is particularly challenging in initiatives that are driven by families but that focus on the person. Facilitators from some initiatives are very aware of the subtleties of the language around power. Negotiating meanings of the word *power* also happens when working with the community. The Halifax Metro Independent Living Resource Centre, for example, spent many hours working with a community coalition educating and negotiating the meaning of *consumer control* and *independent living*.

As people act on the language and meaning of "shifting power," there is often an excitement about the possibility of change. For leaders and their allies, values and principles related to "shifting power" seem refreshing and innovative. Issues and struggles are re-framed, and power itself is seen in a new light. For people who have had few relationships and limited access to regular resources in society, it may take time to trust a process or program that claims to be offering genuine choice and control. Once there is trust, broad support for initiatives that build capacity often follows. People begin to have clarity and belief in their voice and their power.[21] The masks we all wear when "power over" is dominant begin to fall away. As we encounter new sides of power and as we recognize the need to shift power, we create the possibility for understanding and experiencing compassion.

Notes

1. This well-known South African proverb was found in Leff et al. (1997).
2. Hillman (1995), p. 2.
3. . Boulding (1989), p. 6.
4. Foucault (1965).
5. Hooks (1984). Also see Starhawk (1987).
6. Prilleltensky, Nelson, and Peirson (2001).

7. Lord and Hutchison (1993). Also see Nelson, Lord, and Ochocka (2001).
8. Janeway (1980).
9. See, for example, Lovett (1996); McGee and Menolascino (1991).
10. To review these studies, see Lord and Hearn (1997). Also see Hofsted (1996).
11. Lerner (1986).
12. Church (1995), pp. 6–7.
13. Church (1995).
14. For examples, see Keiffer (1984); Prilleltensky, Nelson, and Peirson (2001); Charleton (2000).
15. Proulx (1993).
16. McCubbin (2001).
17. There is a rich literature on community empowerment. See Labonte (1994); Laverack and Wallerstein (2001).
18. The Vibrant Communities Project has worked in several Canadian cities using an inter-sectoral approach to building community capacity. For an analysis of research and stories on community change, see the website of the Caledon Institute of Social Policy: <www.caledoninst.org>.
19. James Hillman discusses this fear of giving up control extensively in his book, *Kinds of Power* (1995).
20. Behar (1996).
21. For books that give voice to people with disabilities, see LPD consultants for the brown shoes series, such as Leavitt and Bender (2004).

6

Compassion and Purpose

Leaving Victimhood Behind

When we act out of compassion, we need to understand and see deeply. If understanding is not present, our action will not be authentic.

Thich Nhat Hahn[1]

Many people we meet in New Story initiatives indicate that they previously felt like a victim when they were part of traditional support systems. Sometimes people experience resentment because of how their impairment limits their participation. Other times family members may be frustrated because of the limited support their loved one receives. In many cases, people blame themselves for their situation. Many people are also angry because services they are using for support are less than desirable. In other cases, people indicate concern because they have been waiting for years for community support. In all of these situations, it is easy to feel like a victim.[2]

In addition to individuals and families sometimes feeling like victims, workers in traditional services also indicate that they feel like victims. Some research shows that workers can easily become discouraged and disempowered due to isolation, bureaucracy, and lack of resources. Much has been written about how caregiving and working in traditional services can produce "burnout" and institutionalization of the staff.[3] Support service work can feel heavy, especially when our helping seems futile. When workers and families feel like victims they are likely to become frustrated and lack compassion.

Values such as human rights, social justice, empowerment, and hospitality have been proposed as ways to give us the wisdom to pursue a New Story path, leading to a better life for citizens who require support for social inclusion to be a reality. In order for these values to work, leaders have discovered the need to be compassionate and intentional about how they implement the values.[4] We have much to learn from New Story approaches about the problem of being a victim and how compassion can be a gateway to awareness.

The Futility of Being a Victim

In our work over the years, many people have told us they sometimes feel excluded and victimized. Traditional approaches to supporting people with vulnerabilities create a second layer of victimization over people who already have social barriers to face through no fault of their own. The traditional response to victims is to blame them for being discouraged and unable to crawl out of their sub-standard lifestyle. Their pained language is often interpreted as "poor me" complaints meant to elicit sympathy.

We now understand that when people are treated in less than human ways, for example by being shunted from home to home, this can be quite traumatic. Eventually people feel as if they no longer have an identity as a human being. Over time and with the repeated experience of compliance, this emerges as a self-truth. Often the destruction of dignity is then complete, with such people believing they have little value as human beings. To challenge people by changing any aspect of their living arrangement can initially be frightening. We now know that people, therefore, live like "victims" as a means of self-protection. Breaking this terrible cycle is a challenge to the New Story approach.

People who have been victimized on many levels for long periods of time have difficulty with healthy relationships.[5] When institutionalized, for example, people often struggle with attachment and connections with others. Unfortunately, in traditional approaches with traditional interpretations of victims' behaviour, service providers often have sympathy, not compassion. Sympathy is a lofty and distant position that is not helpful to victims because it focuses on their deficits. Sympathy usually encourages a charity-like "helping" response or a patronizing attitude. Some people comment that this so-called "helping" makes them dependent because it usually takes place when people lack power and control. Some participants describe this process as a vicious cycle of dependency and victimhood.

Jean Vanier believes that one danger with helping is that it can dominate the person being helped.[6] This is because it is not unusual for a division to exist between the individual and the helper. This separateness is part of the reason why there is so much stress between "us," the helpers, and "them" the people who are vulnerable. This separateness also reinforces victimhood because it encourages passivity and because the person already has limited energy or confidence to be engaged. This passivity and separateness is why people who are vulnerable are so dependent on staff and caregivers in traditional approaches. In this way, being a victim leads to "learned helplessness."[7] Another outcome of people being seen as victims is that staff accept the status quo, even if it is no longer helpful. Neither of these outcomes leads to new paradigm values or opportunities.

In a traditional approach, both workers and individuals tend to blame others for unhappy outcomes, rather than focusing on ways to change their situation. This tendency can reinforce victimhood and inhibit change toward the New Story. On the other hand, when people begin to use a social model, it reinforces that vulnerability is socially constructed.[8] As we have seen, this means being aware that social conditions affect people's experience and sense of reality. Although this construct is usually helpful, this focus on the external environment can lead people to an "if only" attitude. "If only that ... service would

Pathways to Inclusion

change, or group be more understanding, or government policy be introduced, my life would be so much better and I would be happier." This attitude may be unconsciously reinforcing the person's unhappiness and feeling like a victim. There is a certain amount of unpleasantness that comes from the experience of impairment or vulnerability, but many times, our reaction results in much greater suffering than is actually needed.[9] This is not to say that societal conditions do not need to change, but starting with our own attitudes contributes to reconstruction. So we need to start at home and ask ourselves, "Are we behaving like a victim or are we using New Story principles to begin the process of change?" This question applies to individuals, families, and facilitators.

In the Welcome Home Initiative in Kitchener, workers and volunteers have been challenged to provide support to people returning to the community from psychiatric institutions. Many people, after months or years of hospitalization layered upon their original illness or disability, have behaviours that are difficult for others to understand. Anxiety, irrational fears, depression, post-traumatic stress, and so forth may result in people avoiding eye contact, showing no interest in others, and having low self-esteem. Welcome Home staff and volunteers had to learn not to take such reactions personally and not to resort to power tactics. Welcome Home has a motto, "You can't change the behaviour, but you can be there with the person and be kind to the person." In a recent evaluation, one thing participants commented on was the non-judgmental approach of staff and volunteers, which evoked compassion rather than sympathy on the part of the staff.

As parents, we have sometimes heard, "It must be so hard to have a handicapped child." People may say this because they know it would be hard for them. But when parents hear this kind of comment often enough, it can be very easy for them to begin to feel "burdened." Families report to us they get this kind of comment or pitying look on a regular basis. Those who have learned compassion, rather than responding like a victim, usually respond to these well-meaning comments with humour, playfulness, or a disarming directness. Although some individuals and workers find it difficult to rise above victim behaviour, there are many who have changed their responses. Despite abuse, neglect, and segregation, many people are surprisingly forgiving, understanding, and compassionate. Some have been able to deepen their understanding of themselves through their struggles and become a more positive person. New Story initiatives serve as a gateway by enabling people to reflect on their wounds, become aware of their victim status, and understand the difference between compassion and sympathy.

Compassion as a Gateway to Awareness

New Story initiatives are based on compassion for oneself and for others, not on the traditional script of blaming. Although building a compassionate society is the long-term goal of many innovations, the word compassion itself is rarely mentioned. It is more the behaviours, language, and approaches to community support and change that point to compassion as a foundation.

The Dalai Lama, well-known Buddhist leader originally from Tibet, often speaks about the meaning of compassion. "Compassion can be roughly defined in terms of a state of mind that is nonviolent, nonharming, and nonaggressive," he says. "It is a mental attitude based on the wish for others to be free of their suffering and is associated with a sense of commitment, responsibility, and respect toward the other."[10] Compassion has a quality of gentleness that enables one to see the human side in the "other" person.

An important component of compassion is mindfulness. When we are mindful and "in the moment," we are not worrying or concerned about self. Compassion for oneself can deepen as we learn to be present with whatever we are doing. As we practise mindfulness, we learn to "let go" of concerns and attachments, such as self-pity. Many people report that mind–body practices, like yoga, meditation, or tai chi help their mindfulness and contribute to their self-acceptance and compassion for themselves.

The process of having compassion for oneself and others also involves making a commitment to being "open." Many wise people have emphasized this message, each in their own unique way. Morrie Schwartz, who was dying of ALS, spoke to his former student and friend, Mitch Albom, every Tuesday about life and dying. Schwartz said, "Only an open heart will allow you to float equally between everyone." Similarly, Edward de Bono stresses that during innovation, dominating ideas can be an obstacle. Alternatives like lateral thinking and openness to change enable people to see and act beyond the dominant idea.[11] We have found that compassionate people have an openness about them.

A shallow understanding of compassion can lead to attachment, sympathy, and dependency. Genuine compassion is based on the recognition of equality and commonality between fellow humans. Compassion reduces dependency by being clear about motivations, purpose, and responsibility. In the compassionate script we see in many New Story initiatives, there is a genuine sense of mutuality and connection among people in the person's life. People learn a great deal from each other because there is less separation of "staff" from so-called clients.[12] William Bennett, a literary critic, believes compassion "is a virtue that takes seriously the reality of other persons, their inner lives, their emotions, as well as their external circumstances ... compassion thus comes close to the very heart of moral awareness, to seeing in one's neighbour another self."[13] A compassionate response can soften people who have experienced bitterness, rejection, and anger in their past.

Genuine compassion is grounded in a focus on the other person, not on one's own self-interest. John Ralston Saul says we live in an era of self-interest, where individualism and the profit motive are often seen as acceptable values driving society. Ralston Saul warns that people who believe they know the "truth" might see compassion as a sign of weakness.[14] In the initiatives, we found staff and volunteers to be generally compassionate and committed to equality in relationships with the people they support.

Sharron Garrah, a former employee of an Independent Living Resource Centre, is now a user of the organization's services. Being a user has given her a new outlook on the role of staff. "Your focus definitely shifts from providing to receiving services," says Garrah, "and you become very conscious of others' styles of providing service." Because of her unique experience, Garrah is now able to see the importance of advocating for positive support relationships between staff and users. She believes that a person with a disability has a key role to play in shaping the relationship, and she thinks the Independent Living movement provides the framework for this to happen. "Independent Living is about creating a life for yourself," she says. "You determine what that is. It also means understanding your responsibilities and your right to make choices, and knowing you will be respected for those choices. We are just average people, living average lives, feeling our way through life."[15] It is much more challenging for staff to take a compassionate stance when they have not walked in the shoes of the person they are supporting.

As we talked to and observed people living at NABORS in Toronto, it felt as if the relationship between individuals and their personal assistants was a compassionate dance. Together they collaborate to ensure the dreams of the person are implemented. In some cases, we noted that the worker was invisible, standing behind the person, as the individual worked or played independently. At other times, the worker may be symbolically in front of the person, as options and alternatives are presented and supported. There are also times when the worker and the individual may work side by side, such as when cooking. The support relationship demands a delicate balance between listening to verbal and non-verbal communication as well as compassionate understanding. The support person acts as an extension of the person. The personal assistant is sensitive to how the person would do something if support were not needed and then does it that way. Personal assistants at NABORS describe their role as "helping the person to do what they want to do," another way of saying *they* support self-determination of participants.

We have personally found that quiet time, meditation, times in nature, and times with friends who are vulnerable have motivated us to think about what it means to be human and compassionate. We have come to realize that the basis of our humanness is our *connectedness*. Many people are in programs and services that are organized in ways that disconnect them from themselves, from nature, and from others. It is difficult to be compassionate about someone's situation if we feel disconnected from them. Our work has shown that participation in New Story approaches enables people to develop purpose, build connections, and gradually leave victimhood behind.

No Purpose without Compassion

An important part of New Story approaches is helping people develop purpose. When people have purpose, they feel good about themselves and can leave victimhood behind. In the ini-

Pathways to Inclusion

tiatives, the strategy of helping someone develop purpose is linked with compassion because agendas are set with the person, not for them. Facilitating the development of purpose is the opposite of compliance. It involves engaging the person in a relationship and then supporting personal choice and direction.

The power of purpose is becoming well recognized in social science and practice. Daniel Pink, in his new book, *Drive*, summarizes the research on what motivates people.[16] In addition to autonomy and mastery, purpose gives people meaning and is highly motivating. New Story leaders understand that purpose matters, and they encourage people to seek goals that are personally meaningful. The New Story work of "building good lives in welcoming communities" is grounded in words that keep us focused on a purposeful vision.

The recovery movement in community mental health has been instrumental in enabling people to focus on a sense of purpose and ways they want to be engaged. As a leader in that movement, Patricia Deegan has expressed so eloquently that the goal of recovery is not normalization, but the "goal is to become the unique, awesome, never-to-be repeated human being that we are all called to become."[17] Having a unique purpose contributes to this goal.

Developing a purpose that is nurtured by compassion begins with listening and creating opportunities for dialogue. Encouraging dialogue and reflection is very different than the needs assessments that often dominate traditional services. Needs assessments are usually about a search for deficits, problems, and particular issues that need to be addressed. Since it is so easy to judge, listening is an important vehicle for creating an open or responsive heart. In New Story approaches, time for conversing is about getting to know the person's gifts, strengths, dreams, and hopes. It is also about a mutual journey of change. Leaders and workers are driven not by programs, but are oriented to the individual, relationships, and the community. This makes listening an essential first step to understanding. Although finding time for dialogue is not easy in our rushed society, there are ways. These include honouring the person's choice in terms of where and when to meet and talk, finding time to walk together in the community and nature, and gathering friends together to think about a person's strengths, purpose, and direction.

Noticing Personal Reactions

John Lord — I remember the discomfort I felt as a graduate student when I had my first visit to an institution for people with "chronic mental illness." The barren wards, the dulled gazes from over-medicated patients, the lack of any meaningful activity, and the nursing staff huddled in their stations seemed like a page out of Goffman's classic book *Asylums*. At first, I was uncertain about the source of my own discomfort. Did I feel guilty? Did these people really belong here? Was I outraged at such deprived conditions? Was I judging? A fellow student further opened the window on my feelings. "You can see now why the institution will always be needed," she remarked in an offhand manner. I was stunned at how easily my fellow student was making assumptions from "what is," rather than from "what could be." I began to think about what it meant to be human. People were living in sub-human conditions. If we could be clear about our universal understanding of humanness, could we not create contexts whereby all citizens could live as human beings? Fortunately, my fellow student and I were able to have a genuine dialogue about her questions and mine. By exploring the nature of each of our assumptions, we were able to analyze reality and explore how people were suffering in that context. This kind of experience and reflection helped deepen my commitment to a better quality of life for everyone.

Reference: I. Goffman, *Asylums: Essays on the Social Situation of Mental Patients and Other Inmates* (Garden City, NY: Doubleday, 1961).

Pathways to Inclusion

Blair Grove, formerly a facilitator with Community Living St. Marys, Ontario, assists people in clarifying their purpose and goals. He talks about the context of listening. "I see my role primarily as a listener," says Grove. "I am trying to enable the person's voice to be heard, because so often people I support do not have any voice or control in their lives. I often just hang out and do things the person likes to do. I have found it critical to ask the right questions at the right time, questions that open the heart. When my heart is open and really listening, it can be pretty magical." Grove believes the role of professionals is to facilitate, not program. In doing this, they have to bring compassion into their role, because that is how we honour gifts and capacities.

The idea of the reflective practitioner is a practical one that is experienced in New Story approaches and will be explored in subsequent chapters. A reflective practitioner is mindful and principle-driven.[18] Reflective practitioners are sensitive to any tendency to devalue themselves or the person they are supporting. They work intentionally to bring compassion to themselves and others while reflecting on what they are constantly learning. With training in New Story values, people can notice when the values are being experienced or when they are being perverted. They encourage themselves and others to reflect on these things. This stance enables individuals to have greater opportunities to develop purpose.

Person-centered approaches are a central value that honours each person as a unique individual. People connected with New Story initiatives have demonstrated how developing purpose with individuals is intricately linked with a person-centered process. While many of us take the purposes in our lives for granted, fulfilling basic needs and survival are a dominating purpose for many citizens.[19] The experience of the initiatives is that many people do not readily identify dreams, goals, and purpose without encouragement and support to do so. As Blair Grove's story illustrates, this is a deeply personal process for both the person and the facilitator. This process is infused with compassion and creates opportunities for people to be able to develop a sense of direction and purpose.

Compassion and a sense of purpose are two ways that New Story values are expressed. As Jean Vanier has said, in some ways the work of discovering values is a rediscovery of the humanness of each person.[20] For individuals who are experiencing vulnerability, this means being connected with people who genuinely respect diversity and value individuality. Over time, many people begin to see that life can be different and that they can leave victimhood behind. This is not easy in systems where people may be treated as commodities, and where choice and purpose are not within reach. Engaged compassion is, therefore, important for the person and others in his or her network of support.

Engaged Compassion: Expressing the Values through Action

We have been impressed with the compassionate qualities of people involved with New Story approaches. We have come to think of their actions and initiatives as reflecting a stance of "engaged compassion."[21] Engaged compassion is about expressing values and vision through compassionate action. This concept is related to the phrase we used earlier, "walk the talk."

Engaged compassion challenges victimization. We have learned, however, that engaged compassion is not just unconditional acceptance. Rather, to be engaged and compassionate is to be sensitive and gentle when that is required, but to be a warrior, advocate, and organizer when something else is required. Robert Hill recalls the role that his friend Tracy Vesina played during his manic-depressive episodes. Living in the same apartment building, they had become very good friends. When Hill was having a difficult time, Vesina was supportive through the entire period, even making him dinner each night. After a few weeks, she made an agreement with him. She would prepare a decent lunch for him each day, but otherwise he was to look after himself. Hill said, "She looked after me as if I was alright, but she was cool, and I wasn't to be emotionally dependent. As a result, her friendship and support helped me to maintain a sense of dignity and control." It would have been easy for Vesina to feel sorry for Hill and for Hill to feel like a victim, as so often happens in relationships where one person is caregiving for another.

We have noticed that many people working in the initiatives are also demonstrating the New Story in their own personal daily lives. Many people we met have developed close relationships with citizens they support. Larry McNamara, who works in a supportive housing project, took Robert French with him on his vacation. French is non-verbal and spent years in an institution curled up on a mat. McNamara is very sensitive

Pathways to Inclusion

about French's need for comfort related to his complex disability. On their vacation, they flew up north and then took a car around the countryside for a few days. McNamara is committed to French, and he notes that they understand each other and really enjoy being together. There is obviously a deep respect between these two men.

In the initiatives, close relationships can sometimes lead to friendship, whereas in traditional services friendships between staff and "clients" are discouraged. Ram Dass and Paul Gorman have written in *How Can I Help?* that genuine helping comes when we begin to see ourselves beyond separateness.[22] Engaged compassion leads to more trusting, open relationships that are based on respect and reciprocity, not just on a "taking care of" mentality. Jane Hildreth, a staff member with Waterloo Regional Homes for Mental Health, recalls her experience with a participatory research project in her community:

> We were all on an equal footing. Instead of being labelled as consumers, family members, staff, and research members, we became [equal] committee members. The personal element remained for the full two years (of the project). We kept our personalities part of the committee. We shared birthdays, losses and illnesses ... The committee members became a gauge for me. I trusted people to tell me honestly if I was not walking the same walk as I talked ... (I learned that) relationships that are developed through work activities can be stepping stones to new ideas, contacts for help, and supports for the future.[23]

These kinds of collaborative experiences act as a microcosm or example for what is possible in the wider society as we struggle to build compassionate communities.

In New Story initiatives, we found that leaders' awareness of self-interest, individualism, and separateness highlights the need for engaged compassion. In many traditional human services, achieving independence is regarded as a goal. However, we have learned that when independence is not paired with interdependence, the New Story can never be achieved. It is important to emphasize that independence is about personal control, having a voice, individual rights, and self-determination. However, engaged compassion teaches us about the value of interdependence and stresses the important role of family, friends, and community.[24] By being engaged with others, we learn compassion for them and, in turn, compassion for our-selves. Two ideas, independence and interdependence, shine brightly as symbols of engaged compassion for self and others.

The presence of people who are vulnerable in the commu-nity has a tendency to draw out the softer side of others. Peo-ple often report that a person with intense support needs has "touched" someone they know. We think of Katrina Voller, an older woman who had a stroke. Voller does not communicate with words, but she has a wonderful smile. When Voller under-stands or likes what someone is saying, she puts her head back and smiles deeply. If she does not understand, she leans for-ward and frowns until the person explains it better. Voller will slow you down and challenge you to be alive and clear. She will draw compassion from you.

In some of the best inclusive settings we have visited, gen-uine compassion is evident as people with differing gifts learn, work, and play together. When such settings welcome diversity there is potential for people to learn how to value difference. Morrie Schwartz, the dying professor in *Tuesdays with Morrie*, drew compassion from many people with his humour and posi-tive approach to life. It is significant that when Schwartz was asked on national television what last words he had for millions of viewers, he said, "Be compassionate, and take responsibility for each other."

We have often thought about what it would mean to have a truly compassionate society. Essentially, the New Story values explored earlier would be alive and practised by everyone. Compassionate citizens would be engaged with neighbours and co-workers. They would embrace diversity and difference and see giving and supporting as an honourable act of joy, not a burden. They would have empathy for others, find time for reflection, and advocate for change. Compassionate citizens would be mindful about acting in the world, caring about the little things and the big things while working in solidarity with each other. Leaders suggest there are a multitude of personal actions that can be initiated by compassionate citizens in response to oppression and social devaluation. Compassionate citizens would see opportunities to work together and would speak out about the values that are required to build inclusive communities. Service systems would also understand that they should no longer have a monopoly on people's lives. They would be actively supporting separate, inter-dependent functions of the New Story, including independent facilitation, individualized funding, and strong family networks. Service systems in such a community would be person-centered and collaborative. The ethic of caring and compassion would be central to their mission.

Compassion: A Path to Strengthen the Heart

Several studies have shown that compassionate and caring people enjoy better health and well-being. A 30-year study found that people who have an altruistic lifestyle — i.e., where they help others — lead healthier and happier lives.[25] There is also evidence to support the physical and emotional benefits of a compassionate state of mind. People who feel compassionate toward themselves and others are more likely to have peace of mind and happiness. David Spiegel, in his book, *Living Beyond Limits*, describes a study of women with breast cancer who participated in a support group that shared openly. These participants lived twice as long as women with breast cancer who did *not* participate in such a group. In his latest book, *Love and Survival*, physician Dean Ornish shows that there is a strong scientific basis for the healing power of caring, love, and intimacy.[26]

All these studies suggest that an open heart and compassionate living are beneficial to our health and well-being. When we are willing to let down our emotional defences, we allow ourselves to be emotionally vulnerable. This can be difficult, however, if safety and security are issues. Parents of children with disabilities have often been challenged to open their hearts, a sometimes frightening prospect. Twenty years ago, when we were at the hospital for the birth of our youngest child, we began talking with the woman in the next room, who was distraught. She had just given birth to a baby with Down syndrome. Her husband was adamant that they were not able to bring the baby home. The baby was being kept in the nursery, and the mother was not encouraged to breastfeed. Meanwhile, we were happily bonding with our new baby, breastfeeding, and calling family and friends with our news.

We heard the parents' concerns and told them that we had a child with Down syndrome. We said it could be challenging at times, but the joy we had with our daughter made it all worthwhile. The mother was curious and asked us lots of questions when her husband was out of the room. Later that same day, our daughter Karen, who was five at the time, visited the hospital dressed in her favourite smocked dress made by her aunt. We introduced her to this new mother, and Karen's smile captured her heart immediately. As we were leaving the room, we could see a tear running down the mother's face. Soon after, Karen also met the father, who then began asking us questions. The next day, we provided the family with resources and names of people in the community who could assist them in getting their baby's life off to a good start. As we left the hospital that afternoon, we noticed that the mother was nursing her new baby and that the father was much happier. Both had a look of love on their faces. In that moment, we knew the power of compassion.

Building compassionate and caring communities will take much more than a few innovative initiatives. Yet insights from these initiatives can extend our understanding about what these communities might look like. In the New Story community, compassion will replace the sympathy and fear often evoked in the old paradigm. Compassion says with words and deeds that "you matter" and that you do not need to suffer injustice. Compassion that begins with deep listening can form the basis for developing a sense of purpose. It can also contribute to collaboration and reconciliation. People in our midst who are at risk must be part of any struggle that claims to be concerned with caring communities. However, ordinary people must also become engaged, whether as neighbours, friends, city planners, or politicians. All of us could use a strong dose of compassion toward ourselves as an important antidote to the negativity toward difference in our culture. Compassion for fellow citizens will follow.

We conclude this chapter with a summary of *Child Honouring*, a worldwide initiative that was started by Raffi, a Canadian singer and entertainer. The covenant and principles of Child Honouring form the basis of compassionate relationships and compassionate communities. The principles are respectful love, diversity, caring community, conscious parenting, emotional intelligence, nonviolence, safe environments, sustainability, and ethical commerce.[27]

A Covenant for Honouring Children

by Raffi

We find these joys to be self evident: That all children are created whole, endowed with innate intelligence, with dignity and wonder, worthy of respect. The embodiment of life, liberty and happiness, children are original blessings, here to learn their own song. Every girl and boy is entitled to love, to dream, and belong to a loving "village." And to pursue a life of purpose.

We affirm our duty to nourish and nurture the young, to honour their caring ideals as the heart of being human. To recognize the early years as the foundation of life, and to cherish the contribution of young children to human evolution.

We commit ourselves to peaceful ways and vow to keep from harm or neglect these, our most vulnerable citizens. As guardians of their prosperity, we honour the bountiful Earth whose diversity sustains us. Thus we pledge our love for generations to come.

Notes

1. Hahn (2000).
2. For a discussion of victimhood, see Saleebey (2006).
3. Malash, Schaufeli, and Leiter (2001).
4. Compassion is noted in some important Canadian literature such as Nelson, Prilleltensky, and MacGillary (2001).
5. For more discussion on the self-fulfilling prophesy and on being a victim, see Malik (2003). See also Marinelli and Orto (1999).
6. Vanier (1998).
7. For a discussion on learned helplessness see Peterson, Seligman, and Maier (1995).
8. For a discussion of the social model and social construction, see Berger and Luckmann (1966).

9. There are a number of important books on mindfulness and compassion in the Buddhist tradition. See, for example, Chodron (1991); Goldstein and Kornfield (2001).
10. Dalai Lama and Cutler (1998), p. 114.
11. See Albom (1997), p. 128; de Bono (1999).
12. For a link between clienthood and compassion, see Prilleltensky (2005).
13. Bennett (1993), p. 107.
14. Saul (2001).
15. Sharron Garrah, quoted in the Independent Living Centre of Waterloo Region Newsletter, *The Forum*, November (2002): p. 3.
16. Pink (2009).
17. Deegan (1996), p. 92.
18. For more thinking about reflective practice, see Pinkerton, Dolan, and Canavan (2006). See the journal *Reflective Practice*.
19. Raphael et al. (1996).
20. Vanier (1998).
21. For commentary of the roots of the concept *engaged compassion*, see Dass and Gorman (1987).
22. Dass and Gorman (1987).
23. Nelson, Lord, and Ochocka (2001), pp. 261–263. Also see Scott (2000).
24. Condeluci (1991).
25. Spiegel (1993).
26. The following books report on several studies on the benefits of compassion. Dalai Lama and Cutler (1998); Ornish (1997); Spiegel (1993).
27. Raffi Cavoukian is a well-known Canadian singer and songwriter, particularly for children; see Cavoukian and Olfman (2006).

Part 3

Strategies and Pathways

Inspirational Leadership

A Key to Innovation

Inspirational Leaders practice the generosity implied in Aquarian power and assume their true role as loving teachers, coaches and spiritual guides to those they lead. Their aim is not to control others, but to liberate the greatness that is naturally within them. The Aquarian leader archetype is a giving leader ... [and] asks others, "How can I be of service to you?"

Lance Secretan[1]

The development of social innovations requires inspirational leadership. Without people with vision and strategies, it is virtually impossible for good ideas to be created or implemented. Leadership has been shown to be one of the key elements for sustaining innovation in the non-profit sector.[2] Inspirational leadership likewise has been central to the development of the New Story approaches, and in fact, many people in these initiatives have played leadership roles. At the same time, it is well known that many forward-thinking undertakings die or lose their innovative edge over time. Margaret Mead's famous quote on leadership speaks poignantly to leadership and innovation: "Never doubt that a small group of thoughtful, committed citizens can change the world. Indeed, it is the only thing that ever has."

We will explore the leadership of individuals and small groups who are moving toward the New Story. Sometimes this leadership is in the context of starting a new community initiative or organization, while other times it involves changing the values and direction of a traditional organization. We find that leadership in both these kinds of endeavours is visionary and inspiring. While common leadership elements exist across initiatives, concrete strategies often vary. For example, the executive director of one of the large organizations we studied has a very different role and set of skills than the facilitator of a grassroots initiative working with 15 families. However, both leaders of these very different organizations also have much in common. They work from similar values, are strategic in how they proceed, are strongly committed to the people being supported, and engage people in the change process.

The leadership we see in the initiatives is what Peter Block calls stewardship, where purpose, power, and rewards are shared widely.[3] Those involved in governing roles are stewards of a precious resource that is all too often not available to citizens who are vulnerable, nor to their allies. Leadership in these initiatives is crucial because people's hopes and expectations have been raised by the vision of the New Story. They have much to lose if leadership does not flourish. People will be disappointed if desired outcomes are not realized. Leaders must rise to the occasion by inspiring and mobilizing people to make progress on many difficult fronts.[4]

Leaders with a Cause: Values and Vision Come Alive

The values and visions described earlier are the foundation for building the New Story — human rights and social justice, diver-

Pathways to Inclusion

sity and person-centeredness, participation and empowerment, and community and hospitality — and are more than mere words. We find that these values are alive in the hearts and minds of the leaders in the initiatives. It is leadership that moves the values and visions into action. When combined with compassion, the values and principles reflect a way of being, which is much more than just a set of procedures. In studying and working with innovations over several years, it is clear to us that most leaders have a cause that embraces the values.

Lance Secretan says that a cause "connects us from our present reality to a richly imagined future."[5] We have found that a deeper cause sustains leaders and also encourages others. The passion for a cause tends to be contagious and focuses outward toward building an organization, community, and society that is truly inclusive. What strikes us repeatedly is how leadership in New Story initiatives is different than what we often see in more traditional non-profit organizations, where efficiency, service delivery, and programs usually guide implementation. How different for a leader to focus on gifts, citizenship, collaboration, and connecting people to community, *and* inspiring others to become engaged in this cause.

Marlyn Shervill, from Windsor–Essex Brokerage for Personal Supports, lives the values and believes deeply in a cause. Shervill works tirelessly for persons with disabilities and their families. Her work is about listening and about helping people plan for a full life in the community. As a leader in her organization, she constantly reminds people through her actions that the power of each person matters. She emphasizes that we need to do "whatever it takes" to assist people in living their dreams. Shervill stresses that her "cause of building an inclusive community that welcomes citizens, requires work on many different levels." Engaging others in this cause means inspiring her staff and being vigilant with service providers who can "get in the way of the values." Shervill also finds time to serve as a volunteer advisor to Windsor–Essex People First, a self-help group of people with developmental disabilities. Shervill says this work feeds her soul because she has a chance to hear people's life stories. She believes that "community living for all" must be based on the experiences and stories of people themselves. Shervill says, "We need to constantly be finding ways for people to tell their stories. It is an incredibly powerful way to learn and a constant reminder of what the values and the cause are all about."

In promoting their vision and cause, leaders in New Story initiatives express their values and vision through their words and action. They walk the talk. The *use of principles* is one way we can see the values come alive in day-to-day work. Staff members in the Foundations initiative, for example, show that adherence to principles is one way that consistency is maintained. Beth Hancox, a facilitator, passionately expresses the view that "it is very important to always come back to principles. When you do that," says Hancox, "you always come back to families and individuals, their voice, and their capacity to be able to solve problems."

Interestingly, the most effective leaders are not always those in a position of authority. It is not unusual for new organizations that have been innovative since their inception, such as New Frontiers in London or NABORS in Toronto, to have more than one community volunteer who is a "champion" of the values and vision. These individuals remind others of the guiding principles and play key roles in keeping the initiatives on track in the early years. It is also important to emphasize that not all leaders who inspire are dynamic and charismatic. One parent who worked for years on an innovative initiative described the leadership style of the executive director as, "very quiet and methodical, yet we always know where she stands. She takes direction from people, listening and responding, and she is incredibly reliable." Although people with different types of personalities can be leaders, we find that "feeling the cause and the values in the gut" is common to most leaders.

Developing a New Initiative Demands a Special Touch

What do we mean by *a new initiative*? Several New Story initiatives started from scratch. Usually this involves a few people in a local community identifying a need that they believe can best be addressed by organizing a group to develop an innovative initiative. Although all of these new projects began as small, local initiatives, over time some have become more established, and some are now sustained, larger organizations. Others, however, have remained small with fairly insecure funding. There are several lessons we can draw from working with and studying these new initiatives.

The source of leadership for developing a new initiative can come from individuals, family members, community members, or a combination of all three. In many of the initiatives, the passion of families fuels the idea of starting a new initiative. What is it about families that their passion fuels such leadership? Is it the frustration they often experience with trying to influence traditional services? Is it the isolation they feel and the need to connect with others? Is it compassion for their sons or daughters or spouses who often have their vision thwarted? Some of the new initiatives began with family members connecting with one another. The Durham Family Network, for example, began more than a decade ago when a few families decided to start meeting on a regular basis. Families soon discovered there was great strength and learning possibilities from working with each other. What started as one network of five families has grown to more than 15 separate networks involving more than 80 families.

Another source of leadership comes from citizens who themselves have experienced vulnerability. Most innovations either have these people in key leadership roles or include them as an integral part of the planning and development phases. The Independent Living Resource Centres are a particularly instructive example of such leadership, both in terms of project development as well as partnership building with other sectors in the community. Vic Willy, former Executive Director of the Centre for Independent Living Toronto, for example, played a major role in developing the Centre. He also worked with others to advocate for direct funding for people who require attendant services in Ontario. Once the government approved the Ontario Direct Funding Project in 1993, the Toronto Centre became the sponsor of the province-wide initiative. Willy's leadership, both as a person with a disability and as the executive director, was instrumental in bringing this idea to fruition.

Individuals and families play major leadership roles in the development of new initiatives, often with the support of other skilled community members. These individuals act as role models, help the groups with strategies, or provide inspiration for new ideas. A few initiatives, such as Project Friendship in Prince George, British Columbia, and Brokerage for Personal Supports in Windsor, Ontario, were started by community leaders, but quickly drew in individuals, families, and other

Pathways to Inclusion

community members to become part of the vision. In other cases, individuals or family leaders invite a community leader or a supportive professional to assist with initial planning and strategy development. Such facilitators share the values of the group and are skilled at listening deeply as they support people to plan what they want to do. Sometimes in such community processes, what people decide to do may actually differ from what they initially thought they wanted. Understanding the entire context enables the "outsider" to see patterns and capacities that others may not see. An effective outside facilitator will ensure ownership by the group by asking the right questions, rather than by proposing solutions.

Another lesson we can draw from these new initiatives is that *collective approaches in leadership help ensure that the initiative builds capacity and becomes sustaining.* In some new initiatives, the passion of a founder may be vital to get a project off the ground. Other new initiatives begin because of the collective wisdom of individuals, families, community members, and employees. Regardless of where the source of leadership comes from, in the end, different sources of leadership must work together to sustain the initiative. In several New Story initiatives, shared leadership creates possibilities for collaborative problem solving. Hands-on, co-operative leadership is also required to keep initiatives going. People who understand the value of shared leadership in the early stages are able to move smoothly through later stages of project development and implementation.

Leaders in several of the new initiatives we studied have a common approach to their leadership styles. People who are in formal leadership positions, such as a co-ordinator or an executive director, operate less from the top, and more from the centre of their organizations. Top–down leaders are found most often in traditional settings and tend to guide all planning and implementation. Leaders from the centre are more able to understand the value of shared leadership and collaborative problem solving. They tend to facilitate, distribute power, and encourage everyone to be creative. In the book *Web of Inclusion*, Sally Helgesen emphasizes that relationships are key in organizations that work more like a web than a hierarchy.[6] Revisiting our quote at the beginning of the chapter, we see that an Aquarian leader is a supporter of teams and open to change, rather than implementing control mechanisms that focus on lowering costs or reducing risks. The person says, "I am your leader. How can I serve you?"[7] In this sense, the leader moves from the top to the centre through a process of engaging others.

A new, small Independent Living Resource Centre in Ontario reflects this way of working. A co-ordinator and four staff members, all persons with disabilities, initially played a lead role for each of their program areas. As a busy drop-in resource centre, it was initially understood that the lead person would not always be available to respond to people who dropped in. So staff members would play various roles and seek out the lead person if they needed support. Over time, people developed expertise in their area. Staff meetings were originally seen as an opportunity for each person to report on their area. As people learned through day-to-day experience more about the roles of other staff, the staff meetings became more creative and free-flowing. New initiatives that are committed to shared leadership and openness are able to "play" more easily with ideas and implementation. When the staff learned about the web metaphor, for example, they embraced it as a way to operate internally as well as with the wider community.

Another lesson learned is that *initiatives partner and collaborate with effective sponsoring organizations and funders who support innovation.* Leaders in New Story approaches are often strategic about how they develop their initiatives and who they chose as partners. Many funders, whether government or foundations, require small, grassroots groups to work with incorporated sponsoring organizations. For one project, Foundations, this requirement created a dilemma because available sponsoring agencies were all traditional and somewhat uncomfortable with innovation. For others, such as Options in Toronto, the sponsoring agency has been highly supportive and collaborative. Options in Toronto operates within the Family Service Association, which is a good fit with the values and principles of the New Story.

Some projects refuse to use government funding and have developed their own non-profit enterprise. PLAN in British Columbia has followed this route. It has obtained multiple sources of funding over the years, including fees from families, grants from non-profit foundations, and corporate dollars. PLAN, which is having success with its approach to personal support and future planning, recently sponsored the develop-

Pathways to Inclusion

ment of 10 new locally based initiatives across Canada. PLAN has been very entrepreneurial, developing partnerships with the private sector around specific issues of concern to its members. For example, PLAN has played a key leadership role with the Registered Disability Savings Plan, in collaboration with partners such as the Royal Bank.

Finding government funders that support innovation is not easy. It took NABORS several years to become established as a program within the Ontario Ministry of Health and Long-Term Care. Similarly, it took years for the Personal Communities Project in Alberta to become sustaining. Effective, persistent internal leadership and a supportive civil servant inside the Alberta government enabled the initiative to eventually be accepted. Leaders of new initiatives understand that they are often in a minority but must be able to work with more mainstream sponsoring organizations and funders. This dilemma is a challenge for social innovators. They understand that it takes time for the principles and values of innovations to become more widely accepted by funders and mainstream community organizations. Living with this dilemma is one of the leadership challenges of building New Story initiatives.

A lesson can be drawn from the fact that, in *developing a new innovative initiative, leaders build in time to clarify concepts that are important.* In the early years of NABORS, there was much negotiation about the meaning of concepts such as *intentional community* and *support circles.* To their credit, NABORS' leaders took the time to negotiate the meaning of concepts and develop forums whereby concept clarification became an ongoing process. John O'Brien has called this the process of addressing problems where negotiation is used to solve problems.[8] This is an important part of leadership that brings people together to reflect on different understandings. Most leaders in New Story initiatives feel comfortable knowing that the meanings of concepts might change over time; they base their reflections on a clear set of principles and on the lived experience of the people that the undertaking is designed to benefit.

We believe that clarifying concepts and negotiating meanings in an ongoing manner is a strategy that enables grassroots initiatives to become sustaining, longer-term innovations. We see this in small family-led initiatives, such as NABORS and New Frontiers, in several Independent Living Resource Centres, and in the Canadian Mental Health Association Framework for

NABORS: Lessons from a New Initiative

NABORS (Neighbors Allied for Better Opportunities in Residential Support), started in the early 1990s, is an association comprising 12 people with disabilities, their families, and friends. NABORS was the outcome of a small group of families and friends who wanted to create an "intentional" community that would enable 12 individuals to live in two Toronto housing co-operatives. The idea was to split up or de-link housing and support, with a separate board of directors for the support component, which was NABORS. The founders, who were strongly committed to community alternatives, expressed deep concern about the exclusion, lack of choice and control, and segregation associated with most human service systems. They decided to build their new initiative on the values of community, self-determination, and person-centeredness.

Dialogue was critical for this group in the development of their proposal. Peter Clutterbuck, board chair in the early years, emphasized, "We felt that co-operative living and our rather early weak notions of 'intentional community' would create conditions and opportunities for our supported members to make friends and build relationships where they live." As the small group talked together, their ideas became sharper, implementation strategies evolved, and various roles and responsibilities were identified. In the development stage, weekend retreats were held with potential co-op members to help citizens understand the values and principles that the early leaders were striving to establish. Gillian Chernets, a parent leader of NABORS, emphasized that "these retreats were an important part of developing intentional community."

Over a period of years, proposals were written and re-written, new families became involved, co-ops were chosen and developed, and funding was finally secured. Chernets also explains that a small pilot project that helped a woman move from an institution to the community helped build the group's confidence. She

NABORS: Lessons from a New Initiative (continued)

explained that "the group experienced a long, arduous journey before finally reaching its goal. The scope of community building that was required to build strong relationships is quite substantial."

In the early years, there was an important mix of leadership within NABORS. Families played a key role in defining the values and vision. Chernets, a critical "keeper of the vision," had been a founder and leader of Toronto Citizen Advocacy for more than a decade, and knew what it took to develop a complex initiative. The 12 individuals and their families participate regularly in membership-based policy making. These meetings create a sense of community for determining priorities and directions. When you see 30 people spend two hours on a Saturday reflecting on their lives and their future, it is easy to become an advocate of small-scale initiatives that allow full participation of members. The role of volunteer community members, such as Peter Clutterbuck, is critical in the development of these kinds of innovations. Clutterbuck has a great deal of planning and systems expertise, having worked for years at a policy institute, and at the time of NABORS' development, was a senior staff member with the Toronto Social Planning Council.

Interestingly, when we first visited five years after the organization's inception, it was difficult to identify one or two leaders. Many people were sharing the leadership and providing inspiration. The 12 supported members provided leadership by identifying key issues that needed to be addressed. Although families continued to play leadership roles, their voices were more in harmony with their relatives'. And it was not unusual for a friend of a supported member to play a leadership role in facilitating meetings or helping to solve a co-op issue. This is the special touch of leadership, the capacity to live stewardship where everyone feels a sense of ownership, participation, and power.

Reference: J. Lord, *The NABORS Experience: Lessons in Community Building* (Toronto, ON: Greendragon Press, 1998).

Support projects. Brenda Zimmerman reminds us that bureaucratic initiatives do not work because they cannot sustain innovation.[9] The metaphor of "planting seeds" is relevant here. As
we saw in several new initiatives, leadership and the right conditions enable the initial seeds and ideas to grow and become
self-sustaining over time.

*Leaders do not try to plan everything, but rather create an
atmosphere of "learning as you go."* This is another lesson of
new initiatives, even though there is a strong tendency among
leaders to want to plan. Value-based planning in the development of new initiatives certainly helps them develop functions
and structures that are a good fit with the values and principles. Although planning is valued in new initiatives, there is
also a resistance to planning too much. As one co-ordinator put
it, "We find that we often learn by trying new things in
response to families and individuals." Research supports this
idea that action and learning often come before intentional
planning.[10] The development of support networks is an interesting example. In the early stages of some new initiatives, including Options in Toronto, it was assumed that the development
of a support circle should precede any individualized planning
and support development. As the initiatives evolved and facilitators learned from families, however, facilitators found that
immediate support issues often needed to be addressed prior to
the development of support networks. Initiatives use these kinds
of insights to adjust their assumptions and directions.

Leaders in new initiatives try to balance the need for planning and clear goals without being too attached to outcomes.
Although everyone we met would say that positive outcomes
are important, one key part of many innovations is to get
people to stay focused on good process. Several initiatives
emphasize outcomes as a way to get staff to understand the
importance of such domains as "citizenship," "having friends,"
and "participating in community activities." Yet, it is the principles, processes, and "how to's" of relationship building and
community connecting that are paramount to outcomes actually
happening. Often people have to "invent" new ways of working
because there is simply no research or guidance on how to do
the innovative work. Most leaders encourage this on-the-ground
innovation and use these lessons for reflection and the development of new principles. Several leaders use the motto "Learn

as you go" as a guide to remaining committed to good process while being less attached to outcomes.

Evaluation and ongoing reflection are important parts of learning as you go. Leaders understand that there must be regular check-ins and feedback opportunities if an innovation is to grow and change. Westley, Zimmerman, and Patton have a wonderful phrase to describe this process in their book on innovation, *Getting to Maybe*. "Standing still" is a metaphor for taking time to reflect on how things are going. These authors also outline the importance of developmental evaluation as a tool for assessing process and progress in the development of innovations.[11] Others have described the importance of building a "learning organization."[12]

We are very impressed with the quality of leadership exhibited in new initiatives, which has enabled us to witness these important lessons. And as we mentioned before, in most cases, these leaders are ordinary people. Whether leaders are individuals, family members, or community members, ordinary people rise to the occasion and take responsibility for carrying dreams forward. The special touch of leadership shown by many people reflects deep compassion and commitment. As one person told us, "You can count on these leaders," which sums up why New Story approaches ultimately have an impact on the wider community.

Revitalizing a Service Organization

Transforming an "old story" service agency into a New Story organization is difficult, and we have observed many attempts at transformation that have been unsuccessful. Leaders in New Story approaches are aware of the pitfalls when embarking on a change process. We tracked six service organizations that transformed or revitalized themselves in recent years. In all cases, these organizations changed toward the values and vision of the New Story. There are several common themes across the six organizations in terms of leadership and the change process.

First, *interest in transforming an organization usually begins with conversations about discontent*. Conversations about concerns are initiated from several different sources, including individuals, families, workers, or leaders themselves. For example, a leader from one organization that has been transforming itself describes the way she began to notice discontent. Wendy Czarny has been executive director of Waterloo Regional Homes for Mental Health Inc. since its inception in 1980. In the late 1980s, she realized that expansion of the organization had taken away some of the intimate ways of working. At the same time, she noted that her organization's approach was "no longer a good fit" with current trends and research that were starting to emphasize inclusion and empowerment. Czarny recalls having many informal conversations with individuals, staff, and volunteer leaders about these issues before actually working with her Board of Directors on a change strategy. These early conversations included those people being supported, which ensured that an accurate understanding of the nature of their discontent was being raised and that any change would include their concerns. "Beginning with conversations" is an important theme in other settings as well. A leader within a branch of the Canadian Mental Health Association points out that this is important because it is how you find unexpected allies. These allies may come from inside the organization or may be community members who are supportive of impending change.

Another theme common to the six service organizations that we tracked was that *leaders need to start "where people are at" and create an open process for learning.* One leader notes that starting where people are at requires a commitment to honour the reality of people's lives. It is challenging for leaders to balance accepting "what is," while at the same time creating opportunities to reflect on "what could be." Leaders observe that if people experience good process, they can share their concerns and fears about change in a safe environment. In working closely with these progressive organizations, it seems that their leaders are being compassionate to people's struggle with change.

Years ago, Archie Dowker, executive director of South-East Grey Support Services, instituted yearly reviews by external consultants to create a more open process with individuals, families, and staff. Over a period of years, the feedback from this review process, combined with Dowker's leadership, enabled South-East Grey to become a highly participatory, open organization. When Community Living St. Marys considered shifting from traditional programs to an individualized, holistic approach, the board and members held a series of meetings to hear people's concerns, reflect on the issues, and set directions. They also began to conduct regular training sessions for everyone to learn about new possibilities in areas such as values, person-centered planning, and support-circle development. The experiences of these two organizations confirm what the literature on organizational change shows: open processes that promote participation and that start where people are at produce leverage for change and the high probability that people will take ownership for the change.[13]

Another common theme in the change process is that *leaders use the need for paradigm change as the lever for organizational change.* Effective leaders from organizations that have been transformed understand that the passion for change must be grounded in the need for a new paradigm for their organization. Too often, change that occurs in human service organizations is done for reasons other than shifting to the new paradigm and, as a result, often fails to make real differences in the lives of the people being served. When Doug Cartan arrived at the Brockville and District Association for Community Involvement, he soon concluded that his organization was doing too much and getting too large, and that this interfered with making progressive changes. In order to be more focused and change toward the new paradigm, Cartan and his board decided to "focus more on the individual." This necessitated that the Association "spin off" housing to a separate organization. This organizational change enabled the transformed organization to be more creative with its use of resources. Staff became facilitators of an individualized planning process that was consistent with the new paradigm. The purpose of the transformed organization also became clear to everyone.

In order to effectively use the new paradigm as a lever for organizational change, these six service organizations all implemented processes that engaged people in new ways of thinking. In one large mental health agency, Waterloo Regional Homes for Mental Health, a year-long strategic planning process was designed to create a learning organization, enhance "consumer" direction, and provide more individualized support. In order to ensure that this process resulted in a paradigm shift, a few conscious strategies were followed, including utilizing an external facilitator who brought a strong set of values and "lateral" thinking. The outcome of this strategic planning

Community Living St. Marys: Lessons from the Evolution of a Progressive Service Organization

Community Living St. Marys has provided supports and services to citizens with disabilities since 1962. St. Marys is a small community of 6,300 people in southern Ontario. It is on the Thames River, located between the larger communities of London and Stratford. Throughout the 1960s and 1970s, the services offered by Community Living St. Marys included education and a sheltered workshop. In the late 1970s, the agency began to support 20 individuals in their homes through a provincial program known as Supported Independent Living (S.I.L.). In the early 1980s, the agency facilitated the return of several individuals from institutions where they had resided for a long time. Due to a severe housing shortage, the agency created an incorporated company that included housing in the form of a duplex, a fourplex, and a sixplex.

In 1983, the St. Marys Association for Community Living began a process of reshaping itself into an organization that provides supports and services in more non-traditional ways. The impetus for these changes began in the early 1980s, as senior staff and board members were exposed to new ideas about community integration. A former staff member reflected on this period as an "era of reflection and learning." Much dialogue ensued, and by 1983, the executive director and board were ready to engage the members in a process of change. In a series of meetings with families and individuals, a number of changes were initiated. As so often happens with New Story approaches, a clear set of values became the foundation of the new paradigm changes. These values included a commitment to community participation, integration, and person-centeredness in the provision of all supports. At the time, these leading-edge changes were insightful and progressive.

Staff at Community Living St. Marys embraced the new values and the new direction. By 1988, great strides had been made toward the replacement of their congregated settings. Individualized supports were becoming the norm, as people began to experience much more participation in the full range of community opportunities available to all citizens. However, by 1990 the staff and board recognized that some of the problems they were still experiencing might be the result of the way they continued to structure their agency with separate residential and vocational services. There was also the recognition that planning with individuals *and* providing their services often created a conflict of interest. A full-day meeting with members fleshed out the principles that would separate planning from the direct supports people required.

In the new structure adopted by the agency, two distinct divisions were created: a support services division and a planning and community development division. The rationale for the separation of planning and support services was threefold. First was the reality that when planning and support service are combined, it is less likely that genuine options will be presented to the individual and family. Second was the need to build a culture of planning and advocacy that sees Community Living St. Marys services as only *one* option, with the community as a resource being widely available. Third, a more autonomous and valued planning enterprise would support linkages with other organizations and assist people to think creatively during the planning process.

Building the capacity for planning support has been an ongoing process at Community Living St. Marys. Leaders within the planning and community development division have refined their facilitation approaches and the agency has responded by ensuring that each person being supported has an individualized budget that describes their support goals and costs. Facilitators are committed to "community as a first resort" and are creative in the way they help people build a life in community. By 1996, the last remnants of congregated, traditional services had disappeared. Closing of a shel-

Community Living St. Marys (continued)

tered workshop and ending congregated housing gave facilitators and the people they supported a deeper commitment to the new paradigm and the energy to pursue community alternatives.

Community development has been an important part of this new approach. St. Marys not only helps people find opportunities in the community, but it works with others to change community conditions. Community Living St. Marys did not buy housing, but it helped create co-op housing for those who want it. It does not have a van, but helped set up a mobility bus service available to the whole community. In the process of community development, facilitators have become quite skilful at inviting others in the community to collaborate for change that will benefit all citizens.

In 2008, Community Living St. Marys embarked on another stage in their evolution. Years earlier, the leaders had realized that they had reached the limit of effectiveness with their internal planning and facilitation. Collaborating with three other community agencies in Perth County, St. Marys saw an opportunity to build *independent* planning and facilitation. Leaders of the four organizations worked with disability and family leaders for almost a year, crafting the values, principles, and functions that would guide the new "facilitation entity." Each organization contributed resources, and with the support of the government, launched a new independent organization in the spring of 2010. Driven by families and people with disabilities, the mission of Facile, the new organization, is to use facilitation to enable people to build rich lives in community.

The St. Marys example illustrates the importance of being open to learning and that paradigm change is an ongoing process. Interestingly, change-oriented leadership within St. Marys has rested within the hearts and minds of many people — individuals, family members, staff, facilitators, and board members. This may indeed be its most impressive lesson of all — inspirational leadership now permeates the whole organization.

process was effective organizational change with clear principles that reflected new paradigm values.[14] In a Canadian Mental Health Association in southern Ontario, a pilot project related to "community connecting" was initiated and then used to move the innovation throughout the entire organization. This organization found that having small but noticeable successes with the new paradigm builds confidence and skills among staff.

Resistance to change is minimized by New Story training and putting the right people in place was another common theme among the six organizations we tracked. "Change is challenging," explains John Jones from the Canadian Mental Health Association, Grand River Branch. Jones found that the process of change to revitalize his organization was difficult for some staff and volunteers. As a strategy to deal with resistance to change, he stresses that it was critical "to relate everything we did back to the new attitudes and values." All leaders in the revitalization initiatives note that because people need to change attitudes *and* practices, the change process takes time. Jones reflects on the time it takes: "I was thinking of a three-year process: one to think about it and develop a philosophy, and the second year, implementation, with the third year to tidy up. That was unrealistic. We could have spent three to four years on implementation."

All leaders emphasize that listening and dialogue are helpful in overcoming resistance to change. Some leaders recall the hesitation from senior staff when implementing the new values and a new vision. Regular meetings, open dialogue, and starting where people are at were keys to getting everyone on board. One executive director noted that two senior staff moved on to new jobs at other agencies when it was clear that they were uncomfortable with the directions in which the changes were heading. This underscores the importance of getting the right people in place to make the paradigm shift. One executive director admitted that she waited too long before making changes in her senior staff team.

Training in New Story values and practice is strongly emphasized by all six organizations we tracked. There are two kinds of training, the first being of a more general nature about trends in the field. Leaders find it is often useful to do this even before much planning is under way. The second type of training is more specific to the principles and goals related to the organization. "We recognize that a substantial amount of time was invested in training with our staff before initiating our new direction," says Archie Dowker from South-East Grey Support Service in Markdale, Ontario. "A lot of training was directly related to the philosophy we operate with. We also sensitize staff to the issues that families have encountered in the past and are currently encountering on a daily basis." Brockville and District Association for Community Involvement and Community Living St. Marys also continue training individuals, families, and staff with workshops, speakers, and practical training events being held on a regular basis. These training events tend to emphasize the components of social inclusion, including person-centered approaches, connecting with community, and how to build on people's strengths and gifts.

The themes described in the preceding pages work together to "build momentum for change," as one leader put it. When collaborative change processes are put in place, it creates a context for people to get engaged with the new paradigm. Some staff immediately get excited about the possibilities, and training events create interest among an even larger group. Perhaps what is most interesting is that as momentum is built, the actual direction of the innovation may shift somewhat because more people are now involved in the process of change.

All six organizations we examined have been able to shift toward the new paradigm to varying degrees. For a short period of time, two of the organizations attempted to keep some parts of their organizations embedded in the traditional paradigm. For example, while working in the new paradigm with individualized supports for some individuals, these organizations initially kept their traditional segregated residential and vocational programs open. Fairly quickly, these organizations realized that this would not work. The leaders found it was counter-productive to try to operate two different paradigms in the same organization. As one executive director from one of the transformed organizations said, "It is hard enough to maintain the innovative stuff, without having traditional programs in the same office. We learned we all needed to be on the same page with the same principles."

In summarizing the lessons from these organizations that have transformed themselves from traditional agencies to New Story approaches, they all have similar outcomes resulting from their efforts toward change. All organizations developed clear values and principles, shifted power and participation to people who require support, offered more individualized planning and support, enhanced connections to community and personal support networks, and created more participatory management. These outcomes, the result of much hard work and creative leadership, are changes to which any organization could aspire.

The Personal Nature of Leadership: Women's Ways of Working

Leadership in New Story initiatives generally has a personal touch. We did not observe old-style leadership, where decisions come down from the top with no input from employees or from people being supported on the organization's directions. Rather, what we saw over and over are leaders who have personal styles that are very nurturing. This style is more often attributed to the way many women in leadership positions work. The personal nature of leadership is reflected in the fact that 70% of the "official leaders" of the New Story initiatives are women. This is an important finding, since between 50% and 75% of non-profit sector employees are women; 54% of all volunteers are women; and in certain areas, the gender breakdown is 80% to 90% women.[15]

What is it about the role of women that makes their leadership so important in creating new paradigm approaches? First, women tend to be more social than men, and many are superb communicators. As Carol Stephenson, Dean of the Richard Ivey School of Business has written, "[Women] speak clearly and honestly. They listen with intent and invite feedback ... This honesty and openness engenders trust, reinforces relationships, and secures employee loyalty."[16] This empathy for others contributes to women's skilful relationship building. Many leaders are family members and know full well what it means to struggle.[17] As one mother indicated, "My own experience with adversity makes it easy for me to stand with people in their adversity." Female leaders we got to know were very good at relationship building and were comfortable creating open environments for people to learn and change.

Women in New Story initiatives often hold the values and the vision. In our case study of Community Living St. Marys, where inspirational leadership permeates the whole organization, most of the leadership roles related to carrying the values and vision over the years have been by women. Even larger organizations that have made new paradigm values central have created opportunities for women to take on extensive responsibility. Women's ability to encourage others to contribute is also reflected in these approaches. Community support co-ordinators at Waterloo Regional Homes for Mental Health Inc., most of whom are women, have a lot of freedom to provide leadership with people they support. Their commitment is to self-determination. They are able to be very creative in how they support personal recovery. In evaluations done at Waterloo Regional Homes, people being supported say what they like is the fact that co-ordinators listen, are very helpful with planning, and are available when needed. The nurturing aspect of women's ways of working is surely a factor in this success.

Concluding the chapter with this section on women's way of working sends a powerful message about inspirational leadership being a key to innovation. It reminds us that much of what is still occurring in our communities is stuck and in need of rejuvenation. Inspirational leadership reflects new ways of working in the world. Leaders in New Story initiatives reflect a strong commitment to teamwork and collaboration. In fact, collaboration is both an internal and external principle. As an internal principle, staff and people being supported collaborate on a wide range of community issues. As an external principle, collaboration means that initiatives work with others in the community to find solutions to some of the barriers that exist for social inclusion to be a reality.

In some settings, it is difficult to know who the official leader is because organizational leadership rather than leaders are nurtured. So often when we think about leadership, we think of a person, but our work is teaching us that leadership is a shared process, and that innovative initiatives themselves can be thought of as being a leader.[18] In this way, leadership contributes to social innovation and makes a real difference in the lives of citizens who are struggling with inclusion.

Notes

1. Secretan (1999).
2. Light (1998); Foster (2000).
3. Block (1993).
4. Heifetz and Sinder (1988).

5. Secretan (1999), p. 69.
6. Helgesen (1995).
7. Secretan (1999), p. 43.
8. O'Brien (1989).
9. Zimmerman (1991).
10. Lincoln (1985).
11. Westley, Zimmerman, and Patton (2006).
12. Senge (1990); Yukl (1998); Yukl (1999).
13. Block 1993); Faber (2002).
14. Lord et al. (1998).
15. Malloux, Horak, and Godin (2002). In another study, three-quarters of all paid employees within the sector, women represent a clear majority; while looking at the caring industries alone, women represent over 80% (health, education, and social services); see MacMullen and Schellenberg (2002).
16. Stephenson (2005), p. 1.
17. Panitch (2003).
18. Hutchison et al. (2007); Hutchison et al. (2007); Arai et al. (2008).

8

"It's My Life"

Building on Dreams and Gifts

Communities can sustain themselves in a meager way with the absence of gifts, but thrive with the presence of gifts. If we acted on this idea, citizens now at the edges would be welcomed not as an act of charity, but out of the wisdom that every person has a significant contribution to make to his or her community.

Bruce Anderson[1]

Andrew Bloomfield was given an opportunity to leave the institution where he had stayed part-time for several years. People might have assumed that he would move to a group home run by a community agency. Bloomfield and his family had other ideas. Bloomfield's combination of disabilities, abilities, and motivations were so distinctive that planning for his future called for a personalized plan. It was one that would be based on his dreams and the supports he would require. Today, Bloomfield lives in his own home in Guelph, Ontario. Over the years, we have had an opportunity to get to know Andrew and his family. He has an active support network of family and friends. He participates fully in the planning and implementation of his supports with the help of facilitated communication. And most important, he contributes to his community.

Sadly, many people are unable to live as Andrew Bloomfield does because their lives are controlled, shaped, and directed by others who practise the old story. Nobody listens deeply to their dreams or imagines how different a New Story might be. At the same time, we now have a multitude of people like Andrew Bloomfield who *are* living their dreams. With their dreams as the foundation for planning their lives, they are not unlike other citizens in terms of where they live and whom they live with, daily rhythms, relationships, and hopes for the future.

How do any of us build a good life in a community? There are many ingredients, including goals, relationships, and resources. New Story initiatives are teaching us that people also need things beyond what we typically consider ingredients for a good life.[2] This is because the traditional paradigm has limited people's possibilities. People who have experienced the New Story identify several ways that vulnerable people can begin to live the "good life." Dreaming, participating in decision making, building on strengths and gifts, accessing independent planning and facilitation, acquiring individualized funding, and being creative in implementing supports are all important. These ideas work together to create conditions and opportunities for people to experience citizenship.

The Power of Dreaming: Enabling People to Find Their Path

When Martin Luther King said, "I have a dream," he was talking about the hope in all of us to experience dignity and community throughout our lifetime. Unfortunately, when people experience compliance they have little chance to either dream or participate. Shifting power to supporting self-determination honours what one person exclaimed to us, "It's my life." The value of authentic self-determination is paramount in New Story initiatives; people are encouraged to dream and participate fully in creating their own lives.

This idea builds on a growing body of research that shows how autonomy (self-determination) is a key element in motivation.[3] If we want to engage someone in a change process, we need to provide opportunity for the person to fully participate in the process, with as much autonomy as possible.

Self-determination is a process of people determining their own needs and interests. Individuals make decisions about their life choices and the type and quality of support they want. They use words like "I decide;" "I choose;" "I am heard when I am speaking up." We have learned a great deal about self-determination in recent years. We know that all human beings seek their own path. When we listen deeply, persons who require significant support are able to express their desires and dreams. To dream is to envision yourself in a different place and state of being. John Ralston Saul says that to dream is to expand the imagination in ways that enable us to be full human beings and citizens.[4]

Dreaming is powerful because it often begins a journey full of intent. Intention is about expressing our will or desire related to who we are, who we want to become, and ways we want to be engaged in life. Without intention and purpose, life lacks meaning. Judith Snow, a wise leader who has influenced many people to begin to dream, says that being intentional enables people to begin to gain control of their lives. Snow sees dreams as intentions that are freely chosen. Snow also points out that in our culture, dreaming is often seen as an activity, something you do. She notes that in cultures that are more conscious of their relationship with the earth, dreaming is seen as a form of awareness. It is more like seeing or finding one's balance. Like all living organisms that are part of nature, intention and self-determination are a natural part of the web of life.[5]

The idea of being intentional about one's future requires a different frame of mind from the usual mechanistic approaches we often use. Many people tell us that they never knew how to dream until they were connected with others who were learning the power of dreaming. In conversations about the importance

Pathways to Inclusion

of dreaming we are discovering a profound truth. People do not dream about programs and services — they dream about a life in community full of things that really matter to them. Most people dream about ordinary things that can make a good life, such as having a home or participating more fully as members of a community.

The process of each person finding a unique path begins through creative ways of enabling dreams. As Goethe said, "Whatever you can do, or dream you can do, begin it. Boldness has genius, power and magic in it." How to assist people to dream and to find that boldness is not as easy as it sounds. The process of dreaming can unlock energy people did not know they had and can sometimes be frightening. Managing risk is an important part of the process. Becoming aware of possibilities is part of the puzzle of building a life in community.

Carl Hiebert, an author and photographer from Waterloo, Ontario, reminds us how much risk there was following his spinal cord injury. Although Hiebert continues to use a wheelchair for mobility, he flies an ultra-light airplane and takes photographs all over the world. Hiebert says that the greatest quality one can display is courage, the willingness to take risks without knowing the outcome. Visualizing, which can help people dream, is vital to any goal or recovery. "Visualize success," says Hiebert, "Visualization is the formation of mental images. Scientific studies have shown that our central nervous system does not know the difference between a real and an imagined experience. What we believe to be true can easily become so ... By imagining success, we subconsciously begin to believe we are actually capable of accomplishing it."[6]

People learn more about dreaming by attending workshops or conferences. Exciting opportunities arise when these educational opportunities bring together those who have already learned about dreaming with those who have not yet been through this process. Keeping Your Dreams Alive is an educational initiative developed in Ontario with People First and other disability groups. It includes several workshops that explore questions such as the following: What is a dream? How is the past important? What is most important in your life? How can you create your dream? And, who can you count on to assist you? Richard Ruston, past president of People First of Ontario, is a frequent facilitator of Keeping Your Dreams

Alive.[7] He says that the process has been very empowering for participants: "It has helped them express wishes, dreams, and ideas that have been held inside for a long time."

Dreaming is like a vision that is often the surface of a deep tapestry of hopes. It is important to understand that dreams exist within a broad context. When a person has a dream or an intention "to move away from home," "to regain my life as a painter," or "to have fun with friends," this can be understood at one level as a direct wish. However, there might be a different meaning that needs to be explored to assist the person to realize their dreams. If we only focus on "moving away from home," we might miss deeper insights about the person's desire to gain personal space and independent relationships. It is important to explore the broad context of a dream and the underlying motivations and experiences.

Garth James is a 20-year-old man with vital energy and a love for life. His autism makes it difficult for him to focus on tasks or relationships for any length of time. After finishing high school, he spent most of his days playing on the computer at home or pacing up and down in his parents' living room. As part of the Foundations project in Kitchener–Waterloo, James connected with a facilitator who encouraged him to think about what he really loved. What were his passions? If he could dream, what would he want to do? At a small gathering with James' mother and two other relatives, James blurted out that he really wanted to be an astronaut. While his family members chuckled at the idea, the facilitator wisely asked James some important follow-up questions. "What is it about being an astronaut that is exciting for you?" James thought for a few moments and then said, "Science ... Travel." The facilitator's question was beginning to unravel some of the motivations and context related to the dream. The facilitator realized that James' love of science and travel would be vital to exploring and actualizing the dream. Everyone present slowly realized that there are many different ways James might be able to experience this dream without actually putting on a space suit and flying to Mars.

We are also discovering that dreaming happens best within the context of relationships. Dreaming by oneself might be considered fantasy, while sharing dreams and intentions with those whom you trust creates a base for participation and contributing. "Dreaming within the circle" becomes a metaphor to replace the machine-like, traditional system that prefers certainty and compliance.[8] There is a natural uncertainty to this process of dreaming, and supporting intentions can be unsettling. However, members of the person's network need to be open to a different future of whatever possibilities arise. Marc Gafni points out that our role is to be a witness which involves seeing, hearing, and understanding.[9] This work suggests that when supporting another person's dreams, we have to set aside our preconceived notions of the person, and focus on people's goals and capacities. Relationships also create conditions for the co-creation of dreams and intentions. Joan Sutherland, a Zen teacher, says that "our individual dreams ... are touched by the dreams of others, and that is how our common world is made."[10] This "relational" process of dreaming and exploring intentions enables us to move away from "fixing" the person to "building a *pathway* with the person." The dream or personal vision often begins this process of creating a meaningful life.

We All Have Gifts

Much of our life with our daughter Karen has involved reminding ourselves and others of her gifts and contributions. This may seem like a strange preoccupation, but it is an essential conversation to have over and over, especially as children grow and new gifts emerge. In our culture, once a person has been labelled, it is far too easy to ignore the gifts or possibilities for contribution. The traditional, "old story" paradigm continues to be so much a part of our culture that deficits keep on guiding much of our thinking and acting.

Judith Snow believes that "all individuals, regardless of their differences, must be regarded as an unusual gift, not a burden, to the broader social structure. People must see that differences do not have to be fixed or cured. Instead, each individual's gifts must be discovered, accepted, and shaped."[11] Bruce Anderson points out that our gift is a passion that we feel strongly about.[12] Our gift is not just a list of strengths, but a deeper sense of who we really are.

In her book, *What's Really Worth Doing and How to Do It*, Judith Snow describes giftedness as something that is part of all humanity and every person.[13] Snow challenges us to see disability and chronic conditions differently than in the past. Our historical descriptions tended to categorize and devalue. Instead of seeing our daughter Karen as "slow," "retarded," "handicapped," and having "special needs" or "Down syndrome," the challenge is to focus on her capacities. For some families, this idea is new even today because they have been socialized to see severe disability and chronic conditions as negative, debilitating, and limiting. In this sense, the very idea of "giftedness" is not only startling but also ironic. Things are not always what they seem. For example, certain persons may not appear to have strengths. When strengths are not obvious, the challenge is to discover the person's gift. In order to see people's gifts, people in initiatives say they "spend more time with the person," "really listen," and "pay attention to subtle signs of interests and strengths." We are learning that quality of life is enhanced by focusing on gifts rather than limitations.

Harvey Bristel loves to walk. As a child, he would be seen walking in his neighbourhood and dropping in to visit people. Some people did not appreciate his presence, while others welcomed him. Often his parents would resort to locking Bristel up in the house to limit his walking. Over time, he became depressed because he could not express his need to walk and meet people. Eventually his family gave up and put him in an institution. After spending years there, he moved to a large city where he was able to live with the support of a small innovative initiative. It soon became obvious to people that Bristel's gifts included walking and connecting with people. He is now able to walk miles each day visiting his favourite places and delivering packages to people's homes for a personal courier service.

Harvey Bristel's story is a typical example from New Story initiatives where deficits have been turned into strengths. Gifts are used to build capacities during employment, school, leisure, and other community participation. A genuine focus on strengths helps to define a person's identity. Carl Jung said that personal meaning in life comes when we embody what is important to our being. Bristel's walking is part of his being and his identity.

When focusing on a strengths approach, language takes on new meaning. The language we use to describe people or concepts needs to reflect their gifts and capacities. New Story initiatives strive to ensure that new concepts are embedded in language which emphasizes strengths. Many words are used that reflect gifts such as *capacities*, *strengths*, *abilities*, and *contributions*. All these words have become cornerstone values for the way these social innovations work in the world.

Types of Gifts

In New Story initiatives, we learn that gifts have a variety of meanings related to identity. Initiatives recognize that each person's gift and identity is unique and related to their strengths and interests. First is the *gift of presence*, which means that the person's presence is enough to engender smiles, hospitality, or relationships. It is not necessary for someone to do something extraordinary in order for their personal gift and strengths to be recognized. The young woman in the wheelchair with the radiant smile who hands out programs at our local theatre brings the gift of presence to that experience.

Second is the *gift of participation*, which means that the person's participation in community life is an expression of their interests and strengths. Participation can range from recreation to sports to culture to civic responsibility: Harvey Bristel's love of walking is an example or Karen Lord's regular participation in a drumming circle in our local community. In some cases, the gift of participation enables people to build a leisure identity.[14]

Third is the *gift of contribution*, which means that people are contributing their gifts to the life of their community and beyond. Many people have a particular gift that enables them to inspire others. Judith Snow, Catherine Frazee, and Carl Hiebert, all people we have talked about, are examples of citizens who have moved way beyond their disabilities and vulnerabilities in terms of impact and contribution. Many other citizens who are hardly noticed in their daily lives are bringing comfort and compassion to others in ways that are making a significant contribution.

Although people in New Story initiatives experience these types of gifts, the reality is that any one person can move from one to the other depending on the situation. Each person's identity is strengthened by having opportunities to express his or her gifts in all of these ways.

Using a Strengths Approach

As explored previously, *independence* has been a commonly used word in the fields of disability and aging for more than 20 years. Typically, the deficit perspective on independence is equated with "being able to do things yourself." This view reinforces that if you cannot do it yourself, you cannot be independent, and therefore having a disability or being old and frail is a burden.[15] A strengths approach first re-frames independence as a process of having choice, freedom, and control over personal experiences. The tension of these differing viewpoints on language is reflected in the York Region Alternative Community Living program, where frail elderly persons are able to live on their own with support. One tenant explained, "The idea [of being independent despite our frailties] is fantastic ... You have your freedom and yet you have care and support when you need it." In this strengths approach, people with complex disabilities can experience independence by directing those who provide the support they require. In the world of disability, the Canadian Association of Independent Living Centres and its affiliates across Canada have long been proponents of this strengths-oriented view of independence.[16]

One way strengths' language is embedded in New Story practice is through the intentional use of principles. New Frontiers in London, for example, has nine guiding principles. One principle that is based on a strengths and capacities perspective states, "Each person's individuality, their unique gifts, talents, preferences, and differences will be honoured." Similarly, Deohaeko Support Network, an innovative family-driven housing project, has a principle that states, "We believe in our sons and daughters — they have gifts to offer and we believe that community is stronger and better for all when our family members are included."

More and more individuals and families are beginning to understand the importance of person-centered approaches that build on strengths. As this happens, they are able to take it upon themselves to develop guiding principles for how they want their lives to look. The experiences of two persons reflect this trend. Joel Pott, a young man in his twenties, lives with his family in Brockville and has been associated with the Brockville and District Association for Community Involvement for some time. One of the basic principles in Pott's plan affirms that "decisions regarding choice of activities must take into account

Pathways to Inclusion

Pott's aspirations and be made by Pott and his support circle."
Similarly, Andrew Bloomfield has parents and friends who have
helped him build a life in his own home since 1997. In a document called *Planning with Andrew: Individualized Service and
Support Plan*, there are a number of principles that serve as
strength and gift strategies for anyone in a relationship with
Bloomfield:

- Focusing on him as an individual human being with a distinctive combination of needs and strengths
- Facilitating his efforts to do what he knows makes sense and
  is necessary, rather than just prompting him to conform to
  others' expectations
- Supporting him with regular structure, consistency across all
  parts of his life, and continuity in objectives and skills from
  the past into the future[17]

Principles for individuals and organizations help ensure that
people's strengths are combined with their dreams to create
meaningful goals and activities.

Strengths-based, person-centered approaches can be very
empowering for older couples when one spouse is experiencing
dementia. In such situations, the caregiving spouse often
requires regular respite as a way to enhance their health and
well-being. The Alzheimer Society of Hamilton Halton has
developed a program called "Supporting Couples to Remain
Together." In this initiative, a facilitator meets with each couple
and establishes a relationship, becomes aware of the couple's
strengths and situation, and explores needs and wishes. Based
on the premise of "respite as an outcome," a variety of individualized supports are available to assist each couple. These
include ongoing facilitator support and counselling, and access
to a small respite fund that can be used for a variety of things
that either spouse may require.

Participation in community life is another important way
that persons in the initiatives are sharing gifts and making a
contribution. However, all initiatives have learned that mere
participation in a leisure program or volunteering on a community board does not ensure that full participation will happen.
When gifts, high expectations, and intentional planning are the
focus, the meaning of participation deepens and creates more
potential for change. Participation in a yoga class becomes an
opportunity for people in the class to learn about the New

Story. Authentic relationships are more likely to emerge from these situations where gifts are noticed and nurtured. When participation is based on gifts and community, capacity building of all members of a group or neighbourhood occurs.

It is important that the planning process takes two things into consideration when thinking about participation: connecting people with places that build on their interests and dreams; but also finding settings that demonstrate commitment to capacity building. Gifts can lead to community and relationships when there is the capacity for ongoing connections and involvement. This has been demonstrated over and over in New Story initiatives. For many people, the opportunity to participate is enough. Mark McCormack from Prince George Project Friendship had an accident when he was 18 that left him paralyzed and unable to walk. Barely recovered from his accident, he saw a poster advertising the B.C. Games for the Physically Disabled. He was inspired and decided he would pursue the path of participation in sports. For the past 20 years, he has been an active participant in all kinds of sporting activities in his community. McCormack has a strong sense of purpose and belief in his own gifts and in what he is doing.[18]

In the gifts approach used within New Story initiatives, there is recognition that strengths are not just identified, but they are also developed and nurtured. Sometimes dreams may seem far in the future. Barb Kinney from the Personal Communities Project in Alberta had a dream to be a teacher. Since Kinney's developmental disability made it somewhat difficult for her to attend college, Kinney and her network thought hard about ways she could teach. Building on her gift of swimming, they found a YMCA that was interested in supporting her to learn to teach young children to swim. She was paired with an experienced swimming teacher who became her mentor and model.

Recognition of strengths can contribute to *capacity building* and enhanced participation over time. Our daughter Karen's experience with drumming is a prime example. When Karen was in high school we noticed she began using a large plastic water bottle for drumming. When her friends came over, they wanted to "play" too, so we collected a few more water bottles. Later, a friend, Amanda, from work noticed Karen's interest and suggested we buy a drum. It started with a small bongo and later progressed to a large hand drum. Amanda was a drummer herself and started inviting Karen over each week for drumming lessons and playing with her children. Karen got so excited that she eventually took African drumming lessons from another teacher. A few years later, Karen's facilitator noticed there was a new "drumming circle" in town, and Karen joined a weekly group in a nearby cultural centre. In the summer, she also attends a drumming circle at Kitchener's Victoria Park. This past summer, Karen went with her personal assistant/drummer friend to a weekend drumming camp on Lake Huron. Recently, Karen became a drummer for our local community band, which plays weekly at retirement homes and other community settings. Drumming has been a very important part of Karen's "leisure identity" and has played an important role in expanding her social network.

There is a strong learning element to the gifts approach. Self-determination and learning are central to everyone's life path. "We *all* have strengths and gifts" and "We can *all* contribute" is almost a mantra that we hear over and over. Whether in language, principles, or reflective practice, there is an earnest attempt to honour the identity of each person. And opportunities to extend that identity through the identification and nurturing of gifts and strengths are evident.

The more challenging part of the New Story is finding places and people in our communities that also embrace such a welcoming approach. According to people in · the initiatives, these welcoming settings do exist, although it might take time to find them. The way people are introduced in a new setting can sometimes be a factor in their acceptance. When persons are introduced with mention of their gifts and strengths, reciprocity more than likely is returned. As many families tell us, they only talk about the disability or vulnerability of their family member *after* they have shared the person's gifts and strengths.

In the New Story, leaders embrace the process of finding places and people that welcome gifts. John McKnight and Peter Block, in their book, *The Abundant Community*, point out that every community has "connectors," people who believe in the power of the neighbourhood and who know how to link others together. In many ways, this is the community development work of the New Story, where we seek out natural connectors. They can help us to know our neighbourhood and identify the gifts and strengths that exist.[19]

A Powerful Combination: Independent Facilitation and Planning

We have spent a lot of time listening to, being with, and supporting persons and families who are seeking a full life in a community. Many years ago, we began to realize the benefits that people derive from having such support from people or initiatives that are not part of the established service system. Whether it is one family helping another or a facilitator who is independent of service agencies, people appreciate having someone who can assist them with planning a good life in their community. The inspirational leaders we talked about earlier recognize the value of creative planning. But they are also beginning to understand why the New Story needs to embrace independent facilitation and planning. This practical concept builds on the idea of leaders and organizations thinking and acting like a social movement.

A simple definition of independent facilitation and planning is people having access to a facilitator who provides planning and network support that is independent or "de-linked" from direct service-providing agencies, both traditional and innovative. As the New Story emerges, people in the social innovations are realizing that traditional planning is inadequate. In traditional planning, people must choose from a limited range of program options offered by that service. In other words, traditional service planning limits possibilities for people pursuing their dreams. Alison Ouellette, a parent leader whose son has received facilitation support from Windsor–Essex Brokerage for Personal Supports, says that "planning is the new program."

The type of facilitation support available to a person in the New Story means that "I have someone in my life that is freely available to listen and support me in my quest for self-determination and citizenship." Many people long for such a source of guidance.

The facilitator works for the person, without a conflict of interest, although self-reflection is always needed to safeguard the facilitator from having too much influence or power. A facilitator assisting people in making key decisions must not have a vested interest in that decision. This issue of conflict of interest has been exposed in a variety of contexts beyond human services, most notably when politicians use their affiliations with the corporate world. Expecting the person to choose

The Reflective Facilitator

Facilitation is the art of supporting people with effective process, communication, and reflection. Facilitation is often described as a process that makes group process and decision making easier. To facilitate also means to "draw out" and to create hospitable settings for conversation and dialogue.

Several New Story initiatives have created the role of facilitator. In many ways, this is a reflective role. Facilitators bring to their work strong values, a commitment to self-determination for all citizens, and a belief in building vibrant communities. Facilitators who are trying to nurture New Story principles play a variety of roles, which include the following:

- Being mindful, in the moment, and aware of context
- Nurturing good process with groups and individuals, listening deeply
- Helping people to dream, build on strengths, and plan their future
- Helping people to build relationships and networks
- Connecting people with resources and meaningful places in community
- Negotiating and brokering for people who have individualized funding
- Collaborating with diverse groups and individuals in community
- Building capacity of community at all opportunities

Note: For more thinking about reflective practice, see J. Pinkerton, P. Dolan, and J. Canavan, *Family Support as Reflective Practice* (London, UK: Jessica Kinsley Publishers, 2006); the journal *Reflective Practice*; and L. Chenoweth and D. Stehlik, Implications of Social Capital for The Inclusion of People with Disabilities and Families in Community Life, *International Journal of Inclusive Education*, 8 (2004): pp. 59–72. Also see Ram Dass and P. Gorman, *How Can I Help: Stories and Reflections on Service* (New York, NY: Alfred A. Knopf, 1987).

from the facilitator's programs is a prime example of such a conflict. In addition, when a facilitator feels allegiance to both the person and the agency, the facilitator will feel torn and be in a conflict of interest. John McKnight says that many human services have become corporate-like in structure and operation, with the accompanying outcomes of clienthood, compliance, and loss of identity.[20] This provides all the more reason for examining the issue of conflict of interest. Some approaches, such as Windsor–Essex Brokerage for Personal Supports, reduce conflict of interest by implementing "unencumbered" planning. The person is able to receive planning support and facilitation without any pressure to select one agency or program over others. This means the person is free to choose the most suitable option for meeting his or her needs or desires.

Independent facilitation and planning has evolved from several developments that began in the 1980s. Pioneers at the time realized that community services seldom provided individualized support. In response to this concern, approaches like individualized program planning and case management became part of the human service landscape. Like many new ideas at the time, these approaches were usually added on to existing agency structures. Case management tended to be primarily concerned with planning *for* people and managing their programs, services, and daily routines. Critics also pointed out that early work on individualized program planning did not lead to significant changes in people's lives as citizens in community. By the 1990s, many social innovators realized that an individualized plan by itself was insufficient. Facilitation was linked with planning and slowly became part of a desired vision.

It is important to stress that the *process* of planning is seen as more important than the "plan" itself. Independent facilitation assists people in identifying and implementing their dreams. Early facilitation work at Community Living St. Marys also focused on community development as a way to address the barriers and challenges being faced by people. Individualized planning and facilitation are now seen as one integrated approach in many New Story initiatives. This approach, despite research showing its worth, is often compromised by those who believe that their existing agencies could incorporate or "add on" this service.[21]

When there is a focus on good process and facilitation in New Story initiatives, more attention is paid to building a good life rather than on placement. The latter is common practice in the old story. People with the innovations understand that building a life is different from finding a placement in a program or service. The metaphor of the waiting list reflects the traditional paradigm where persons and families must wait, often for years, for the supposedly right service, professional, or intervention.[22] Yet waiting usually reinforces compliance. It assumes that existing services and supports will work for the person. Sometimes they work, but often times they do not. In reality, waiting is disempowering and creates dependency. In New Story initiatives, the assumption is that people require dialogue, facilitation support, and control over the planning process and its outcomes. They do not need a placement and certainly not a waiting list. In this way, independent facilitation stays focused on what the person decides he or she needs and wants as well as attaining conditions and opportunities afforded other citizens. Shifting power to individuals and families helps balance the power already invested in organizations.

Facilitation Issues

As we begin to deepen our understanding of how independent planning and facilitation works, several issues emerge from the initiatives. *The first is how persons and families choose their facilitators.* In most cases, facilitators are assigned, not chosen by persons or families. However, because of the focus on empowerment, changes can be made in facilitators if the match is not suitable. Increasingly, persons and families are demanding more choice in their facilitators. Community Living British Columbia, an entity that provides planning and service support to people with developmental disabilities, has developed 17 community living centres throughout the province. Each centre includes several facilitators who provide independent planning and facilitation to people who desire such support. In addition, however, individuals and families have the option of choosing their own facilitator and receiving payment to hire such a person.

Durham Association for Family Respite Services in Ontario promotes planning and facilitation support by inviting people to choose their own facilitator. Their brochure on person-directed vision planning states that, "You may want to lead the planning yourself, or you may want to invite a family member, friend, or broker/facilitator to help you with the planning process." Barb Leavitt, a facilitator from southwest Ontario, emphasizes that the fit between a facilitator and the person is critical: "There needs to be a trust relationship between the facilitator and the person and it needs to be long term ... People need someone to walk with them through difficult stuff." Whether facilitators are chosen or assigned, there needs to be a period of time for trust to develop. Clearly, some progressive organizations and many families feel that this trust has a better chance of succeeding if they play a role in choosing the facilitator.[23]

Dialogue is a word you hear often within New Story approaches. Facilitators use dialogue and deep listening, not just discussion and debate. Many people in New Story initiatives can recall countless meetings where discussion and debate was the norm. Such communication is dominated by the presentation of various positions or viewpoints on issues. Dialogue, on the other hand, is a process of deliberate listening and the building of genuine shared insights, rather than position taking. When working with a person and his or her network, we often see facilitators respectfully listening and honouring different voices.[24] Families for a Secure Future describes the importance of "fostering meaningful dialogue" and assisting groups to create opportunities where "families/friends can talk about what really matters to them," and "assisting individuals and family/friends to reflect on their values and what it takes to have a good life." Reflecting a person's dreams, strengths, and issues is important in building a meaningful plan. Many people underestimate how much work is involved in building a process and a plan that lead to citizenship. Dialogue with others around a person's dreams creates a context for inviting people to participate in the life of the person. The Support Clusters Project, for example, found that effective dialogue moves planning groups away from professional domination and, in some ways, blurs the boundaries between professionals and users.

John O'Brien says that dialogue within person-centered planning increases uncertainty within service systems, which is a good thing. This happens by strengthening people's alliances, clarifying interests and goals, and energizing new demands on service systems. O'Brien points out that person-centered planning is often misunderstood and seen as a series of meetings designed to produce a static plan.[25] A commitment to ongoing dialogue helps minimize this misunderstanding. A plan should never be considered a "done deal." Rather, facilitators and participants work together, constantly reviewing and renewing goals and opportunities. Facilitators say it takes months of ongoing dialogue to deepen a person's pathway to inclusion. For people who have been quite isolated, there is often no goal, perhaps just a faint intention. Facilitators walk with people as they explore these possibilities. We often see this exploration; a person has a glimpse of being able to sing or dance, gradually finds ways to express the voice or move the body, then eventually connects with a choir or a dance group. To some, it appears that this result just happened, but we know that developing these pathways to inclusion takes a lot of dialogue, experimenting, and community development.

It is often said that information is power. It may seem surprising in this information age that many persons and families lack reliable, useful information. On the other hand, facilitators in New Story initiatives have vast amounts of information about their communities. They are also well connected with people and places that can provide information. Ana Vicente, manager of the Options program in Toronto, says that "The facilitator needs to be very well informed about their community — knowing the clubs, the churches, schools, everything that is out there, and to know how these contexts relate to the person's strengths." Since facilitators work from values and principles, they can help people discern what information is most relevant. One value or principle that we often hear is "Community as a first resort." In practice, this means that having knowledge about regular, community-based information is paramount for facilitators. This is in contrast to services or resources designed *only* for marginalized persons.

As persons and families move away from "waiting for services," they also require information and knowledge about many things beyond services and programs. People might need information about facilitation, person-centered planning, how to build a support network, or initiatives and policies that fund individualized supports. Alice Quinlan, a mother whose son receives facilitation support from Windsor–Essex Brokerage for Personal Supports, says that the right information was very empowering for her at the time when she began planning to improve her son's life in the community. Ultimately, the goal of information is to empower people to make meaningful choices.

Seeding and Supporting Independent Facilitation

The following summary identifies themes and insights gathered from eight communities in Ontario that have been engaged in New Story work of "seeding and supporting" independent facilitation.

Get Started

- Identify one or two New Story champions who understand the power and importance of independent facilitation.
- Support the champions to build a cross-sector steering group; be sure it is family and person-driven, but also have facilitators, service providers, and community members in the group.

Build Capacity

- Spend time having conversations about the elements of the New Story and the role that facilitators play in the community.
- Identify the values and principles that you want to drive independent facilitation.
- Organize a training event on independent facilitation so that the Steering Committee and the wider community become aware of the knowledge, principles, and skills that facilitators need.
- Coordinate educational opportunities so that families, providers, and community leaders become aware of the potential of independent facilitation. Education can include PowerPoint presentations, evening round-table conversations, and stories from facilitators and people who have utilized facilitation.

Create Functions and Structure

- Identify facilitator functions that are needed to guide the facilitation work, such as getting to know people and communities, identifying strengths and gifts,

Pathways to Inclusion

personal planning, connecting with community, and building capacity.

- Figure out the structure of the new entity and how it will impact on the community. The "independence from service provision" is a key part of the structure. In Ontario, these new entities are playing multiple roles, including providing facilitation support to agencies, individuals, and families. Some are intentionally focusing on facilitating family groups in neighbourhoods.

Mobilize Resources

- Create resources to launch the new entity. This might entail some community agency and government funds, but will likely also include fund raising dollars, purchase of service agreements, fee for service with families, and crisis support work.

Independent planning and facilitation should be designed to create safe places for people to co-create pathways to community, based on shared reflections about dreams, strengths, and appropriate community information. In the Foundation Project in Kitchener, facilitators are knowledgeable about community-based literacy opportunities. As one example, they supported three people to participate in literacy groups offered to the general public.

As mentioned, *planning and facilitation support should be independent from service provision.* Facilitators need to be located within organizations or places that are not tied in any way to service organizations. The reality and politics of this principle illustrates how difficult this is to achieve. Community Living British Columbia will be critical to watch over the next few years, with its facilitators located in community living centres and paid directly by government. These facilitators are clearly separate from service providers but not from government. A few small organizations in Ontario have been able to build the capacity of independent planning separate from service provision. As examples, Windsor–Essex Brokerage for Personal Supports is an autonomous independent planning organization. Options in Toronto is embedded within a larger organization, Family Service Association of Toronto; however, it does not provide any direct services to people with disabilities.

Since the publication of this book in 1997, several communities in Ontario have been initiating and supporting the development of independent facilitation. Some of this work began through a three-year project called Modeling Innovation and Community Change.[26] We have also been involved in several other communities through the Facilitation Leadership Group. In the focus box on the previous pages, some of the key insights from this work of "seeding and supporting independent facilitation" are outlined.

There is focus in the initiatives on building the capacity of the person and the community. We learn that when people's dreams and gifts are central, the facilitation support can be transformational. When time is taken to listen deeply and to explore people's aspirations, there is a strong social learning component. Relationships and alliances are strengthened, and there is a focus on building the capacity of the person, family, and community. Ana Vicente, manager of Options in Toronto, stresses that the facilitator knows which strength areas the person would need support to develop and creates opportunities that enhance the possibility of inclusion. Vicente notes that "approximately 87% of people we support use supports for community involvement, whether it is recreation, employment, education, or volunteering. It is only a small number of people who use specialized day programs and congregate services."

Barb Leavitt from Community Living St. Marys points out that "the facilitator's role is not just planning, it is also building capacity of the community." For example, several years ago, St. Marys discovered that many people with disabilities were limited in their options because of poor public transportation. They decided to do some community development work with the broader community. This eventually led to the municipality offering improved access to public transportation — a benefit to everyone in the community.

Only a few New Story initiatives have developed the capacity to implement independent planning and facilitation, while several others are moving toward this goal. This is an important social innovation in the way it advances the new paradigm, although it is clearly not easy to implement within current human service systems. To do so requires significant shifts in thinking, policy, and resource allocation.

Individualized Funding: Individuals and Networks Control Support Resources

Building a life in community requires intentional planning, committed people, and access to valued resources. In traditional systems, resources are generally tied to service organizations. In turn, people using these services have few choices in terms of where they live or what their personal supports may look like. In most homecare programs, for example, people receiving support usually have little say about who or when staff come into their home. The New Story focus on dreams, gifts, and person-centered plans demands that we re-examine the way resources for support are organized and allocated. The practice of individualized funding is growing in many jurisdictions across Canada as a way to ensure that persons and their networks have control over valued resources in the community. Several initiatives have been involved with individualized funding.

Individualized funding got its start in Canada when a group of dedicated families brought their sons and daughters home from the Woodlands Institution in British Columbia in the late 1970s. These families convinced the provincial government that funds for supports should be "attached" to each person coming out of the institution. Since that time, a variety of groups have developed their own unique approach to individualized funding. For example, in the mid-1990s Alberta passed legislation that made it possible for people with physical disabilities and people with developmental disabilities to access individualized funding. In 2002, the United Kingdom expanded individualized funding to include older adults who were frail.[27]

In the past decade, we have learned a great deal about individualized funding and how it can be most effective. We now know that individualized funding works best when accompanied by some form of independent planning and facilitation,

Windsor–Essex Brokerage for Personal Supports: Lessons about Independent Planning/Facilitation and Individualized Funding

In the 1990s, leaders in the Windsor and Essex County area of Ontario began to reflect on how to make the supports they offered to citizens with disabilities more personalized and more reflective of the values of self-determination and citizenship. Several people from the disability community started to meet with family leaders and directors of four major organizations. In an initial initiative called Innoventions, the purpose was to identify key factors that would enhance disability supports and the participation of persons and families.

Early in the planning, the Windsor–Essex Steering Committee realized that the traditional approach to service delivery was deeply flawed. Malcolm Jeffreys, the executive director of Community Living Windsor before his untimely death in 2003, coined the phrase "benevolent model" to describe the existing system. It was characterized by community agencies holding most of the power and the decision making about supports for people. In what Jeffreys called the "empowerment model," it was seen as critical to separate the functions typically embedded in traditional organizations. The Innoventions Committee proposed that the main existing system functions — service delivery, advocacy, independent planning and facilitation, and allocations of individualized funding — be separated. In some cases, they were also restructured and reassigned to other organizations.

Work continued during a restructuring phase in the late 1990s. In the restructured system, Community Living Windsor and other service providers maintained service delivery, such as the operation of residential and vocational services. Advocacy was seen as the responsibility of self-help groups of people with disabilities, including an active People First group. Advocacy was also done by family self-help organizations, such as the Windsor–Essex Family Network. Independent plan-

Pathways to Inclusion

Windsor–Essex Brokerage for Personal Supports (continued)

ning and facilitation was offered through a new organization called Windsor–Essex Brokerage for Personal Supports. Allocation of individualized funding became the responsibility of two new affiliated committees organized by the regional government office of the Ministry of Community and Social Services. A priority panel that includes family and broad community members reviews people's requests for individualized support and funding. The priority panel sets priorities without consideration of money. An allocations committee then makes the final decisions about allocation of funds based on the priority panel's recommendations, people's budgets, and available funds. Early in the restructuring, the agencies in Windsor–Essex County also made a commitment to portability of funding. All agencies now have a portability clause in their contracts with the government, further contributing to flexibility of disability supports. *Portability* means that persons and families may move their support dollars to another organization or community if they wish.

Windsor–Essex Brokerage for Personal Supports plays a critical role in this restructured system because of its potential for assisting people to build a good life. According to many people in the area, the organization built a positive reputation within its first two years. A comprehensive evaluation conducted by the Roeher Institute confirmed that people who had used the independent planning support had high degrees of satisfaction and had very positive outcomes. The project became an ongoing support once established by the government. Windsor–Essex Brokerage for Personal Supports, known as Brokerage, is described in its brochure as an organization that is a support in the community for people who are looking for a different way to work toward their goals. "Dedicated to maximize self-determination, it was first set-up to be the primary and dedicated resource for unencum-

Windsor–Essex Brokerage for Personal Supports (continued)

bered person-directed planning support and facilitation in Windsor and Essex County."

Although established as an organization to provide planning support, Brokerage for Personal Supports is seen as playing other valuable, related roles. The provision of information is crucial, and Brokerage believes that people and families need good information and good advice in order to make decisions. With highly personalized and accurate information, persons and families are better equipped for the future. Brokerage also works toward strengthening people and families and assists people with a variety of tasks related to planning and individualized funding. These include negotiating, writing contracts, building support networks, and hiring staff.

System redesign in Windsor–Essex is far from perfect. However, in its separation of functions and in the development of the Brokerage organization, it has contributed immensely to our thinking about the possibilities of the New Story. Catharine MacQuarrie, a woman from the town of Essex, captures the importance of both changes when she says, "We don't know what we would have done without the assistance of Brokerage for Personal Supports and also Windsor–Essex Family Network. It took help from both organizations to make a difference for my brother. Brokerage facilitated the ongoing planning process, provided mediation, and is writing our contract with the agency. The Family Network helped strengthen us so we could effectively champion what changes my brother needed in his existing supports. We feel that there is some hope now."

Reference: Roeher Institute, *Windsor–Essex Brokerage Pilot Project Evaluation Report* (North York, ON: Author, 1999).

Pathways to Inclusion

ensuring the support plan be based on dreams, strengths, personal goals, and directions of the person.[28] As explored above, this ensures that there is an ongoing process for dialogue and change. It also creates appropriate infrastructure supports for individualized funding.

One of the most important outcomes of individualized funding is supports that are flexible and geared to the person.[29] The Ontario Direct Funding Project, for example, enables people with physical disabilities to access individualized funding for attendant services. The planning and facilitation support comes from nine Independent Living Resource Centres across the province. People develop a plan and are eligible for direct funding if they can direct and manage their own system of support. Once people receive their direct funding they hire their own personal assistants or support workers. They also have flexibility with scheduling them for the hours that work best for their lifestyle. Flexibility is further enhanced by the fact that people can use their attendants at home, at work, and on vacation. Evaluation results of this initiative show that people are more empowered, engaged in the community, and satisfied with their lifestyles than they were prior to their involvement with Direct Funding.[30]

In addition to increased flexibility, many people tell us they find it liberating to have individualized funding. They are free from a reliance on traditional services and afforded more control in their life choices. In communities where all the agencies that provide support services work from the traditional paradigm, the availability of individualized funding creates a valuable option. Families that have built an inclusive community life for their son or daughter find individualized funding offers the chance for this enriched life to continue into adulthood. Far too many young people with disabilities who finish high school are faced with a life that involves either sitting at home or within a traditional day program as a last resort.[31] Individualized funding and strong facilitation within the Foundations program has been a powerful impetus for young people and their families to build life goals and community connections in ways that are meaningful to both. In this way, individualized funding, when combined with independent planning and facilitation, has been able to build capacity of people and their networks.

Creative Approaches to Direct Support

Building supports on dreams, strengths, and intentional planning is a key part of the New Story for persons and families. In addition to independent planning and facilitation, many people require direct support in their lives. Personal assistants who provide direct support is one mechanism that is vital to the implementation of the New Story. In the old story, support workers provide support to the person in ways that are directed by the agency. As we have seen, this kind of agency-directed support works for some people, but for many people it simply is not personal or individualized enough. We learn from the initiatives that the use of direct support often requires creativity. Creative supports for people often emerge from "outside the box" thinking that accompanies strong independent facilitation.

New Story principles shift the role of the personal assistant. Remember that person-directed planning created a plan outlining how a person could establish a good life. The role of the personal assistant is to carry out the person's plan under the direction of the person. Some individuals also need others in their network to play a role in directing the personal assistants. These workers are typically hired by the person and their network. When supports are based on an individual's plan and direction, and when we have the "right" facilitator and personal assistants, we can say that we have the conditions in place for creative supports to be implemented.

Creative supports in the New Story generally have three components. First, the *purpose* of supports is clear — to build a good life in the community for people who have been segregated or, in the case of an older person, to continue to experience quality of life. In the "old story" the purpose of supports is often protection and passivity. As we explored earlier, there is power in purpose. Intention creates opportunities and possibilities. The second component of creative supports in the New Story is that support is based in *relationship*. Judith Snow says "the support relationship is like a dance" where both the person and the personal assistant are moving in the same direction but the leader is clearly the person. The initiatives honour that support is always embedded in relationship. The third component of creative supports is that support is about *process*. Consider the simple human activity of helping someone go shopping. If there is a belief in self-determination and community, much creativity is required to ensure that shopping includes choice, control, and full participation of the person.

The support relationship is influenced by the history and experience of both the person receiving support and the people who are providing the support. Since the benevolence of "doing for" is often the experience of both the person and personal assistants, change may involve a period of re-learning and living with tensions. Our work with several initiatives suggests three stages in the support relationship. The first stage is *connecting*, where the two people begin to form a relationship. The second stage is *learning*, and involves a period of time for the personal assistant to learn how to best respond to the person's directions. Respect is central to the support relationship. When this is present from both people the learning process can be fairly rapid. The third stage is *flowing* and describes the mutuality of understanding that exists when the person and the personal assistant are working well together. The importance of connecting, learning, and flowing for all support relationships confirms the importance of people and their networks having choice and control over who plays that role in their lives. Does it make sense for an agency to send a worker sight-unseen to a family supporting a person with dementia?

Issues that need attention in the support relationship will vary depending on whether or not that relationship is a formal (paid) relationship or an informal (family or friends) relationship. Regardless, in the New Story there is dialogue about these issues and sometimes a mediated process with a facilitator to resolve power issues that might emerge between the person needing support and the workers. To prevent issues from getting to that point, it is usual for people with personal assistants to have regular team meetings along with the facilitator. This helps ensure that everyone is on the same page in term of goals and processes. We also find that team meetings offer a space for the group to be creative in thinking about how to enhance inclusion and participation.

While the old story became fixated on traditional concepts, such as group homes, long-term care facilities, and sheltered employment, there is a danger that the New Story will become fixated on other things. As an example, some initiatives struggle with how to move beyond one-to-one support issues, where it may be assumed that a person always needs a worker in their life. Leaders are recognizing that direct support can be individualized in many different ways and that one-to-one support is only one variation. These initiatives seek to connect people with natural supports in their communities. Yet leaders of initiatives also know how difficult this can be. Earlier, we explored Garth Jones's dream of being an astronaut and his love of travel and science. Jones's network learned that he loved to travel on the train to Toronto and that he regularly watched science programs on the Discovery channel. The facilitator asked some further questions: "What places and what people would support Jones's dream and his love of science and travel?" It did not take long for the group to generate lists of people who would support his dream. Over the next few weeks, the personal assistant worked closely with Jones, introducing him to people on the list. Although few of these early connections worked, Jones then met a physics professor at a local university. When Jones talked with the professor, he discovered that this professor worked with telescopes. This eventually led Jones to the lab where a graduate student showed Jones how to use the telescope. This kind of intentional planning, facilitation, and direct support is helping initiatives discover the power of natural supports in helping people build a life in community. As this story illustrates, it is often a time-consuming and uneven pathway.

Time for Common Sense

Common sense about building a life in community is partly about applying the same standards or expectations that we have for *ourselves* to *others*. If being able to dream is fundamental to people's well-being, then we must assume the same is true for people who are vulnerable. This means we must listen to people's dreams and support their choices and preferences. Recent research shows that many people experience both internal and external barriers to living their dreams.[32] While these barriers are addressed in some initiatives, the reality is that many barriers are systemic and difficult to change. Common sense will certainly help to change the way society begins to address these barriers. In addition, common sense in a democracy is about honouring people's choices, and it is also about what is right. Common sense is also about equity and ensuring that people are not discriminated against because of age, disability, or other factors. Addressing these barriers is a long-term struggle that involves significant policy change at municipal, provincial, and federal levels.

Although most of the innovative work related to gifts and person-centered planning has emerged from people with disabilities, the insights can be applied to any area of vulnerability. With frail elderly persons, for example, housing and support are seldom de-linked. This means that planning usually revolves around the "best placement" for the person. Instead, attention needs to be paid to existing strengths and supports that could be built on, so that people could remain in their own homes. The expansion of homecare is helping Canadians think about and plan ways to keep frail seniors in their own homes. But independent planning and facilitation, along with individualized funding, would greatly enhance the capacity of homecare initiatives. A few small initiatives, such as the York Region Alternative Community Living program in Ontario, demonstrate that "aging in place" is both possible and practical when seniors and their families are offered facilitation and person-centered planning support.[33] A recent Canadian study shows that intensive case management, which has some of the attributes of independent planning, contributes greatly to the life of elderly people who live in supportive housing. The research found that regular visits from a facilitator enhance people's well-being and social connections.[34] Applying this kind of research and common sense across service systems would expand the New Story.

Building on dreams and gifts will require common sense to counter a strong deficits approach that continues to dominate disability and aging policy making. It would be wise to examine other communities where "differences" are recognized as a natural part of life. One example is a small island called Martha's Vineyard, off the coast of Massachusetts, where a community used intuition and common sense in its approach to about a third of its population, which was deaf or hard of hearing. In *Everyone Here Spoke Sign Language*, Nora Groce describes how, over time, almost everyone on the island learned sign language.[35] In Canada, the percentage of the population made up of baby boomers, while less than 30%, is certainly substantial and could make a difference in how the New Story evolves for older adults.

With common sense, is it possible that the paradigm may shift even more than is currently being conceptualized? In many ways we are only beginning to uncover insights into what might be possible. Think of how communities could change if they took seriously the dreams and goals of all its citizens. Think of how communities would change if they honoured the participation and wisdom of elderly citizens.

Fortunately, the commitment to person-centered approaches is gradually moving beyond small, individual initiatives. As some of these initiatives have become established programs, new approaches are visible in small pockets throughout Canada. British Columbia's implementation of system-wide independent planning and facilitation, the growing awareness about the possibilities of "aging in place," and more creative use of homecare are other signs that the New Story is starting to evolve beyond a few innovations. Several communities in Canada are also beginning to take seriously the notion that social inclusion requires collaboration and new kinds of social networks.

Notes

1. Bruce Anderson, "The Rules We Live By", Number Five. Community Activators website: <http://www.communityactivators.com/the-rules#>.
2. The phrase "a good life" was used by Al Etmanski in his book about planning with people and families; see Etmanski (2000).
3. Pink (2009).
4. Saul (2001).
5. For more about Judith Snow's contribution to our understanding of the importance of dreaming, see Killoran (2002). Also see Pitonyak (2007).
6. Hiebert (2004), p. 2. His photography books to date include *Grand River, This Land I Love, Where Light Speaks, Us Little People,* and *Gift of Wings* <www.giftofwings.ca>.
7. Ruston and Powell (1995).
8. Falvey et al. (1997).
9. Gafni (2001).
10. Sutherland (2005), p. 72.
11. Judith Snow, quoted in quoted in Langley School District #35 Student Services BD Department Newsletter, *Ain't Misbehaving,* 4, 1 (October 2006): p. 3 <www.sd35.bc.ca/programs/SocialResponsibility/Newsletters/Sept06.pdf>
12. Anderson (n.d.).
13. Snow (1994).
14. McGill (2002).
15. Minkler (1990).

16. Canadian Association of Independent Living Centres. See their website <www.cailc.ca>.

17. Bloomfield, Bloomfield, and Bloomfield (n.d.): p. 8. For additional practical lifestyle planning process, see John Lord's website <www.johnlord.net>; go to publications, Lifestyle Planning.

18. Project Friendship in Prince George has a website filled with stories of people who have overcome great odds in their quest for citizenship and participation. See <www.projectfriendship.com>.

19. McKnight and Block (2010).

20. McKnight (1995).

21. For a review of 10 projects in three countries that make independent planning and facilitation a priority, see Lord, Zupko, and Hutchison (2000). For a more thorough analysis of the politics of independent planning, see O'Brien (n.d.).

22. Waiting lists are one of many complaints that people have of our human services. See Pedlar and Hutchison (2000).

23. For a review of person-centered planning and research, see Holburn and Vietze (2002).

24. David Bohm, a physicist, has done some seminal thinking about dialogue and its importance in relationships and innovation. See Bohm (1996).

25. O'Brien and O'Brien (2002).

26. Modeling Innovation and Community Change was a three-year initiative designed to develop community readiness, strengthen autonomous groups, and build sustainable new paradigm approaches in three communities.
See <www.modelingcommunitychange.com/>.

27. See research by Tim Stainton, Individualized Funding presentation to a policy forum on funding approaches for developmental services for the Ontario Ministry of Community and Social Services, Toronto, Ontario, March 30, 2005.

28. Lord (2006); Lord and Hutchison (2008).

29. Lord and Hutchison (2003); Hutchison, Lord, and Salisbury (2006).

30. Roeher Institute (1997).

31. Hart (2001).

32. See, for example, Sundar and Ochocka (2004).

33. Heumann and Boldy (1993).

34. Lum, Ruff, and Williams (2005).

35. Groce (1985).

9

Social Networks

Expanding Capacity through Relationships

In our loneliness and isolation, there is a deep longing, a yearning ... to be connected to a larger whole, to not be anonymous, to be seen and known.... It is deeply satisfying to experience meaningful connection with others. We hunger for that feeling of belonging.

Jon Kabot-Zinn[1]

It is challenging for any of us in this highly urbanized, consumer-oriented society to experience fulfilling relationships. People of any age can experience isolation and have few relationships, especially people who have typically been excluded from community life. In light of this reality, there has been an extraordinary movement over the past 20 years to assist people to intentionally build social networks.[2] *Social network* is a term that refers to all the important relationships in a person's life, both formal and informal. When social networks and relationships are supportive, researchers call it *social support*.

Research on social networks shows how our personal behaviour and attitudes are shaped by people in our networks. Interestingly, it is not just immediate friends, but friends of friends (our broader networks), that influence who we become, the kind of jobs we find, and the type of leisure we pursue. People with rich and varied connections have increased opportunities for participation and contribution. This new research on social networks shows how a network approach can enable us to influence and to engage people in supportive ways.[3]

There is recognition that friendships are lacking in many persons' lives because of isolation and dependence on formal services and staff. Attention to social network development has the goal of strengthening relationships and friendships. As Judith Snow says, "The only disability is having no relationships." This movement toward seeing relationships and networks as a critical part of a community's social capital is growing in importance. Many areas of vulnerability are being impacted by this movement, including aging, disability, and chronic conditions.[4] Desmond Tutu from South Africa claims that "a person is a person through other persons. We can only be human, only be free, together."

Social support in the form of social network building is recognized as a strong determinant of both physical and mental health. Building relationships in a community is a core idea for action in almost all New Story initiatives. It is clearly understood that isolation and loneliness must be addressed for people's quality of life to be improved. Some initiatives were in fact formed for the sole purpose of building social networks with people. In the New Story, people are less reliant on formal, traditional service structures. Social network approaches, when combined with independent planning and facilitation, are a central mechanism for bringing the values and visions to life.

Major Approaches to Network Building

Social networks are built or strengthened in New Story initiatives primarily by using one or more of the following approaches: informal connecting, network analysis, circle approach, and associational approach. The network and circle are powerful metaphors for building a society with inclusion and diversity as the foundations. Regardless of the strategy chosen, research shows that concerted effort is needed to create strong social networks, especially with people who have limited or no family connections.[5]

A widely recognized approach to building social networks is *informal connecting*. In this approach, the person and the facilitator are constantly looking for ways to expand the person's network. It usually involves looking for hospitality and relationships in the neighbourhood or in expanding relationships in the family. There is no attempt in this approach to formalize relationships but to build on any interest and connection that may be developing naturally. Sometimes there are shopkeepers who are very supportive who can become part of a person's informal network. In smaller communities, people in the initiatives tell us that most people they support now have strong informal networks and they are "known" in the community by lots of fellow citizens. Facilitators admit that building informal networks takes time and that "asking" is a key strategy for connecting. One organization we studied, the Welcome Home Initiative, uses informal connecting when it works with people leaving psychiatric facilities and assists them in identifying and strengthening potential networks. As David Schwartz has written, promoting asking can have huge effects on connecting and relationship building.[6]

Another approach to network building involves *network analysis*. Building a social network begins by first identifying the major areas of a person's life. School, work, volunteer work, neighbourhood, and church are common areas. Each of these components of the person's life becomes a potentially rich source of relationships. The planning process in this approach helps the person create a relationship map that identifies the current status of relationships in each area. For example, at the workplace it might be determined that there are two people who have shown an interest in the person; however, neither of these relationships has sufficiently evolved into what would be considered a friendship. Strategies are discussed to help make this happen. The Personal Communities Project in Alberta used this approach with new participants to help people think about potential areas of their lives where friendships could be nurtured. The paradox of network analysis is that the practical aspect of it requires us to show interest in people in our network. In a recent book called *Loneliness*, the authors show how reaching out to others in simple ways can trigger connections.[7] Network development is all about "we," not just "me." By engaging with others, perhaps with a simple question or comment, we find that most people naturally respond. Network analysis can assist us to be intentional about our connecting strategies.

Another approach widely used to strengthen people's social networks is the *circle approach*.[8] This approach embodies the native concept that a circle represents wholeness and the belief in the power of a circle or community of people. A circle usually comprises friends, family members, or sometimes other acquaintances. Each circle is known by a different name, depending on its purpose. Sometimes it is known as a "support circle," a "support cluster," "personal network," or a "microboard."

A support circle is a fairly formal network that meets as a small group on a regular basis and ensures that the person is surrounded by family and friends. Judith Snow created one of the first circles in Canada. She named it the "Joshua Committee" to signify that it also had the capacity to break down walls and barriers. The focus of a support circle can be on support for the person and sometimes the family. A support cluster is very similar to a support circle, but has one fundamental difference: professionals who are involved with the person are intentionally included, which is similar to the strategy called "wrap around." A personal network consists of the person's friends, and the focus is primarily on the person and their relationships and friendships. Microboards are yet another variation, where a small circle of family and friends join together with the person to incorporate a non-profit society in order to have the legal mandate to receive support funds and make decisions with the person.

A facilitator is often invited to assist individuals to build their circle. People often begin with a small group of friends and family and, with the assistance of their facilitator, learn to ask others into their network. Several New Story initiatives have shown leadership related to the development of various types of circles. For 20 years, Planned Lifetime Advocacy Networks (PLAN) in British Columbia, with affiliated groups across Canada and beyond, has been supporting families to develop personal networks with their loved ones. NABORS has been instrumental in building support circles with its members for more than 15 years. Vela Microboards in British Columbia has been supporting small groups who become incorporated entities for more than 15 years.[9]

Social network development can also occur through what has become known as the *associational approach*. John McKnight's work related to building the capacity of community is often credited for the development of and increase in popularity of this approach. The associational approach focuses on ways of connecting or bridging people to community associations or groups.[10] This is based on the belief that community associations, because of their more informal nature, provide untapped potential for inclusion and relationship building. More informal groups such as churches, community centres, and clubs tend to be welcoming and hospitable. Their social component and looser structure contribute to their informality compared to more formal settings. The groups are particularly useful because they attract people based on common interests. These groups are available for all citizens to participate in precisely because they are based on voluntary participation and shared interests. In the New Story initiatives, people are assisted to find these places of hospitality in their communities. Several initiatives focus on people's gifts and strengths related to their interests as a way to identify places where the person will be accepted and welcomed.

Although these four approaches to networking can be seen as distinct, they are often used in combination. This happens over time as people realize the limitations of any one approach used alone. The key seems to be having a "relationship lens" on the life goals and issues of the person, ensuring that all efforts will contribute to the New Story. Much of the traditional literature on social networks emphasizes the "provision" of social support, as if the person is somehow a "recipient" of support.[11] Social networks we have experienced have more of a quality of "connectedness" and "mutuality." People participate with the person in the things that matter to the person and to the network members.

A Meaningful Process to Building a Network

We have found that there is a common process that captures the essence of network building through our work with several initiatives. While specific strategies for building a network will vary with each person, this common process involves awareness, invitation, facilitation, mapping, dialogue, monitoring, and sustainability. This approach to intentionally constructing social support also raises a compelling point about the nature of acquiring knowledge. Typically, knowledge is seen as individual-oriented and expert based.[12] Members of support networks, in contrast, experience knowledge as collective and experiential. This different knowledge base is what grounds this work in community, rather than in systems of expertise.

The starting point for building a network is gaining awareness and understanding as a basis for commitment to a network approach. Although recognition of the value of relationships and networks has grown in recent years, many individuals and families lack awareness of its benefits and potential. Families often see their life with a person who is vulnerable as a burden rather than as a catalyst for expanding community. Some families also embrace a "myth of autonomy," believing they have to manage everything "on their own."[13] These beliefs create barriers to network building. Too often we do not allow ourselves to connect with our friends and acquaintances and involve them in ways that address our fears, struggles, and hopes.

It sometimes takes quite a bit of dialogue with individuals and families to show the power of planned network building. A jolting experience in our own family got us on the path of awareness and commitment to a network approach. One day when our daughter Karen was in grade 6, we were walking with her at school and almost everyone we passed said, "Hi Karen." This was remarkable because Karen had been in that school for two years and had never been invited to a party with any of her classmates. This experience reminded us that people can be an acquaintance to many, but not necessarily more deeply known or included. Shortly after this experience, we decided to intentionally build a support network with Karen. We invited a facilitator to assist us, discussed it with family and friends, and involved the school principal in the planning. We decided to begin by having the facilitator talk with a few of Karen's school acquaintances. The principal then called a meeting where Karen's relationships were documented in the form of a

The Process of Network Building

- The interested person and the family *gain awareness* and understanding of network building as a basis for making a commitment to a network approach.

- The person, family member, friend or facilitator *extends invitations* to others to be involved in a network.

- The interested person and the family engage someone who can *assist with facilitation* of the network.

- Existing relationships and networks of the person are *mapped*, sometimes by making a pictorial representation or map of current networks as a basis for expanding connections.

- *Places in the community* where the person can participate are identified by the network: places that would understand and support the person's dreams and goals to participate.

- *Celebration* of key events, like birthdays and holidays, is built into network relationships.

- *Ongoing monitoring and follow-up* is an important role of those involved in a network.

- *Sustainability* is the final component of the process of building a network.

"Map" or a visual representation.[14] Karen, the facilitator, parents, siblings, one other adult friend, four classmates, and the principal attended. What happened in the meeting confirmed what many families have learned. People genuinely liked Karen, but needed some support and suggestions on how to include her more in their lives. This first meeting grew into Karen's support circle, a group of committed family and friends who continue today. They walk with Karen in her life journey as an

Pathways to Inclusion

adult and support her as she makes decisions about her dreams and goals.

Our insights from this experience parallel what many New Story initiatives have learned. Before one intentionally begins to build or strengthen a network, you must first bring it to your consciousness. With awareness of the importance of relationships, you will soon begin to notice possibilities for network building. The uncle who has long shown interest in his relative, the neighbour who shows she cares, or the person in church who always asks questions about the family, all become potential members of the network. As awareness grows, the implementation of network building may go in different directions. For example, different individuals may favour one of four approaches mentioned. Some people immediately take to the idea of a formal support circle that includes peers and family, while others may not. Another area where differences might emerge is in people's opinions about meetings. Some people intentionally hold regular meetings with a person's network in the early years to build a strong base for the future. Other people prefer not to have regular network meetings but are interested in more informal approaches. For these people, a network approach may simply mean being aware of key people in their life and receiving support to nurture those relationships. In that case, the facilitator assists the person in "holding the connections together." Typically, independent facilitators have network development as one part of their role. However, Options in Toronto has a network builder/facilitator whose sole responsibility is to work with individuals and families on network building.

The next aspect of the process involves extending invitations to others to be involved in a network. People vary in terms of whom to have in their network. They normally have a combination of friends and family. Sometimes people choose to have their network include only peers and no family. PLAN has found this approach can be very empowering for the person when developing personal networks as it affirms personal choice. Sometimes "asking" people who are outside the family to get involved is a challenge. A woman who had built a support circle with her brother, Tom Clancy, says that "asking" was the most difficult part: "We just didn't think that others would be so keen to be part of my brother's life." Yet hospitality is central to building a support network and a good life in community. People were asked to be part of Clancy's network, not to "help" him but to participate in his life and to be part of his community. This mutuality is empowering for the individual when they see others showing such interest in them. But it is also empowering for the invited people when they realize that their participation is needed and valued. This mutuality of networks is captured by John Ralston Saul, who says, "There is no idea of society more ancient than a circle of friends. And there is nothing more predictable than the discovery that the one in need is somehow helping the others."[15]

The Support Clusters Project in Kitchener learned early on that the person and family do not have to do all the asking. This initiative was designed to help families that were struggling to build a support network. In meeting with Trevor Jones and his mother, Elaine, their aspirations and hopes for an expanded network were explored. They both identified a few people in *his* network who might have the potential to be involved. Mrs. Jones could not think of anyone to ask among her friends. "There is no one" she said abruptly. "The only people we do anything with are some other couples we go dancing with every month at the Legion, but I would not want them involved in any of these issues." Mrs. Jones finally agreed that her friend Martha could be asked to be part of her son's network group. "But I do not want to ask her," Mrs. Jones said emphatically. When the facilitator asked Martha to be part of the support network, Martha was "honoured to be asked" and "excited about being involved." This invitation began what would become a long-time commitment to the support network of Trevor Jones, including Martha playing a leadership role.

The interested person and their family engage someone who can assist with facilitation of the network. Facilitators can be paid or volunteer and seem to function best when they are independent of formal services and systems. Peter Dill, a long-time facilitator of support circles in Durham, says the development of a support network is often difficult, but "the path is rewarding." Dill emphasizes that the support network is a journey involving time, commitment, and consistent facilitation. Facilitation does not have to be a formal process. Sometimes a family member or friend can play the role of facilitator.

At first the facilitator assists the person and family to extend invitations. As the network develops, the facilitator creates opportunities for group development among the network members itself. The facilitator assists the members with good group process and encourages them in their sense of belonging to a community vision. Leaders note that membership cohesion happens in a number of ways. Storytelling in the early meetings helps the group learn to listen and laugh together. Food always helps create hospitality and a sense of comfort and enables people to get to know each other in an informal atmosphere. As a sense of belonging deepens, a network is formed to support the person's vision and become the "holder of the person's plan."

Facilitators assist the individual, family, and friends to work together as a team. Together they craft goals, directions, and activities that ultimately enhance the person's quality of life, citizenship, and participation.

Judith McGill from Families for a Secure Future says it is important for facilitators to deepen conversations initially with the person, the parents, and siblings and later with friends. Network meetings are valuable in encouraging dialogue because time is taken to listen and to try to understand the expressions and the choices being made by the person and the family. Facilitators use network meetings to go beyond family concerns and serve as a base for thinking about how the person's dreams and goals for a "good life" can be realized. As relationships are strengthened, dialogue often moves to exploring how "community" can be used to enable the person to fully express his or her identity. As one example, the Support Cluster Project finds that most of their networks create the base for increased community involvement. Enabling this to happen is where an effective facilitator becomes so important for networks. Facilitators who truly understand the New Story are able to keep network members focused on community and its seemingly limitless reservoir of resources. As McGill says, "meaningful conversation and dialogue help family members to re-imagine possibilities."

An important role for facilitators is "working across differences" and ensuring that the voice of people is central within networks. Human services generally focus on either the family or the individual, but the network approach focuses on both. While this has merit and richness for creating community, it can also cause strain if the parents and their adult children have very different views of what is possible or desirable. Many facilitators admit this is a challenge that must be faced. We find in initiatives that parents tend to favour more protection and support while younger people more often favour choice and increased opportunities. Research shows that elderly people are often resistant to having support services come into their home, even though their children may be strongly in favour.[16]

Linda Perry from Vela Microboard Association says that facilitators and networks need to work really hard in the beginning to get the principles right for how they are going to work together. Microboards have the advantage over some other initiatives because their mandate is the development of support networks in which the person has a large amount of say and control. The reality in some initiatives, however, is that the parent may be heard more than the person. Barb Leavitt from Community Living St. Marys emphasizes that it is a tricky balance for facilitators. "It is our job to enable the person to be heard," says Leavitt, "but not at the expense of relationships within the family." Facilitators need to be patient with the family member who is overprotective but most also be very creative in seeking solutions so that everyone feels it is a win-win situation.

Relationship mapping is another important part of the process of network building. Some facilitators assist the network in making a pictorial representation or map of current networks as a basis for expanding connections. Most people are surprised that there are so many people in their lives and that they have lots of "potential relationships." Pat Simpson from the Support Clusters Project is a typical example. When Simpson's networks were explored she realized that in fact she had four networks. She had a community/neighbourhood network that involved several places in the community that she regularly visited, including a market, drugstore, and coffee shop. In each of those places, Simpson had at least one person with whom she felt a good connection. She also had a family network that included her parents and several cousins that she liked but seldom saw. She had a friendship network that was quite small and inactive but potentially included two good friends. Finally, she had a professional/service network that included a current personal assistant, chiropractor, counsellor, and two former personal assistants who dropped by occasionally.

Like Pat Simpson's networks, most of us have networks with various strengths and weaknesses. To begin building a more intentional network, people in the innovations are encouraged to choose a few people whom they like and trust and where they think a relationship could be strengthened. Simpson's network map helped her and her family see possible relationships that could be strengthened. Simpson chose her mom, sister, aunt, a former worker, a former teacher, and two friends to form a more formal circle. She also agreed that her mom's best friend could be part of the circle. Although starting with a small group seems to work best, Linda Dawe from the Deohaeko Support Network admits that "as a parent I can be overprotective. The key is to have enough people involved so parents don't dominate." Mapping and building a network is not something that happens overnight. Starting slowly and gradually adding people is part of the process. "We build people's relationships and capacity slowly," says a facilitator with the Toronto Options project.

We find that when people are asked to map the people in their life, they almost always name people who see their strengths and gifts. In her book, *Loving Kindness*, Sharon Salzburg tells the story of how one African tribe responds to individual transgressions.[17] When a person in the tribe has been accused of some wrongdoing, the person must sit in the centre of the village, surrounded by tribe members. Each person who knows the individual then describes a gift or strength of the accused person. This storytelling includes details of positive things that the person has done. This event might go on for hours or days. At some point, the person is welcomed back into the tribe with a celebration. Like this African story, New Story initiatives that map networks are committed to surrounding the person with others who see and embrace the person's gifts and strengths.

Places in the community where the person can participate are identified by the network. These places benefit from people who understand and support the person's dreams to participate. These places and people are everywhere, but the challenge is to find real hospitality. People have had success participating in a wide variety of community associations. In a recent study we completed on four of the sites that provide facilitation and network development, we found people with disabilities were engaged in a wide range of community and leisure experiences.[18] The key to enhancing community connections is first identifying places and people that would understand and support the person's dream. When Adam Danko from the

Options Project in Toronto first identified gardening as an important part of his dream, the facilitator and his network listed several places (e.g., garden stores, local parks) and several people (e.g., his aunt, a neighbour, store manager, landscape architect friend) who would likely understand the dream. This process gradually enabled Danko to find the right place in the community that reflected his interests. Danko's network spent many hours finding connections for him. As a result of this work, he ended up doing volunteer work with a landscape architect and working part-time with a local gardening store.

While New Story initiatives have success in connecting people with a range of community associations, they have less success in finding people within associations who can build connections and relationships. Such a connector can be important in being a bridge for the person in a new setting. Project Friendship intentionally does this kind of connecting work. When people first met Terry Gangnon, it was apparent that he had a fascination with trains. The local railway museum was contacted to see if it needed any volunteers. The hope was to create an opportunity for Gangnon to develop relationships and be around trains. A museum director gave Gangnon a tour of the museum and later arranged for Gangnon to have a ride on one of the locomotives. Gangnon was thrilled and after that began to spend every Friday afternoon at the museum. A supervisor ensured that Gangnon met everyone, and before the summer was over, he knew all the tour guides and the crew. Gangnon was included in all the museum events and activities.[19] In some ways, Gangnon's experience can be considered an ideal example of a leisure identity because he was effectively supported in expanding his interest in something he loved and had relationships nurtured at the same time.[20]

Another variation of this approach is occasionally used. Sometimes members of support networks attend community events and activities with the person. This works well when both people have a common interest. Our daughter Karen often attends yoga class with one of her best friends, Amanda Soikie, who is an important part of Karen's support circle. We have found that this approach increases the likelihood that Karen will meet others since Amanda acts as a bridge to other people in the group. Another deviation from this approach is when someone with an interest is connected with a mentor. Spark of Brilliance, based in Guelph, Ontario, works with peo-

Pathways to Inclusion

ple with mental health issues. It offers workshops on a variety of visual arts. When someone shows an interest in a particular art, it is often one they had been involved with prior to their illness. They can then be connected to a local artist. This connection often becomes a mentoring relationship as the artist encourages the person to pursue art to the best of his or her ability.[21]

Celebration of key events, like birthdays and holidays, is built into network relationships. Most of us celebrate from time to time with family and friends. Many people who have been isolated need support and encouragement to rekindle their spirit of celebration. This may begin with a small number of people from the person's network being invited to a birthday party. Facilitators report that networks celebrate lots of things — the anniversary of leaving the institution, the beginning of a new season, the birthdays of everyone in the network, or other special occasions. Once the spirit of celebration takes hold, the person and their network have more opportunities to build hospitality. One facilitator notes that "it was like hospitality enabled us all to deepen our connections with each other." This insight is central to the growth and development of networks. They not only deepen relationships for the person, but they enlarge the relationships and connections of all network members. In this way, when we intentionally develop networks with vulnerable members, we actually build capacity and connections for the whole community.

Ongoing monitoring and follow-up is an important role of those involved in a network. Support networks, because of their ongoing nature, are in an ideal position to oversee how things are going with the person. However, governments and community agencies usually assume that monitoring of service quality needs to be formal and managed by a service system. Individuals and families with active support networks are teaching us that monitoring for quality assurance is also about ongoing, informal, individualized attention. In some initiatives, facilitators and families talk about this regularly and have simple ways to review how things are going. These conversations are vital to the health of a support network since they often uncover things that one person alone may not have noticed. These monitoring approaches assist the network in being mindful about all aspects of the person's life. Circles, for example, play an important role in the implementation and monitoring of person-centered plans developed with the person. Like most support networks, members of our daughter's support circle not only care about Karen, but also watch out for her, participate with her in achieving her goals, and talk with her regularly. Although she has some paid support people in her life, friends and family are connected with Karen on a regular basis.

Sustainability is the final component of the process of building a network. Ana Vicente from Options in Toronto reminds us that support network development is intense work. "A support circle is constantly changing," says Vicente. "The same way that people's lives go through different phases, networks go through different phases." Vicente and other leaders note the need for networks to be constantly renewing themselves. The facilitator plays a key role in noticing issues or discerning when a network might be "stagnant." The Support Clusters project shows dramatically how important facilitation is to sustaining networks. When the funding for facilitators ended after more than two years, most support networks lost their intensity and significantly decreased their participation.[22] The other factor that increases sustainability of the support network is the extent to which someone plays the role of champion. The champion is usually a family member or friend who reminds network members of their important role and encourages ongoing communication and connection among members. In this sense, there is a connection between sustainability and renewal.

As people using network approaches learn how to make them more sustaining, there is a greater likelihood that networks will be seen as central to the New Story. We learn from the initiatives that networks expand the citizenship of people. They make life in a community possible and they enable relationships to grow and prosper in ways that previously people never thought possible. There are hundreds of small groups across the country constructing social support with citizens who require network support. They show everyone that families and communities can play a more significant role in safeguarding the quality of life of our fellow citizens.

It is important to stress that social network interventions *do not* eliminate the demand for formal, paid support. Citizens with extensive support requirements continue to require both formal *and* informal support. In the field of aging, there is currently considerable focus being paid to the caring capacity of the informal networks of frail seniors. While some of this dis-

Pathways to Inclusion

Story of Lisa Pieniazek and Her Support Circle

For more than 20 years, Lisa Pieniazek from London, Ontario, has had an active support circle. It all began when Marilyn Haywood started working with Lisa when she was one of many people in Ontario being supported to return to the community from institutions that were closing. The Ministry of Community and Social Services sent Lisa's mother a letter promising Lisa a "community placement." After Lisa's "placement" in a large residence, Marilyn was recruited by the Ministry and became involved. When Lisa did not cope well with the change she was returned to the institution. The Ministry program supervisor's direction was clear. "Get Lisa Out!" A medical condition proved to be one of the reasons for Lisa's challenging behaviours and eventually resulted in surgery and admittance to yet another institution. Marilyn realized that she would need to use a creative approach to address Lisa's long history of complications, disruptions, and isolation.

It took some time for Marilyn to figure out how to proceed. Marilyn recalls visiting Lisa in the institution and asking the staff what Lisa was interested in, and staff said they did not know. This was telling because it showed how Lisa's life was devoid of connection and relationship. Marilyn then approached Lisa and her mother, Gemma Pieniazek, with a New Story question. "Once I would have asked, 'What can I bring to Lisa, as in what program would best meet her needs'" says Marilyn. "But instead, I asked, 'Who can I bring to Lisa?'" Marilyn's idea was to invite people she knew and others who knew the family into relationship with Lisa in the form of a support circle. While Gemma supported the idea of building a support network, like many families she was initially hesitant. Gemma admits that "at first I was rather skeptical; I didn't think people would come through with their commitments. I didn't think a support circle could happen, but it has."

In the first year, the support circle focused on building what might be considered a better future for

Story of Lisa Pieniazek and Her Support Circle (continued)

Lisa. Support network members recall "kitchen table talks" and many planning meetings that considered what Lisa's home might look like, whether she should have roommates or not, and how to introduce her to community life and neighbours. Early on, support circle members agreed on one key strategy — that each member would introduce Lisa to members of their own network. This turned out to be a significant insight even though it did take time to reap the benefits. This idea of borrowing the network of another person has been used in other initiatives as well.

Lisa's story is intricately linked to the development of New Frontiers, a small innovative organization in London, Ontario. Lisa's support circle struggled in the early years with finding an effective community organization that could support Lisa. The circle members realized they needed to be part of a larger group that shared their vision. The possibility of becoming part of a new organization both challenged and pleased the support circle. Lisa and her family began to meet with other families to discuss "the formation of a new organization that would see people as individuals and their family and friends paramount in making decisions along with the supported individual." New Frontiers was born in 1990 in a similar way to NABORS in Toronto and the Deohaeko Support Network in Durham Region. Families made a commitment to a New Story organization based on the concepts of support circles, individualized support, and individualized funding. Once New Frontiers was in place, Lisa and the other supported individuals began to grow in leaps and bounds. Lisa became much happier, busier, and more independent.

The members of Lisa's support circle have played various roles over the years. They interviewed and hired a co-ordinator and all personal assistants. They felt they now had the tools to ensure Lisa's dreams could be realized. In the early years, they still had to advocate for Lisa with unresponsive government and community agencies. They did a lot of planning, which resulted in

Pathways to Inclusion

Story of Lisa Pieniazek and Her Support Circle (continued)

Lisa having a rich life in community. For example, they assisted Lisa in becoming an active volunteer at a life-long learning centre. As well, Lisa delivered Meals on Wheels in her favourite mode of transportation, the automobile. The support circle members were Lisa's friends. Each circle member had a unique relationship with Lisa. Some had built their relationship on common interests, such as road trips, going to a cottage, and sharing dinners. Some families spent time with Lisa, giving her the opportunity to make friends with lots of children. The young people who met Lisa 20 years ago are now married with their own children. Lisa has been present at wedding showers, weddings, baby showers, and, sadly, some funerals.

Over time Lisa's support circle became vibrant and sustaining. A staff co-ordinator now attends support circle meetings and keeps circle members current about issues affecting Lisa's quality of life. The circle meets informally, at social gatherings, birthdays, and drop-ins to visit Lisa. Despite the number of supports and services in her life, the circle provides an important safeguard for Lisa because of its focus on relationships and community. Circle members believe the number of friends and family who care about Lisa is the best protection for her today and in the future.

The circle is also a way to build capacity and community. Although Lisa is not someone whom people initially view as able to contribute to her community, it was reasonable to assume that Lisa, like most people, would like to do this. With help from her circle, including her caring family, Lisa is now a member of her church, a volunteer, a friendly neighbour, and a small business operator. Many people in her community know her. They attend her birthday open house each year. Lisa now has friends outside her support circle. They have a different role in her life than circle members but are also very important.

Marilyn Haywood continues to be part of Lisa's circle as a friend. Marilyn and Charlotte Dingwall, a

Story of Lisa Pieniazek and Her Support Circle (continued)

long-time circle member, reflect on the lessons learned in the process of building a support circle with Lisa. Networks grow, they say, "when everyone deeply respects the person and the family." Although support circle meetings were important in the first few years, Marilyn and Charlotte note that "we do not have what we call meetings anymore. We will if it is ever needed. That is our commitment to Lisa. However, it is more natural now, more casual and less intentional." They also point out that they did not ask people to make lifelong commitments to the circle. "We know from our experience that if you ask people to do one or two small things, they will likely agree. But guess what? They stay!" They stress the importance of celebrating events regularly, such as birthdays, holidays, and key milestones. This year, the celebration will be for Lisa's 20 years with her support network. Marilyn and Charlotte note the importance of being creative with individualized supports and of working hard to keep everyone focused on "community as a first resort." Finally, they emphasize the value of having a sense of humour, playing together, and laughing.

Lisa's support circle shows that when people make intentional commitments to others, they build community. Support circles create opportunities for people to come together, grow together, and share life. All the members' lives are now deeply connected, even though it started with one person. The support circle continues on through a second generation of people that have come to know Lisa. Members' children have known her all their lives. Important lessons that stand out for Lisa's circle are how to really listen and how to act on what's been heard. The development of New Frontiers as a social innovation is a central outcome of this network development.

Sources: S. Joyce (Ed.), *Collages: Sketches of a Support Circle* (London, ON: Realizations, 1993); New Frontiers, *Stories of New Frontiers Support Services* (London, ON: New Frontiers Support Services, 1995).

Pathways to Inclusion

cussion is long overdue, some of it assumes that informal networks can provide much of the support, rather than formal long-term care. While we support the idea of caring networks for seniors, such strategies should always be designed as networks and relationships for health and well-being, not to replace reductions in public sector spending. Rather, expenditures for aging and disability supports need to be reallocated and redesigned to be a better fit with the New Story.[23]

Outcomes That Make a Difference

Several key outcomes are noteworthy from a review of eight New Story initiatives that have a major focus on building support networks or support circles. They demonstrate how intentionally building networks with citizens can expand the capacity of the person, family, and community.

Support networks provide people who are vulnerable with more witnesses in their lives. The idea of family, friends, and other citizens being witnesses to the person's life strengthens relationships and ensures the person is noticed in all aspects of his or her being. In this way, support networks contribute to safeguarding the quality of a person's life. If a person is being noticed, it is less likely that bad things will happen. Neglect and abuse occur when people are isolated or surrounded only by formal services.

Support networks create a vehicle for people to express and act on their deep commitment to the person. In several initiatives, support network members talk about the importance of supporting the person to pursue their dreams. People emphasize that network members are present "through good and bad times" and that they are prepared to "advocate for the person." We continue to be humbled by the sense of commitment expressed by families and friends. With our own daughter's network, we have found that friends will be there when called upon and will often go beyond the call of duty. While the commitments expressed by network members obviously benefit the person, it has the added value of being an opportunity for network members to deepen their contribution to community.

Support networks create relationships and "connectedness" that deepen people's community and identity. As Janet Klees

Pathways to Inclusion

from Deohaeko Support Network says in her insightful writing on support circles, "the circle is one way to hold and invite relationship."[24] Out of relationship comes the capacity to care and deepen commitment. We all have support networks whether we have identified them in that way or not. When we have friends who call us or when we have people who invite us to do something with them, we feel included and strengthened. Despite the seeming naturalness of relationships, they do not happen naturally for many of us. The need to be intentional about relationship building is one of the greatest contributions of the New Story initiatives. Research completed with the Vela Microboard Association finds that people's network experience allows participants, their families, and their friends to reconnect and rebuild their relationships.[25]

Network building almost always leads to an increased number of social roles experienced by the person. Each of us participates in a variety of social roles as employee, friend, neighbour, or participant. Consider Jamie Strickland from the Foundations Project. Although Strickland is unable to talk, he can clearly indicate his needs and wants. As the facilitator worked with the network, it became apparent that Strickland wanted to attend church, spend time with horses, and take cooking classes in the community. One member of the network attended the United Church and began to take Strickland with him. Within weeks, the facilitator found a cooking class in a community centre near Strickland's home, and a neighbour in his network began to go to the cooking class as well. This kind of story gets repeated over and over with successful support networks as people experience new roles. In Strickland's case, the role of congregation member, learner, and participant were his first community roles since leaving high school five years earlier. His mother described the network and her son's community experience as a way to "launch him into adult life." This story reinforces the idea that a valued social role can be more important than the actual activity being pursued.[26]

Constructing social support networks enables families to regain their lives by relinquishing some of the caregiving functions. In some cases, people describe their struggles as primary caregivers. Some families find the support networks a safe place to express emotions about that experience. The network also provides a context to collaborate and problem-solve with others and build more consistent approaches with the person.

Pathways to Inclusion

Families then begin to feel that they no longer carry all the responsibility. In this sense, the process of building social support gives voice to the person *and* the family. In some cases, women point to the fact that support is being more shared. Mothers feel less alone and more able to call on others. This is an important insight because informal support arrangements have been shown to typically put more stress and burden on women.[27] This approach is also very promising with children who are supporting aging parents. The difference here may be the collective nature of the interventions and the sense of community reported by many people involved in intentional social networks.

Finally, support networks provide an important mediating structure for social change. *The process of constructing social support enables us to begin to look at how to build the capacity of communities to include all citizens.* In our highly urbanized culture, it is a challenge to break down loneliness and alienation. Certainly it is difficult to do so through public policy related to disability and aging issues that only focus on "more services." The reality is that most citizens who are vulnerable require different services *and* expanded opportunities to be included in community life. What are needed are more intimate structures where people can negotiate and co-create community. The support networks we have studied embrace difference and create community in ways that destabilize the traditional idea that vulnerability means lack of resilience. Such small community-mediating structures illustrate the power of shifting decision making to the individual and their networks. Within the safety of a support network, a person experiences acceptance and value. Those who believe in support networks as a mediating structure for social change stress that everyone in the social network can carry these attributes into the wider world. In social science terms we might say that intentional support networks build social capital. Unlike economic capital, which involves money, social capital refers to trust, participation, and relationships.[28]

In a recent study on *Building Inclusive Communities*, participants across Canada identified "failing social support systems" as a major source of vulnerability.[29] Interestingly, study participants also identified municipalities as "best understanding the social needs of the community," while at the same time recognizing that few communities have the resources to advance a social inclusion agenda. Although building social networks is a central approach to inclusion, it will be a challenge for this to become a priority among policymakers and funders. While municipal and provincial policy can provide support for network development, it is the role of communities and facilitators to seed and support the development of networks in families, neighbourhoods, community centres, and schools.

Leaders need to know that many people feel loneliness at the depths of their being. Isolation and rejection can have a devastating impact and leave people quite wounded. Building relationships and a network with someone can begin to soften the loneliness and slowly build trust. Hospitality is the glue that makes this possible. Networks and genuine hospitality take away some of the loneliness and can also begin to heal some of the wounds that people have experienced. However, we must recognize that loneliness is part of the human condition and that it is natural that some loneliness may always remain. In a profound sense, support networks create hospitality so that loneliness can be accepted and even embraced. Meaningful relationships and participation in networks thereby enhance our compassion for ourselves and for others.

Finally, we want to share a reflection we had when the first edition of *Pathways to Inclusion* was published. We realized that this chapter was somewhat limited for people who wanted to be intentional about building networks and meaningful relationships. We therefore decided to write an entire book on relationship building! In 2010, *Friends and Inclusion: Five Approaches to Building Relationships* was published.[30] The book explores five different approaches (one-to-one, social networks, circles, bridging, and leisure identities) for building friends and relationships as a way of enhancing an inclusive life. What is unique about the book for us was that we wrote it with our daughter Karen Lord, a young woman with Down syndrome who lives in Kitchener. While each approach to building relationships is guided by some theory and research, the real strength of each chapter is that the ideas are grounded in a person's life in community. Karen lives and breathes an inclusive life: she lives independently, works in regular jobs, and is an active participant in many aspects of community life such as her church, neighbourhood, and workplaces, including being a certified yoga instructor. Karen has a strong network of friends that has developed through this rich life in community. We learn how relationship building must be intentional, as we work to re-claim sense of community with citizens who traditionally have been outsiders to community life. This book is an inspiration and testament to the importance of friends in all our lives.

Notes

1. Kabot-Zinn (2005), p. 144.
2. For an insight into social support, see Gottlieb (2000). For insights into social support in leisure, see Coleman and Iso-Ahola (1993). Also see Wasserman and Faust (1994).
3. Christakis and Fowler (2009).
4. For social support in aging, see Chappell (1992); Wenger (1997); Connidis (2001). For social support and disability, see Stein, Rappaport, and Seidman (1995); Prince (1998). For more on the link between social capital and social networks, see Field (2003).
5. Hutchison and McGill (1998); Lord (1999).
6. Schwartz (1997).
7. Cacioppo and Patrick (2008).
8. For more on circles as a form of social support, see Gold (1994).
9. Pedlar et al. (1999).
10. McKnight (1995).
11. See Taylor, Sylvestre, and Botschner (1998). Also see Styan (2004).
12. Gergen (1994).
13. Fine (2004).
14. Falvey et al. (1997).
15. J. Ralston Saul (2005): p. 12.
16. Some research shows that education is a key factor in whether or not elderly people make use of homecare support. See Wister (1992).
17. Salzburg (1995).
18. Lord (2006).
19. Project Friendship Society (1993).
20. McGill (1996).
21. For an interesting glimpse into the arts and disability, see the documentary film by Klein (2006).
22. Ochocka et al. (1993).
23. Keating et al. (2003).
24. Klees (2005).
25. Malette (1992).
26. For ideas on valued social roles, see Wolfensberger (2000).
27. Studies generally report that informal caregiving can take a substantial amount of families' time: 50 hours a week or more if the family member has a severe chronic illness or dementia.

See Arno, Levine, and Memmott (1999). Research also points to women carrying the majority of the informal caregiving; see Statistics Canada, and M. Navaie-Waliser, A. Spriggs and P. Feldman (2002).

28. Chenoweth and Stehlik (2004).
29. Clutterbuck and Novick (2003).
30. Hutchison, Lord, and Lord (2010).

Pathways to Inclusion

10

Together Is Better

The Power of New Story Self-Help

Friendship is born at that moment when one person says to another, "What! You too? I thought I was the only one."

C.S. Lewis

The meeting was very ordinary, but at the same time quite unique. We were present as researchers to explain a study we were conducting with a group of people who all had one thing in common: their mental health issues. The group of 22 people had just finished eating a simple meal together and the room was filled with chatter. As we explained our study to this self-help group, we could sense restlessness in the room. After 10 minutes of the presentation, the hands began to go up. The questions were direct and from the heart of people's experiences. "Why is this study needed when resources could be better spent on support services?" "Whose study is it, anyway?" "How will we benefit?" "How can you assure us that the results will truly reflect our experience?" Group members, as "insiders," understood the questions because of the common experience that led them to initially mistrust people with ideas, resources, and power. The group became more comfortable with us as the dialogue proceeded. However, we realized that we were clearly "outsiders."

Self-help or mutual aid groups, as they have commonly been called, have members with a common condition or concern. They come together for the purpose of supporting one another and often working together for change. We studied two types of organizations that fit in with New Story principles. The first were self-help groups composed of people who are vulnerable. These peer support groups and peer-driven organizations might be senior citizens, people with disabilities, or people with specific chronic conditions. The essence of these groups is that membership and leadership is by people with disabilities or other vulnerabilities.[1] We also looked at family-to-family groups and organizations consisting of family members who are in a support role with a child, parent, sibling, adult child, or spouse. These groups often include friends and other interested community members. The essence of these family networks is that membership and leadership is primarily by family members who in some way have a family member who needs support.[2] Peer support groups might be thought of as primary self-help because they are led and composed of people themselves. Family network groups might be considered secondary self-help because they are run by and consist of families and friends.

In the past 30 years, self-help movements in North America have grown dramatically. In larger communities there is now a group for everyone. In fact, according to some researchers, self-help is the only area of civic engagement that has been growing.[3] While people may be participating less in most aspects of their communities, they are now involved in self-help groups more than ever before. Despite this recent rise in popularity, in many respects the idea of people supporting each other is a return to societies of long ago that found ways to help people with their losses, fears, and suffering.[4]

Self-help organizations address these struggles by creating opportunities for people to ask questions and talk about their common concerns. The nine organizations we studied understand the stark reality that each of us is *dependent on one another* for a variety of needs. Although these groups stress that self-determination is an important goal for people, they recognize it must always be linked to collective responsibility and equality. However, being a self-help organization in itself does not guarantee that the group reflects the principles of the New Story.

Power of Self-Help

Self-help creates space and opportunities for people to share their hopes and struggles. It works on the assumption that giving support is at least as beneficial as receiving support. The grandparent of self-help is Alcoholics Anonymous, or AA. Started in the 1930s, AA began with a strong commitment to egalitarian principles and the belief in people's ability to change without experts. With mutual support as its cornerstone, AA pioneered the idea that all members are equal. This democratization and commitment to equality are key principles that make self-help organizations very different from typical human service organizations.[5]

There is a generosity of spirit that one feels within self-help. This altruism is central to the initiatives we studied, although it is not always clear why people are so willing to help others. Katherine Ashenberg, in her book, *The Mourner's Dance*, suggests that it may be part of an ancient strategy. She points out that in primitive societies, a distressed or troubled person was often ordered to make a meal or do some other good work.[6] Members of self-help groups tell us that they often feel their suffering and powerlessness lessen when they participate in helping others who are struggling. It may be that people's own struggles enable them to be effective in understanding and supporting others with similar struggles. This effectiveness comes with rewards that nurture self-esteem. Similarly, research on chronic conditions reveals how critical it is for people to develop a "positive relationship with their condition," to "let go" of more negative aspects of their past life, and to "take responsibility" for creating their life.[7] Self-help plays an important role in enabling people to move forward in their lives.

Pathways to Inclusion

Telling the story of one's own experience is central to how self-help experiences enable people to move ahead in their lives. In the early stages, people often struggle to find the words to describe their feelings or grief associated with their own personal story. One woman who became disabled later in life told us it took her years to accept her disability. It was only when she joined other women in a self-help group that she was able to begin to slowly pour out her sadness and regret and see some hope. For many, storytelling takes courage. Listening to others tell their stories helps a person piece together what is possible. In such situations, people find they gradually move from shame to acceptance. Storytelling enables people to come to terms with their own situations.

However, a state of acceptance is not the end of the process. We have learned that storytelling enables many people to move past acceptance to being comfortable in challenging existing norms of "difference." Ed Hughes, a long-time board member and leader of Waterloo Region Self-Help, says it took him years to move "beyond acceptance" to where he could understand his vulnerability as a gift.[8] Hughes's story continues: "I find I have become more human than I was before. I like people more than I did before. Perhaps also I have looked at the abyss most people dread, have gone over the edge and swam like hell to the other side, tired but able to climb out." Hughes's reflections echo the self-help movement, which sees hope and possibility in illness and disability. From our experience with several self-help organizations, we also wonder if it is possible that people in these settings find the solace and support needed to allow them to constantly be re-framing their own story.

Self-help serves a vital function. To be powerful and part of the New Story, self-help needs to be autonomous and independent of service organizations. This is because self-help is different than professional support groups offered by many formal organizations. While the latter can serve a purpose, they should not be confused with genuine, "autonomous" groups which are embedded in notions of support and collaboration among people with similar concerns and life experiences. When service organizations try to "manage" self-help, there is potential for conflict of interest. Although *autonomous* is a crucial term for genuine self-help, some leaders stress that the important thing is that their self-help groups be seen and treated as equals to other kinds of professional interventions. Bart Forman from the Canadian Paraplegic Association of British Columbia says that self-help and peer support often fail when they are treated as a "subset" of other professional activities. The key to New Story self-help is that it needs to be independent yet have respectful dialogue and partnership with other groups that are supporting an inclusion agenda.

Self-Help among Peers: Building Identity, Finding Strength

Self-help among persons who are vulnerable includes two types of initiatives. First, there is what might simply be called "peer support." Second, there are organizations that are driven by vulnerable people themselves that offer a unique perspective. These New Story self-help organizations usually offer peer support in addition to a wide range of initiatives, such as education, advocacy, and economic development. We shall explore peer support and peer-driven organizations as windows into their contribution to the New Story.

Peer Support

Peer support usually refers to New Story initiatives where people provide support, mentoring, or education to peers who have similar experiences or conditions. Peer support has been a principle of the independent living movement in Canada since its inception in the early 1980s. In the early years, peer support within this movement consisted mainly of peer support groups. Several Independent Living Resource Centres continue to offer peer support groups on a range of issues. Centres find that peer support programs are popular with some people, especially newcomers to independent living, who have had little exposure to possibilities about inclusion and human rights. Over time, however, some Centres have realized that peer support is more than a program or a group. It was the late Allan Simpson, long-time director of the Winnipeg Independent Living Resource Centre, who coined the phrase "peer support is a philosophy." By the late-1990s, peer support as a philosophy was becoming part of "new paradigm" language. Across North America, a range of organizations began to develop

A Unique Self-Help Experience

Sometimes a peer support group enables people to communicate together in unique ways. Bridges-Over-Barriers in Guelph, Ontario, includes several adults with autism who exchange thoughts and feelings with facilitated communication. Nobody in the group speaks, but facilitated communication allows them to communicate via their keyboards and computers. Facilitated communication is a form of augmentative alternative communication that helps people who have limited speech use a keyboard or point to letters, images, or symbols. Andrew Bloomfield is the leader of this group and his vision is that facilitated communication builds bridges among people in ways that enable them to support each other. Although members of Bridges come from a wide area of southern Ontario, several members were astounded at the first meeting of the group that others used facilitated communication. As Andrew notes in the first Bridges Newsletter, some people thought they were quite alone and unique in needing this form of communication. Bridges facilitator Beth Komito-Gottlieb notes that the more the group meets the easier it gets, "with members pounding away on their letterboards, listening to each other and responding thoughtfully, with little signs of discomfort at being touched or difficulty staying 'on task' as people with autism are reported to be. No signs of cognitive impairment here; no difficulty empathizing with others in this group!"

In 2010, the Bridges-Over-Barriers group published a book called *In Our Own Words*. Edited by Andrew Bloomfield, this resource and DVD outlines the thoughts, feelings, and insights of several members of the group. It is an inspiring document that also highlights some of the ways that adults with autism can be supported with respect and understanding.

Note: For information on the Bridges-Over-Barriers group, which began in 2004, see their newsletter *Bridges Over Barriers*. For their principal facilitator Beth Komito-Gottlieb's challenging thoughts on barriers, see Newsletters 1, 2006 <www.ont-autism.uoguelph.ca/BoB-2006-1.pdf>. To order *In Our Own Words*, visit the Bridges website <www.ont-autism.uoguelph.ca/bridges.shtml>.

peer support initiatives. There was finally appreciation for the idea that people who experienced an impairment or chronic condition could be a support to people who were new to the experience.

Another very successful peer support initiative is sponsored by the Canadian Paraplegic Association of British Columbia (BCPA). The Peer Support Network of BCPA has developed extensively throughout Vancouver and area and is broadening to other parts of the province. It took years to build its membership, and the Network currently has more than 100 peer volunteers. Peer volunteers perform many jobs, including a formal one-to-one match, network events throughout the year, running monthly peer support groups, and hosting a website with many hits a month. Peer volunteer training is another aspect of the Peer Support Network of BCPA that enables peer volunteers to act in mentoring roles with newly injured participants. Mentoring initiatives are often established as a way to intentionally connect experienced people with new people.

Bart Forman, one of the founders of the Peer Support Network of BCPA, points out that knowing how to structure training is a challenge. "Peers are often hesitant to agree to undergo training," Forman notes, "as the majority feel aptly prepared by their life situation to provide support." The relationship between the two peers, which is based on equality, may be affected by introducing training to only one person of the pair. This dilemma has led the Network to pursue alternative approaches to training, including ongoing support and coaching of mentors. The Peer Network program now has a presence in the Vancouver G.F. Strong Rehabilitation Centre so that people with spinal cord injuries get a chance to meet a peer volunteer as part of their recovery.

Research on outcomes of peer support initiatives is quite positive. The Peer Support Network of BCPA had a formal evaluation completed on its program in 2003.[9] Participants who were part of the evaluation reported increased well-being from their participation in peer support. One participant said, "The value of peer support — I see that life goes on, meet with other people, can ask questions, can learn how to get over fears, and discuss medications." Participants also noted that peer support "helps you to build a life," "move ahead with your plans," and "helps me try new things." The Peer Support Network of BCPA Evaluation also notes that peer support builds community capacity by expanding the ways that people participate. This is done by developing skills and knowledge for action. Leadership that enables a community to work together builds trusting relationships that promote creative problem solving and mutual support.[10] Research on other peer support mentoring programs also identifies positive outcomes, but cautions that there is a need for peer mentors to understand their role and for professionals to be supportive rather than directing.[11]

Research with GROW, an international self-help movement, shows that people actually change their world view and increase their self-confidence as a result of peer group participation, and that people who stay in a peer group for a longer time achieve better outcomes.[12] We also found that members' participation with peer support varies in terms of types of supports needed. This finding underscores the reality that peer support participation needs to be individualized and appropriate for the person. Independent Living Resource Centres find that some people prefer peer support groups, others prefer one-to-one mentoring, and still others prefer the informality of being with peers in social situations. This diversity of peer support preferences is one reason that independent, peer-driven organizations makes sense, because they can offer a range of self-help activities.

Peer-Driven Organizations

The peer-driven organizations we studied have various descriptions depending on their area of vulnerability. The Independent Living Resource Centres that involve a range of people with disabilities refer to themselves as "consumer-driven" organizations; the Ontario Peer Development Initiative for people with mental health issues is referred to as "consumer/survivor initiatives"; and People First, a group of people with developmental disabilities, is referred to as "self-advocate" organizations. Despite these differences in terminology, there are important themes that traverse all types of peer-driven organizations.

Peer-driven organizations are run by and for people who have been identified with a particular label, such as *disabled*, *senior*, or *mentally ill*. They are much broader than peer support initiatives but they almost always include peer support as a program and a philosophy. We have been honoured to spend a lot of time over the years with members of these organizations. One of the first things we consistently note is that peer-driven organizations are based on a clear set of values that distinguish them from many human service systems. The Ontario Peer Development Initiative is based on values such as member empowerment and participation through peer support and mutual learning. The Independent Living Resource Centres are based on principles that include peer support, community integration, and participation. We find that people connected with these organizations have thought a lot about values and principles. The process of finding the "right" principles seems to be part of a struggle against the oppression people have experienced. Diana Capponi, co-ordinator of the Council of Alternative Businesses, which works with the Ontario Peer Development Initiative, notes that "the majority of members of our community have learned through being involved in paternalistic systems to internalize concepts of dependency, helplessness, worthlessness, and craziness."[13] Peer-driven organizations create mutual support and effective processes that enable members to "unlearn" some of these dependencies and support people to raise expectations about their quality of life.

Although many peer-driven organizations began with peer support groups as their reason for being, most have evolved and have since developed a range of community activities and initiatives. The Kingston Independent Living Resource Centre, typical of the IL Centres across Canada, now offers a range of core programs to its members. With more than 50 organizations in the Ontario Peer Development Initiative in local communities, most groups now offer some combination of the following program activities: peer support groups, one-to-one peer support, community economic development, education and training, advocacy to create systems-level change, opportunities for members to develop their skills, and the creation of resources based on members' knowledge.

When Barry Savage joined Waterloo Region Self-Help (WRSH), he had been "feeling down and suicidal." He recalls the energy he experienced the first time he went to WRSH and was warmly welcomed by the director. "She just made me feel that I was OK, taking time to tell me about the peer activities I could get involved with. My confidence grew as I started to participate." Recent research with Waterloo Region Self-help

Pathways to Inclusion

and three other Peer Development Initiative organizations confirms Savage's experience. A comprehensive four-year study conducted by the Centre for Community-Based Research and Wilfrid Laurier University shows that participation in peer-driven organizations has extensive benefits. In this study, active members showed a decrease in symptom distress, while those in the non-active control group showed no change. Active members had a significant drop in the number of days they spent in hospital in comparison to the non-active control group, where there was no such reduction. Most important, perhaps, this study showed that active members significantly increased their social support and quality of life over an 18-month period. One member noted, "Overall I just feel better. I don't feel hopeless and unsure of what to do now. Before, it felt like I had no opinions and I'm trapped."[14] A national research study on Independent Living Resource Centres showed similar positive outcomes for individuals. People connected with Centres felt a sense of empowerment as a result of their participation. Members noted they were treated differently by the peer-driven organization, emphasizing the importance of being valued as a human being.[15]

Autonomous peer-driven organizations may at first appear to be quite insular, where people with similar conditions support each other in small groups and mentoring activities. A deeper look, however, uncovers a vast array of community connections. Independent Living Resource Centres, such as the Kingston centre, have established numerous partnerships with other community organizations. These partnerships assist the Centres in connecting their members to the wider community. Often these partnerships are designed to educate the wider community about rights and independent living. Similarly, Peer Development Initiative organizations such as Waterloo Region Self-Help (WRSH), have worked hard with their communities to create community environments that are more supportive for people who experience mental health challenges. The longitudinal study on these initiatives, including WRSH, found an extensive amount of community activity in four areas: public education, political advocacy, community planning, and action research. By far the area of greatest involvement was community planning, where members who sit on committees and local planning groups have an impact on the directions of mental health systems.[16] Having a "seat at community tables" is seen as critical for peer-driven organizations that hope to influence

Pathways to Inclusion

local policy and programs. This political influence of peer-driven organizations is important to note since it stretches beyond the more personal benefits often associated with self-help.

Peer-Driven Organizations Are Different

Our own observations of these peer-driven organizations, along with recent research, point to three things that make peer-driven self-help organizations different from traditional service organizations. It is precisely those differences that make such a positive impact.

First, there is the *atmosphere*. Peer-driven organizations feel different because of their acceptance of vulnerability. As one person at the Winnipeg Centre for Independent Living said, "Not only is my difference accepted, in some ways it is embraced." People in these settings live their pain and struggles in very different ways than in service systems. In one sense, diversity is valued and explored for its meaning and insights. When visiting these organizations, we often experience a welcoming tone, a sense of people all being together in this journey. Members sometimes mention that no one is labelled and everyone with this condition can be a member, regardless of economic status, race, or ethnicity. It is of benefit to note that in such an atmosphere people feel liberated to try things they previously have not had the opportunity to experience.

Second, *leadership and training* are key to making peer-driven organizations work. While leaders of these organizations hold the same attributes of all leaders of innovative initiatives, they also have another quality, the quality of supporting people to challenge the status quo. Richard Ruston exemplifies this quality because of his lived experience and leadership style. He is past president of People First of Ontario, a group of citizens with developmental disabilities. Ruston understands that People First groups are at risk and require leadership and training. During the past few years, Ruston designed and led numerous workshops for members called *Keeping Your Dreams Alive*. Ruston's leadership style is both inspiring and challenging. He demonstrates deep listening skills but also prompts members to explore their dreams and possibilities. Ruston says he is always trying to increase people's assertive communication and to encourage people to feel good about themselves. In many ways,

Pathways to Inclusion

he is assisting members to realize their own "power within" and potential to take on leadership roles. Ruston and his People First of Windsor colleagues recently designed a booklet called *Building Leadership in the Community*.[17] This training booklet is filled with practical leadership ideas that are presented in plain language with diagrams and pictures. Ruston's style reminds us that leadership that is respectful holds all members in positive regard and challenges peers to grow.

Third, self-help organizations create *structures* that enhance equality and participation. Finding the "right" way to organize is sometimes a challenge. In one way, the peer-driven organization serves as a "mediating structure" by being a link between the individual and the broader community. People who have been isolated appreciate the support that helps them build their identity and strengths. The number of community connections and partnerships that these organizations have been able to develop attests to this important role. Some members, however, are less interested in the wider community and more interested in having a place where they can connect with peers. This may involve dropping in regularly, having coffee with friends, or volunteering on a newly created initiative. The structure must also allow for the "give and take" of members. We now wonder if equality is somehow more important than we originally realized. Over the years, we have seen peer-driven organizations struggle and fail, often when leaders forget that members are all equal and mistakenly create a hierarchy of leadership. Their failure is testimony to the principle of equality that members seem to understand intuitively.

Self-Help among Families: Gaining Support and Influence

We recently attended a government consultation meeting in a local community. The meeting was part of a series of Ontario meetings to give family caregivers who are supporting an at-risk family member at home input into issues of family support. During the evening, we observed three or four family members express clear New Story values and perspectives. After the meeting, we introduced ourselves to some of these family members and learned that they were part of a local family network that provided information, education, and support to family members. Learning about this approach was not surprising, since families not connected with family-to-family groups often experience isolation and receive only professional information. The interactions of this meeting highlighted the concept that family networks are an important part of the New Story. Most other families at the meeting expressed traditional views about the kind of supports they thought would help.

Families of citizens who require support to experience social inclusion play a central role in the life of that person. Children with chronic conditions and disabilities depend on their parents for love, support, and advocacy. Children thrive when they are surrounded by informed, committed parents. Similarly, parents provide the stimulus and direction young people may need to begin to build an inclusive life in community as they move toward adulthood. Many persons, as they move through adulthood, continue to need the support of their families. Similarly, older persons who are frail may depend on children and other family members to help them maintain their quality of life. The reality is that families who are not exposed to New Story ideas often have low expectations for their loved one. The old story may be all that people know and, as we have seen, this can have negative consequences for both the individual and the family.

Family Groups — A Powerful Idea

Family groups have proven to be a powerful support for family members experiencing vulnerability. Groups are emerging in several areas across Canada and have been shown to be effective for families facing chronic conditions and disability, mental health issues, and Alzheimer's. Increasingly, professional interventions are recognizing the value of supporting families, and many hospitals, clinics, and community agencies now sponsor short-term family support groups. These education-oriented support groups, usually led by a professional, can be valuable to families who are experiencing recent involvement with vulnerability. However, for chronic conditions and longer-term issues, the ongoing autonomous family group that responds to both personal needs and collective issues remains a powerful idea and practice.

Doreen Williams' son lived in Edgar, an institution in Durham Region in Ontario. Doreen Williams knew that life could

Pathways to Inclusion

be better for Allan. In 1993, Williams joined a small group of families that came together to share their concerns. Most of these family members felt isolated, and many were worried about what the future would hold for their adult children. These family members, mostly mothers, were all looking for answers. Some were elderly and still had sons or daughters living at home; others had children about to leave school, and Williams's son was still in the institution. In July of 1994, after a few general meetings, eight families decided to keep meeting on a regular basis. The group hired Teresa Dale as their facilitator and a family group was born. Naming themselves Family Vision Support Network, this family group met every Wednesday evening for years. More than 15 years later they continue to meet a couple of times a month.

Family Vision Support Network is one of more than 10 family groups that have formed in Durham Region. Although each family group has its own unique identity, the essence of these groups involves relating their experiences and providing family-to-family support. As we have seen, when people tell their own story, they often develop insights about themselves. Teresa Dale, Family Vision Support Network facilitator, says that respectful listening to stories is a key to the family group process. Dale's role is to create opportunities for people to express their dreams and visions for their own life and the life of their loved one. John O'Brien, who has spent time with members of Durham family groups, says, "The facilitators' willingness to avoid the role of expert answer-giver encourages the emergence of people's own voices and directions."[18] O'Brien says that there is a wonderful "simplicity" about family groups, but he reminds us that they are not easy to make really successful.

Facilitators with Durham family groups emphasize five elements that occur in family groups. *Listening* is seen as a way to deepen knowledge and to share stories. *Connecting* is the way to expand relationships and experiences with each other and with key allies in the wider community. *Exploring* is the way to extend choices and to recognize that the group can find possibilities, support, and answers. *Acting* to meet family goals is how the group intensifies the capacity and supports each other. *Reflecting* clarifies understanding and insight about how and why things happen. While family groups work because families support and care deeply for one another, quiet and respectful facilitation enables the groups to continually expand their stories and take small steps that contribute to the lives of their families and members. A recent study shows that members of Durham family groups are highly active in the lives of their family members and that their supported family members are achieving positive community outcomes.[19]

Short-term family groups can also provide practical support and play a vital role in enabling families to move toward understanding and compassion. Such is the case with family groups designed for people struggling with Alzheimer's disease. The Alzheimer Society of Hamilton Halton, for example, provides ongoing family groups that enable family members to share concerns and strategies for how to manage the entire Alzheimer's journey.

The strength of family groups seems to lie in the simple accessibility to others who are facing issues of vulnerability. As one person tells a story of how they are supporting their loved one to be part of community life, they meet others with similar experiences and struggles. Family groups, like all self-help groups, work best when members do not give advice, but rather encourage others to follow their own dreams and purposes. While families each pursue their own path, Family Vision Support Network and other family groups in Durham encourage families to create a support circle with their son or daughter. Some discussion in a family group can then revolve around how to build and sustain a network or circle. Family groups also explore a wide range of other issues, such as support plans, housing, employment, management of funds, and training. Family groups also actively support each other outside of meetings, including writing letters to politicians, making connections, buying houses, and applying for individualized funding.

Family-Driven Organizations

Michelle Friesen is passionate about the role of family-driven organizations as part of the New Story. Friesen is a family leader who believes that family-driven organizations need to be autonomous and independent from the service system. As the lead co-ordinator with Windsor–Essex Family Network, Friesen and her colleagues have worked hard to build a sustaining organization that provides information to families, support from a mentor, individual advocacy, and systemic advocacy.

Although family-driven organizations have been evolving for some time, they grew substantially in the 1990s when cutbacks to social services left families responsible for more and more support. With a focus on family-to-family support and advocacy, family-driven organizations, in collaboration with peer-driven organizations, provide a balance to the more powerful service provider organizations.

The purpose of family-driven organizations is not dissimilar to the goals of peer-driven organizations. Windsor–Essex Family Network's mission is "To empower individuals and their families affected by disability and to enhance their quality of life through information, learning opportunities, mentoring, and community connections." Families for a Secure Future, a provincial organization, has a similar mission statement; "We are a network of family groups, with shared values and beliefs, who are deeply committed to staying connected and doing whatever it takes to support our family member to be a contributing member of their community." These family groups come together to learn and to support one another to take the next step toward imagining and creating a better future for their sons/daughters. Families for a Secure Future is based on the fundamental principle that individuals and their families can define and prioritize their own needs. The Durham family groups explored earlier have since formed into a broader network of family groups, the Durham Family Network. This family-driven organization creates both support and facilitation for family groups to thrive.

Although the goals and values of New Story family-driven organizations are similar, the activities and strategies vary. Durham Family Network and Families for a Secure Future are both deepening our awareness of the value of family groups. PLAN and its affiliates across Canada are family driven and totally independent of government or services. The heart and cornerstone of PLAN is its emphasis on building a network of family and friends around the person. PLAN also helps people prepare for their future with planning and facilitation support, legal advice on wills and estates, and other kinds of education and advocacy. Windsor–Essex Family Network also stresses family education and offers a wide range of workshops for families. Michelle Friesen reminds us that family linking, mentoring, and support are vital for families that are trying to embrace the New Story. "Family to family support," says Friesen, "involves having trained or experienced families teaching other families

Pathways to Inclusion

how to access what they need, and how to advocate for the things that are important." Friesen adds that mentoring is critical and that many families she works with have this natural gift of being able to listen deeply. They support other families but "do not take other people's stresses home, which is a wonderful attribute."

In an aging society such as ours, "family support" is becoming vitally important to the well-being of family members. While family support includes a wide range of supports and services, one way family support is enhanced is through family-driven organizations. Although the research and literature on family support is sizeable, family support is often seen as a narrow set of discrete activities that benefit families. However, recent research suggests that family support needs to focus on ways to enhance enduring and supportive relationships.[20] Family-driven organizations do their best work when they focus on strengthening family relationships and connectedness with others who understand and support relationship building.

Safeguarding the New Paradigm

Autonomous self-help organizations play an important role in the New Story. As might be expected, however, many of these organizations are at risk because of limited capacity to access resources and funding. Although the groups we studied have created overall capacity through strong leadership, they have all struggled over the years with issues of independence and financial stability. Building viable peer-driven and family-driven organizations is not always smooth sailing, often because of the pull of the old paradigm. Indeed, there are many family groups that are embedded in traditional service systems. Simply being a family group does not guarantee a new paradigm. The peer-driven and family network organizations we studied are finding ways to safeguard the new paradigm.

First, peer-driven or family network organizations that have *several functions* are more robust and coherent. It is difficult for people to piece all the elements of mutual aid together on their own. Families for a Secure Future create a holistic, coherent approach by offering family groups, education, mentoring, and network building. Family groups are the first line of support and are seen as a place for families to share the struggles and joys of providing support and encouragement to their family member. Facilitators also assist each individual within the context of their family to develop an individual plan for creating a meaningful life. The plan evolves over time and looks at both immediate and long-term goals and activities. Facilitators come to know the individual and their family and stand by them as they go through numerous transitions in their lives. They are committed to helping individuals and their families develop a broader planning context that usually involves the development of a support network. Facilitators support individuals and families to focus on strengthening relationships and ties to the community. Many individuals and families now have active support circles. Finally, Families for a Secure Future builds leadership through education and mentoring. The organization also hosts regular workshops in a Family Leadership Series.

The reality is that too many family-driven organizations have a single focus. This limits the capacity of these organizations to fully implement the New Story. Most family groups designed to support those with mental health issues stress education of their members. While many families benefit from education about mental health treatments and related issues, it is very difficult for families to translate education into practical everyday wisdom and action. In fact, some mental health family groups have a philosophy that is so counter to the New Story that the education they receive simply frustrates them further. It increases their dependence on service systems rather than helping them see possibilities for self-help and new community partnerships. Alternatively, both mentoring and facilitation help families take the education they receive into their own lives and use it in practical and helpful ways. These elements are creating powerful outcomes for families when combined with New Story principles.[21]

The second way that these organizations are safeguarding the new paradigm is through family network advocacy that is *complementary* to the advocacy of peer-driven organizations. Citizens who are vulnerable often sit at the same community tables as family representatives, whether for planning or governance purposes. Too often, representatives from peer-driven groups feel at odds with representatives from family organizations. We learn from our family groups that, while family issues are vital, people need to work very hard to be sure they are not in conflict with the agenda of peer-driven organizations. Individuals who are vulnerable should feel and experience support from families, whether at home, in community planning settings, or within agency governance. When family-driven advocacy is complementary to peer-driven advocacy, then rights, inclusion, and individualized support in the community *for all* are supported. Such family-driven work advocates for recovery support and ongoing support to be person-directed and to include families and friends as network members if appropriate. When peer-driven and family-driven organizations work from common ground, they create positive and sustaining advocacy and help safeguard the new paradigm for *both* organizations. When peer and family groups are divided, however, advocacy is limited and both groups are more at risk to the power and control of large service systems.

Finding common ground between peer-driven and family-driven organizations is not always easy because they each come from different experiences. Members of family groups often feel cheated by the turmoil they have had to experience. It is not uncommon for family-driven organizations to seek interventions that will make life calmer for the family. Unfortunately, some interventions, such as "forced treatment," while appearing to make life calmer for families, are not always in the best interest of the person. In turn, peer-driven organizations can sometimes bring an "anti-family" stance to their advocacy. This certainly is not helpful when they are seeking the support of family organizations on key issues. The reality is that both family- and peer-driven organizations bring "experiential knowledge" to their communities. Experiential knowledge and "experiential power" are generally not valued by professional stakeholders.[22] However, when peer and family organizations find common ground, their experiential knowledge and power is expanded. It is not uncommon for professionals to take note when they are confronted with this experiential power from people considered vulnerable *and* families. This kind of power helps destabilize the old story and the dominance of professional control.

The third way to safeguard the New Story is for self-help groups to *build safeguards against sliding into segregation* which can happen so easily in a culture that readily congregates people. Since community and social inclusion have been major themes in this book, we need to ask the question: Do peer-driven and family network organizations contribute to community building and inclusion? The answer is complex but we will begin to explore it here. On one level, peers learning from one another in a group, despite its segregated nature, can be a foundation for community inclusion. In these groups, people learn about their rights and about possibilities for expanding their lives. A young man recently joined a self-help group and learned for the first time that his employment in the sheltered workshop was "not inclusion" in the broad community. On another level, dialogue among equals creates an intimate sense of community. This environment can be very welcoming and have the characteristics of hospitality and belonging that are very much part of "community." However, leaders also understand that their groups only create opportunities for people to listen and learn from each other and that these groups can never replace wider, inclusive communities that include all citizens.

This answer makes sense as far as it goes. Yet, leaders also tell us that safeguarding social inclusion and community participation is complicated. There seems to be little agreement on the principles that might enable groups to avoid sliding into segregation and the old paradigm. Some groups do not allow drop-in activities because they might encourage segregation. Others encourage drop-in activities, despite their segregated nature, because they say it is a way to build relationships that foster identity and purpose. Community economic development is an interesting example to analyze. When people themselves organize an economic enterprise through a peer-driven organization, is it segregation or a business venture? Several Peer Development Initiative groups have developed successful economic initiatives, including a courier service and a restaurant. Employees are all people with significant mental health issues. Kathryn Church argues that this form of "segregation" differs from workshops and other congregated activities because people have control over the directions and activities.[23] Furthermore, all community economic development projects that we know are designed to be part of the wider community in some way. A courier service and a restaurant provide a service to the public which reduces the possibility of traditional segregation and congregation. As groups continue to develop criteria to safeguard the new paradigm, there are obviously subtle nuances that require deep reflection. True to New Story ideals, the organizations we studied take the time to constantly examine their principles.

In conclusion, we must return to social inclusion as a way to determine the viability of self-help groups. The success of peer-driven and family-to-family initiatives must lie in the results. If people have inclusive lives, then the segregated nature of their self-help experience is a non-issue. However, if people continue to experience widespread segregation and isolation, then self-help and broader advocacy efforts must continue to work toward social inclusion. Peer-driven and family network organizations play a critical role in enabling individuals and families to celebrate their identity and differences. In doing so, they contribute to social inclusion by building people's capacity for advocacy, empowerment, and participation.

Notes

1. For example, see McColl and Boyce (2003); Hutchison et al. (2000); Nelson et al. (2006); Park, Monteiro, and Kappel (2003).
2. For information on parent- or family-driven organizations, see Roeher Institute (1996); King et al. (2000); Mactavish and Schleien (2004).
3. See, for example, Putman (2000). For an overview of research on self-help, see White and Madara (2002).
4. Ashenberg (2002).
5. Makela (1997).
6. Ashenberg (2002).
7. Grady (2004).
8. Hughes (2006), p. 5.
9. For a complete overview of the Peer Support Network evaluation, see Romilly (2003). To view the website of the Peer Support Network, see <www.peerzone.org>.
10. Romilly (2003).
11. Davidson et al. (1999).
12. Kennedy (1995). Also see Kennedy and Humphreys (1994).
13. D. Capponi, quoted in K. Church, *Because of Where We've Been: The Business Behind the Business of Psychiatric Consumer Survivor Economic Development* (Toronto, ON: The Ontario Council of Alternative Businesses, 1997): p. 6.
14. For a summary of this research, see Centre for Research and Education in Human Services (2004), p. 4; this study was part of a larger research initiative that examined the effectiveness of community-based mental health services. For an overall sum-

mary of that larger initiative, see The Community Mental Health Initiative (2004).

15. Hutchison et al. (1996).
16. Centre for Research and Education in Human Services, *Summary Bulletin*.
17. People First of Windsor (2006).
18. O'Brien (1996), p. 22.
19. Lord (2006).
20. See, for example, Newberry (2005).
21. Heller, Miller, and Hsieh (1999).
22. Newberry (2004).
23. Church (1997).

Part 4

Creating an Inclusive Civil Society

11

Government and the Common Good

Policies and Funding That Work

A policy is a temporary creed liable to be changed, but while it holds it has got to be pursued with apostolic zeal.

Mahatma Gandhi

Government policies and funding decisions impact the daily lives of citizens in many significant ways. Policy can be thought of as a *purposeful framework of principles and actions related to a particular initiative*. As the quote by Gandhi suggests, policy is a creed — a statement of beliefs, hopes and ideas. Policy shapes the process that moves ideas into action. While many human service practitioners we meet do not see the importance of policy, the reality is that almost all of our service structures, organizational approaches, and funding models are based on policy. The impact of policy goes well beyond formal systems, affecting public and private sectors as well as voluntary organizations.[1] Leaders in New Story initiatives understand that supportive policies at the municipal, provincial, and federal levels are important for innovation to flourish.

There are many reasons why effective government policy and funding are important to innovation. First, policy significantly affects the kind of initiatives that get funded and those that go unsupported. Policy, therefore, can be an "enabling mechanism" for innovation. Second, policy can ensure that innovation is valued by assigning resources and support for new ideas. Third, policy making that is flexible enables local enterprise to flourish by emphasizing the value of participation of citizens. Although seldom implemented, "bottom-up" policy development promotes civic engagement in very positive ways. Finally, policy benefits all people when it enables innovation to be sustainable. Only a few New Story initiatives have experienced all of the benefits of effective policy. In fact, traditional policy and funding is so entrenched that many initiatives find themselves constantly "pushing against" current government policies.

Two types of policies and funding impact the lives of Canadian citizens. First, there are the so-called universal health and social policies designed for *all* citizens. Many of these are federal policies while others are provincial or municipal. Effective universal policies support the common good because the well-being of all citizens is enhanced. "Common good" contrasts with self-interest, a perspective that too often drives public policy. At the municipal level, parks and recreation, libraries, and schools are policies based on the common good and are, in theory, available to all citizens. Well-known universal policies in a national context are Medicare and national transportation guidelines. The Canadian health care system is based on the policy and principles of Medicare and a system of funding that enables each Canadian to access health care without any direct payment. Contrast that with the U.S., where almost 50 million Americans have no health care insurance. The stories of despair among Americans who have to pay huge amounts from their own pockets are legend. While the Canadian Medicare system has problems and limitations, we can say that this universal policy clearly benefits everyone.

The second type of policies and funding are "residual" policies targeted for specific populations. These include most provincial policies related to aging and disability. Typically, these policies and funding mechanisms are based on the so-called needs of a particular group. They usually have a set of well-defined procedures and guidelines for accessibility, the maximum amount of support dollars allowed, and length of time support can be utilized. For instance, all provinces have homecare programs with specific guidelines in all of these areas. While some residual policies are effective in getting the right supports to the right people, such policies often have stringent criteria that are stigmatizing or too restrictive to be useful to most people. Regardless, residual policies by their very nature cannot be as comprehensive as universal policies.

Leaders of New Story initiatives tell us that, as much as possible, they avoid getting caught by the limits and constraints of government policy and funding. As social innovators, some leaders do this by being fully independent of government funding and working mostly at the grassroots level. Other initiatives remain connected to government for funding, but find ways of being innovative, despite the limits of residual policies. In this regard, many people have told us what they like about the initiatives is that the policies and the practices are more open and less rule-bound than traditional programs. Finally, there are a small number of initiatives whose innovative work is supported by provincial policies and legislation. There are lessons to draw from all of these experiences.

Policy and Funding: Good, Bad, and Ugly

Government policy and funding has seldom been based on New Story values and principles. A huge service system has evolved that is paternalistic toward many citizens. After searching for support from agency to agency one person declared, "Navigating the system means not necessarily trusting the answer you get." All citizens experience bureaucracy and feel that services sometimes intrude in their lives. While this is true for everyone, it is even more so for citizens who are feeling excluded or vulnerable. Some leaders would likely agree with Albert Camus, who once said, "Government has no conscience. Sometimes it has policy."

Many policies of today were created 20, 30, or even 40 years ago, so it is understandable why they are no longer

Pathways to Inclusion

relevant. We recently experienced the impact of such outdated policy quite dramatically. One of us was in court as an "expert" witness on an issue related to a person's right to genuine choice in his supportive housing. The government lawyer asked, "Is not the continuum of services approach that guides government policy quite rational?" As we have noted, a continuum of services approach assumes that people have to be "ready" before they can move through a series of steps toward social inclusion. Our response in court was that such policy was rational in the 1960s and 1970s when it was being developed. But today, more than 30 years later, a continuum of services approach to policy is highly inappropriate and oppressive.[2] Historical attitudes have undergone significant changes since such policies were first developed so it is time for such policies to change.

The reality is that outdated policy can do harm. Stories abound from participants about how their previous lived experience with policies and programs did not meet their needs. We learn from these stories that the "ugliest" policies are those that are rigid and inflexible. Many policies related to disability, aging, and chronic conditions continue to be based on discrimination and exclusion. For example, although many people live with low incomes, all provinces significantly limit the employment earnings of people who are on a disability pension. Beyond a certain amount, the government claws back a percentage of earned income from a person's next pension cheque or withdraws the pension including its benefits. For almost everyone, this is a real disincentive to work. In another example, many provinces continue to expand the nursing home industry at an alarming pace — this, despite increasing evidence that "aging in place" and home support are very cost-effective and contribute more to quality of life.[3]

John Ralston Saul argues that the common good is increasingly ignored by governments.[4] As we have seen, the common good refers to ideas, policies, and actions that benefit all citizens rather than just a few. When the common good is ignored, accommodations that are required for all people to experience full citizenship are dealt with in minimalist ways. For many New Story initiatives, the dilemma is that policy that supports innovation is often nonexistent, so social innovators have a challenge to find a niche to build creative community alternatives. As an illustration, despite more than 50% of the almost two million adult Canadians with disabilities who are supported entirely by family members, few provinces have any kind of effective family support policies.[5] Michael Prince, policy researcher in the areas of disability and aging from the University of Victoria argues, that "Minor tinkering with programs and structures will simply perpetuate the frustrating pattern seen over the past generation ... Fundamental reforms in several [policy] arenas are essential for advancing the vision of full citizenship and inclusion."[6]

In those instances when governments at any level create good policy, it is possible to see the "right" values and principles upon which policy was developed. Such values and principles empower people to make choices about their lives, to contribute to citizenship, and to access needed resources. The intent of effective social policy is to create a positive future and enhanced quality of life for citizens.

Organizations also need to put in place people-friendly policies as opposed to administratively efficient policies. In a recent study, families being supported by Durham Association for Family Respite reflected on the policies that they experienced.[7] Families that were interviewed had very positive stories of citizenship. The policies of this individualized support program were guided by values of citizenship and participation in all areas of community life. The policies gave families a planning mechanism and time to make decisions about their support requirements, and facilitators understood that they were to be as unobtrusive as possible. The Durham policy includes the following statements:

- We will promote and support that the use of public funds be made available to people based on their unique abilities, interests, talents, and preferences.

- We will work to ensure that people will have opportunities in their community and valued roles which promote self-esteem and self-confidence.

The paradox is evident here where good residual policy actually has some of the characteristics of universal policy. Good residual policies have inclusive criteria on who can receive support. Many initiatives have created such effective policies. Independent Living Resource Centres across Canada serve a range of people in their communities. Anyone with a disability can access support, whether personal advocacy, peer

Pathways to Inclusion

support, or skill development. The welcoming policies and practices of these Centres do not feel bureaucratic to the person
or to the community. Thus, light is shed on the potential of
good policy that frames local policy around the values of inclusion and full participation. The dilemma is that few service
systems or provincial policies have such values and program
coherency.

Policies That Support Social Innovation

We have already explored the question of why policy is relevant to social innovation. Now we can ask about which policies
support innovation and the New Story. The answers to these
questions are complex, since policy and funding approaches are
interrelated. The following policy suggestions are based on our
interpretation of people's experience in terms of what a policy
agenda for social innovation might look like. Taken together,
these policies would contribute to the New Story and the
common good.

Policies That De-link Housing from
Direct Personal Support

In traditional approaches, housing and personal support
are often linked; a person can get housing only when support
is attached. Policies that link housing and support seriously
limit the options available to people who are trying to create
the kind of homes they want. Typically people are offered a
"residential placement" that comes with a certain number of
hours of personal support per day. It is not unusual for such
settings to be staff controlled. People who need support are
unable to choose their own home since there would be no
support available. This limits where people live and who, if
anyone, they want to live with. Furthermore, when housing and
support are linked, people's choices are limited by what an
agency offers them. These traditional approaches are insensitive
at best and dehumanizing at worst.

To create increased options and choice, provincial governments need policy that de-links housing and support. Provinces
that have done this create housing policy designed to increase

access to affordable housing. Some provincial social service departments across Canada have begun to develop such policies in collaboration with their Ministry of Housing. Making affordable housing available in communities makes good sense. There are many creative ways to do this, such as through rent subsidies, integrated units throughout new housing complexes, and trust funds for home ownership. Affordable housing policy should be separate from the policies that provide resources for individualized support. Obviously, both need to be adequately funded.

Through effective policy, provincial governments also need to encourage and support local organizations to de-link their housing and support. Many organizations are hesitant to de-link housing and support because they do not know what de-linking means and are unsure of its consequences. Good provincial policy provides the strategies and resources for community agencies to be able to do this effectively. Some organizations have thrived when such policies are in place. The York Region Alternative Community Living program began to provide extensive support to seniors in their own homes as part of a municipal alternative community living policy. The benefit of de-linking housing and support was also evident within Waterloo Regional Homes for Mental Health. This organizational direction now enables people to receive individualized support in their own homes, a dramatic change that once saw mental health support only attached to group living situations.

Congregate settings like nursing homes and large group homes that attach support to housing are very expensive. The assumption of policies that create these homes is that everyone needs the same level of support, whether they do or not. In 2004, the Ontario Ministry of Community and Social Services funded 13 new group homes around the province, each one with a yearly budget in the range of $250,000 to $350,000.[8] In the New Story, such funding no longer makes sense. There is a social stigma attached to congregate living that decreases people's relationships with their fellow citizens, and it is almost impossible to individualize supports in such settings. People and local organizations need to become skilled at supporting people to create their own homes. De-linking housing and support in provincial policy is one strong incentive for communities to begin such important work.

Pathways to Inclusion

Individualized Funding Policy

We discovered with New Story initiatives that people need and want to have control over the personal supports available to them. Policies that designate funds directly to individuals greatly assist the process of empowerment. Recently we saw our elderly neighbour going around the block in her wheelchair with the support of a worker. How did we know it was a worker? The woman had on a uniform jacket. With individualized funding people are highly unlikely to have their personal assistants wear a uniform at any time. Rather, people can decide who their workers will be, what they will do, and when they will come to assist. While some community organizations are trying to be flexible with the support they offer, in our experience these changes are limited. Organizations are only able to partially shift control due to the nature of their mandate and operating culture. We need policy options that enable people to self-direct with individualized funding, and permit people to gain the control they want.

Governments that develop individualized funding policies know they will not necessarily be appealing to everyone. In some initiatives, about 20% of eligible citizens will access such new paradigm supports, although over time this figure can rise. Initially the Ontario Direct Funding had a very slow "take-up" but by the sixth year there was a surge of interest. Similarly, after 20 years in California, depending on the county, up to 50% of people who access the In-Home Support Program choose to use direct payments. The point here is that governments need policy in place to make individualized funding an option for anyone who wants it, especially since studies are now showing very positive impacts of such policies.[9] Brian Salisbury, policy analyst with Community Living British Columbia, argues that all new government money should be used for individualized funding as one way to shift the paradigm in service systems.

There are diverse opinions about how best to implement individualized funding policy. The first few initiatives in Canada envisioned individualized or direct funding as a parallel approach to traditional approaches. In other words, people who require support can choose whether they want a traditional approach or an individualized funding option. The advantage of a parallel approach is that principles and procedures can be kept totally separate from an agency model. Such policies, when implemented in initiatives such as the Ontario Direct Funding Project, usually begin with small numbers of people, which enables the policy to be implemented carefully and coherently.

Others argue that we are now at a stage of evolution where parallel projects limit the cultural and systemic change in the overall system, which holds a lot of funding for people. This has turned out to be true with the Ontario Direct Funding, which has been highly successful but has had almost no impact on the wider system (which remains very traditional). More recent innovations related to individualized funding are paying closer attention to the whole system in the hopes that shifting the paradigm can have broader impacts. We explore this issue further as part of an analysis of the transformation of service systems.

Individualized funding policy should allow for "a seamless approach" to direct funding. In a recent study with many people who had complex support issues, almost 20% of participants received funding from three or more sources. As several research participants note, this disjointed approach to funding supports is very frustrating since procedures and policies differ for each program.[10] A seamless policy would allow a merging of various funding sources so people would need to apply just once. When the Ontario Direct Funding Project got under way in 1993, many of its first recipients had multiple sources of support funding. These sources were merged. People are very happy with this seamless approach with only one plan, one budget, and one source of funding.

This issue of creating a seamless approach is further complicated in the "old story" by widely differing agency rules. It is possible for a senior who is frail to have a homemaker who is not allowed to do any personal care, and a personal care worker who is not allowed to do any homemaking. Individualized funding gets beyond such "stupid policies" and enables people to direct their personal assistants in ways that make sense and enhance their quality of life. The York Region initiative with seniors recognized this issue early on and built in policies so that people could dictate what and how their workers would support them. Such seamless policies make sense to people and to workers. Michael Prince shows how the emergence of family support in aging policy might enhance more coherent policies.[11]

Individualized funding policy must be carefully drafted so that it is coherent and separate from the traditional service system. In most traditional service systems, allocation of resources is determined by a committee of agency professionals. Allocations within individualized funding policy often utilize a panel of peers and community members to assess requests from people seeking support. Both the Direct Funding Project and the Windsor–Essex Brokerage initiative utilize this type of mechanism. The wisdom of such an approach is that people who are familiar with the New Story and with community options are making the allocation decisions. While such allocation mechanisms are important, leaders point out that individualized funding policy must be accompanied by policies that create meaningful infrastructure supports, such as independent planning and facilitation.

Policies for Independent Facilitation and Planning

Policies are needed that separate planning from direct service provision. As we explored, independent planning and facilitation means that individuals and families have access to a facilitator who listens deeply and assists people to pursue their dreams and goals. Facilitators also provide information and assist with network development, service negotiation (with formal and generic services) and contract development. Our research shows that individuals and families benefit from having unencumbered, ongoing facilitation and planning support and that such support provides "value for money."[12] Similarly, intensive case management with frail seniors or people with severe mental illness have also been shown to be very cost effective.[13] Separating planning from service provision also creates a powerful building block for transformation. As we shall see in the example of transformation in British Columbia, policy for independent planning and facilitation must be based on values and principles of self-determination, empowerment, and citizenship. Provincial policy must create opportunities that enable the facilitator to get to know the person well. Policies also need to address the issue of accessing generic resources in the community as a first resort, such as making use of accessible public transportation or regular recreation services.

Policy related to independent planning and facilitation must also create a structure that ensures consistency and high-quality facilitation throughout each province. Developing the right structure for independent planning and facilitation will require creative thought from provincial policy makers and other stakeholders. One of the issues for policy development is that the traditional system is typically hesitant to give up resources to a new entity. British Columbia was the first province to build a structure for independent planning and to reallocate resources from the traditional system to do so. More recently, New Brunswick has started an independent facilitation initiative, with facilitators housed in offices of the New Brunswick Association for Community Living, a provincial organization that does not offer any other direct service.

It is important that any structure for independent planning and facilitation must have a provincial component that is consistent and coherent with its values and functions. Furthermore, it needs to be able to deliver province-wide training and support to facilitators. Experience in Great Britain, Western Australia, and some American states confirm this important policy direction.[14]

Policies That Nurture Social Inclusion and Cohesion

Social inclusion and cohesion are about how communities work together to include people; they are primarily about relationships, networks, neighbourhood participation, community connections, and government policies. There are many indications that "old story" policies and funding fail to nurture social inclusion and cohesion. Traditional policy indicators include citizens needing to leave their communities to receive the support they require; people being disconnected from relationships and their communities by being "institutionalized" in nursing homes, large residences, and rooming houses; lack of portability of supports, thus denying people the option of moving to a new location and experiencing genuine citizenship; unemployment continuing to be very high for low income persons; and poverty. Governments seldom intentionally address issues of social inclusion and cohesion, yet the experience of initiatives indicates that policies in these areas will be crucial to the further development of the New Story. A recent national study confirms that inclusion matters to Canadians. When asked, people have lots of ideas of how policies could enhance social inclusion.[15]

Factors that nurture social cohesion are similar to determinants of health. Research suggests it is not just funding of community supports that enhances inclusion and cohesion but the right mix of community infrastructures.[16] Consistent with people's experience, communities that provide conditions and opportunities for citizens to volunteer and contribute enhance social cohesion. Communities that create accessible, welcoming community centres contribute to social inclusion. Similarly, communities that are able to reduce isolation of the most vulnerable members enhance social inclusion. Some initiatives have been seeking more commitments from governments and foundations to address the loneliness and isolation of Canadians who are vulnerable. Although there is presently little government support for such initiatives, innovations that build support networks with citizens contribute in significant ways to social inclusion and cohesion. Similarly, research on recovery of people with significant mental health issues shows the importance of relationships and social networks.[17] Research with children at risk also shows the importance of strong, well-connected relationships in terms of children's health and well being.[18]

Policy makers in disability and aging need to consider factors related to social inclusion and cohesion. It may well be shown over time that funding community facilitators will enhance social inclusion and cohesion far more than simply funding direct services. Although governments are often hesitant to fund capacity-building initiatives, the reality is that investing in facilitation and front-end community development pays huge dividends. It also builds on the New Story commitment that people themselves, along with family, friends, and facilitators all have the capacity to build social inclusion and cohesion. All levels of government have a role to play in this capacity building.

Policies That Enable Full Economic Participation

Policy makers, communities, unions, and corporations need to take seriously the capacity of all citizens to contribute economically to their communities. As Judith Snow says, "We live in a culture that doesn't value or understand the power of people who are vulnerable. We are a socially and economically viable population if well supported." To create effective policies that support economic participation means that systemic change must take place. Leaders often point out that this can be accomplished, in part, with the implementation of a dynamic labour market strategy for people who are on the margins. The Independent Living Resource Centres recently completed a six-year project to enable people with disabilities to access the labour market. Reviews of this project showed some positive gains for individuals, including increased full- and part-time employment.[19] However, there were many constraints to long-term employment because of the lack of a coherent labour market strategy. Economic conditions that foster full participation will enhance employability. They will also ensure that adequate accommodations are in place so that everyone can contribute their gifts and strengths to community life.

Policies That Support and Fund Local Innovation

While the federal, provincial, and territorial governments can provide policies that nurture the New Story, local communities also need initiatives that support and fund innovation. Funding of local innovation is one policy strategy for testing new ideas that are central to the New Story. Some of the initiatives we studied began as pilot projects designed to develop key concepts, such as network development, employment support, or independent planning and facilitation. Several projects received funding from foundations over the years to experiment with new ideas. Such funding can be useful for small local groups as well as for service providers who want to try out innovative ideas. Although foundation funding is usually short term, some leaders have been very effective at using such funds to leverage broader community change. Windsor–Essex Family Network, for example, has used several grants to build capacity of families and to partner with other organizations for policy change with regional government.

We have seen the innovative nature of local family and peer self-help groups and the vibrant manner in which they can influence a community. There is no agreement across initiatives as to how such groups should be funded, although there is consensus that their presence is very important. Some groups believe that the best way to support and fund local self-help groups is through the private sector. Planned Lifetime Advocacy Network (PLAN) from British Columbia has used grants from foundations and corporations to support the development of 10 affiliates across the country. While each affiliate works closely with local families to build capacity with family members, all affiliates are closely connected with PLAN for leadership development, and ongoing support. Government-funded policies in this area of family and peer self-help groups, such as the Ontario Peer Development Initiative, provide support, education and, in some cases, economic development.

Provincial and federal governments occasionally fund innovation as part of a strategic direction. The Canadian experience is actually quite positive in this regard. In the early 1990s, the Ontario government created an Innovation Fund for groups concerned with building the capacity of individuals and communities. A small, energetic group of volunteers and professionals in Kitchener–Waterloo, Ontario, received funding for its Support Clusters project. There have been numerous impacts from this three-year project for individuals, families, and communities including research demonstrations with disability and seniors groups. More recently, the federal government created the Opportunities Fund for employment supports for people with disabilities. Although not intended to support social innovation, some groups used their funds in very innovative ways. The Canadian Association of Independent Living Centres, for example, created a project called Navigating the Waters, using the principles of "consumer control" and "individualized facilitation" to guide the project.[20] Several centres have maintained this innovative approach even though the federal funding has ended. In British Columbia, Community Living British Columbia is committed to providing funds for local innovation that can be used by individuals, family groups, service organizations, and interested partners to develop new approaches to providing needed support. From these examples, it is clear that governments at all levels and other sectors of society, such as foundations, can play a key role in seeding social innovation and supporting local enterprise.

Seeding and Supporting New Story Functions

Since 2007, we have been working with several communities in Ontario that have intentionally decided to seed and support *New Story* functions. Two projects especially reflect this important community development work; the New Story Group of Kitchener–Waterloo and the provincial three-year project, Modeling Innovation and Community Change.

The New Story Group of Kitchener–Waterloo began with a few family leaders and community researchers having conversations about the New Story and its implications for policy and practice. Soon the group realized that the foundation of this work was seeding and supporting separate, inter-dependent functions:

- Strong autonomous family and peer organizations
- Independent facilitation that could help people build capacity in community
- Service Providers that are person-centered and open to change

Conversations are central to the work of the New Story group. Facilitated conversations enable families to understand the power of separate functions. Conversations also enable service providers to see the potential of independent facilitation in a transformed system. With recent grants, the New Story Group is now demonstrating independent facilitation and building capacity for an independent facilitation entity that will be launched in early 2012.

The Modeling Innovation and Community Change project is using a similar "seeding and supporting" strategy in three communities. In Brockville, a vibrant, independent family group is being seeded and supported. In Huntsville and area, a local Steering Committee is developing independent facilitation capacity and a family network. In Windsor, which has the Brokerage for Personal Supports project, the community is working on a new human resource initiative. This provides a place for families with individualized funding to access such things as a worker registry, contract support with staff, and ways to manage direct funding.

The diagram, shown in the focus box on the following page, shows the New Story functions. While the development of each one is enhanced through community development, it is important to recognize that provincial policy can contribute to their full development. When combined, they can seed and support the New Story effectively.

Pathways to Inclusion

The New Story Functions

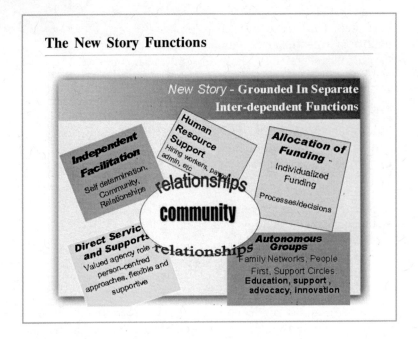

Moving Policy Development toward Genuine Transformation

Although the policy directions outlined above can assist in transforming service systems, few governments have moved toward these policies without significant advocacy and involvement of citizens. Some initiatives have spent an enormous amount of time working with a variety of stakeholders to create progressive policy. This policy work is influencing national, provincial, municipal, and organizational levels, but it has been difficult work because the views and experiences of many citizens have been ignored in the development of social policy for generations. That slowly began to change in the 1980s when the power and voice of people who traditionally had been ignored began to be heard. The International Year of Disabled Persons (IYDP) in 1981 was a significant event that involved the establishment of IYDP committees across the country. For the first time, people with disabilities and their allies had a vehicle to express their concerns.

In 1982, the federal government under Prime Minister Pierre Trudeau entrenched the Canadian Charter of Rights and

Freedoms along with the repatriated constitution. This was an historic event because section 15(1) of the Charter constitutionally protected the equality rights of all Canadians. The Charter provides that "every person has the right to equality before the law and to equal protection of the law without discrimination because of race, national or ethnic origin, colour, religion, age, sex, or mental and physical disability." Not only is the Charter a milestone for minority groups, but the manner in which it developed was also significant. In the first tabled version of section 15(1), "mental and physical disability" were not mentioned. The disability movement was outraged and organized a significant protest that included marches, letter writing, and negotiations with federal officials. The victory that followed gave momentum to the disability movement and to the belief that people could have a say in policies that affect their lives. Leaders of the movement identify this event as a turning point for the involvement of people with disabilities in other policy issues.[21]

In the mid-1980s, the senior citizens movement had a similar experience when the Conservative government of Prime Minister Brian Mulroney attempted to claw back pension funds from elderly people who had income. The proposed policy stated that the only people who would receive the pension would be those who needed it. All across Canada seniors groups met, wrote letters, and were vocal in their opposition. People consciously or subconsciously understood government was trying to turn a good universal policy into a need-based residual policy and fought back. The federal government soon dropped the idea.

Citizen Participation in Transformation

In the shift to the New Story, policy development is vitally important work in system transformation from the old paradigm. In each initiative that has been engaged in such work, the participation of people themselves is central to the development of new policy. In the early stages of these movements for change, there are usually "trigger events" that enable governments, citizens, and advocates to move toward new policy frameworks. Trigger events can be seen as "sparks that fuel social change movements."[22] These events can be unexpected, such as the examples above with the disability and seniors movements, but they are significant because they identify or symbolize a social problem. In terms of paradigms, these trigger events raise broad awareness about issues that previously had been illuminated only by a small group of leaders. The actual trigger events help give the general public language and meaning to the issue.

Examples from two movements, physical disabilities and mental health, will help illustrate the importance of participation of citizens themselves in policy development. In 1987, we were working on the *Review of Support Services for Ontario*, a major undertaking that involved province-wide surveys and interviews with people with physical disabilities as well as with representatives of community agencies and government. "Fear of institutionalization" and "restrictive policies of support programs" were both major themes that emphasized people's strong desire for change. These themes showed the limitations of the "old story" and led us to make more than 40 recommendations in the final report. Some recommendations called on the Ontario government to initiate a project of direct individualized funding as one means whereby people could access attendant services. For the previous two years, the Attendant Care Action Coalition had been lobbying for just such a program. Their advocacy had included some papers that outlined experiences in other jurisdictions. With the release of our report, the Coalition now had research evidence and a trigger event to support its case. Similarly, mental health reform in Ontario was triggered partly by the 1988 Graham Report, entitled *Building Community Support for People: A Plan for Mental Health*. This report highlighted the need for significant changes in ways that mental health supports and services were organized and delivered.

Reports and trigger events by themselves are insufficient to create progressive policy. Momentum, or what some call a critical mass, is also needed to move change ahead. Politicians especially need to feel that there is widespread support for new policy. In the case of mental health reform in Ontario, it was the process of engaging consumer/survivors during the Graham Report hearings that began to mobilize people. Following release of this report, the Liberal government created a provincial steering committee and subcommittees that for the first time gave consumer/survivors and family members a voice in determining mental health policy.[23] In the case of the *Review of Support Services*, our report soon became a catalyst for dialogue

Pathways to Inclusion

across Ontario. Less than a year after the release of the report, momentum began to swing toward the need for policy change. The Attendant Care Action Coalition managed to convince the government to fund a three-day retreat. Attracting more than 130 people, this event built more momentum for the policy change. The disability movement was now on side and many civil servants were enthusiastic as well.[24]

We have also learned that policy development cannot lead to transformation unless there is strong leadership. The Attendant Care Action Coalition and the Mental Health Survivor Movement both had strong leaders who were very knowledgeable about the issues and who could articulate an alternative vision. Both groups became experts at telling their stories, whether to politicians, civil servants, or the general public. Leaders also took the time to build relationships with civil servants. When momentum began to swing in their favour there were civil servants ready to create appropriate policy in collaboration with leaders of the movement. Kathryn Church has written extensively about how "unsettling" this kind of process can be for people in power. Policy makers working closely with people who are vulnerable should have a willingness to change the norms of "discourse" to ways that are undoubtedly much less formal than they are used to.[25]

This policy development work, including trigger events, momentum, and leadership, led to some significant transformation in provincial policy, which has filtered down to communities and services. In terms of Ontario mental health reform, new policies were enacted that created separate funding for people with mental health issues to create their own self-help groups. As we have seen, this funding built capacity for the survivor voice to be more fully developed. Mental health reform also de-linked or separated housing and support dollars, creating more flexibility for individuals and communities to create appropriate, affordable housing. Both of these policy examples, while far from perfect, did give three initiatives a chance to create some innovative approaches in the way they worked. Waterloo Regional Homes for Mental Health, for example, had already restructured its organization and was now able to solidify its individualized support components. The *Review of Support Services* report in combination with the Attendant Care Action Coalition led to legislation and policy regarding adults with physical disabilities who were able to self-direct their support. They were eligible to access support through the new Direct Funding Project. This promising initiative now has the benefit of strong legislation and sound policy.

Role of Governments in Transformation

Policy development work takes different paths depending on the jurisdiction. *Federal policy making* in social policy is complicated because in this area, the federal government almost always works in conjunction with the provinces/territories and social movements. This complexity has seldom achieved positive results for genuine transformation of services and supports. The *In Unison* document published in 1998 by the federal/provincial/territorial governments was the first time there had been a broad-based disability policy framework that included many of the components of the new paradigm. This was also the first time that senior levels of government had made a commitment to a more socio-political or systemic approach to vulnerability and community supports.

The disability movement, while supportive of *In Unison*, has been frustrated with the lack of policy implementation. The exception is in some areas of tax relief for families with a member with a disability. People working at the federal level find it difficult to influence change because a wide number of stakeholders participate at decision-making tables. Another dilemma is that leaders often participate in discussions at the federal level but little of this dialogue and development work filters down to community-based projects. Recent examples in disability and aging have shown that even though numerous national organizations might agree on a policy direction, there have not been any trigger events or momentum to move these common commitments forward in any significant fashion.[26] Michael Prince calls this slow process of policy change "directed incrementalism,"[27] with results that are very modest.

Policy research at the federal level has tended to focus on a wide number of issues, including homecare, employment, transportation, and taxation. This federal policy work can sometimes create frameworks for innovative change. The 2004 Roy Romanow Report on Health Care in Canada, for example, proposes a framework for homecare that would benefit frail elderly citizens. Romanow correctly sees homecare as an essential investment in an aging society. Occasionally, federal government initiatives are actually quite action oriented. In 1991, the federal government initiated a National Strategy for the *Economic Integration of Persons with Disabilities,* with $158 million designated across 10 government departments. Although this initiative ended in 1996, it showed that when leadership and resources are available, governments can create awareness and accommodation for citizens. The federal government continues to fund the main national disability and aging organizations, which enables these groups to hold meetings, write policy papers, and advocate for change. Although senior citizens and citizens with disabilities could benefit immensely from the presence and resources of the federal government, there is little agreement among policy makers and politicians about the role of federal policy making in this area.

In 2008, the federal government initiated the Registered Disability Savings Plan (RDSP). Clearly a New Story idea, the RDSP enables people with disabilities to invest money, which is matched by the federal government. Even a person with a disability who has no money can receive $1000 a year into an account in their name. This federal policy is not means-tested and recognizes that people with disabilities are generally poor and need support to save for the future. The RDSP is designed to be used as a long-term savings plan, since the federal portion of the money cannot be withdrawn for ten years. The RDSP is the brainchild of Finance Minister Jim Flaherty, whose department worked closely with the disability community to draft the details of the policy. PLAN in British Columbia has recently established the RDSP Resource Centre, designed to assist Canadian individuals and families to access the RDSP to its fullest.[28] At the end of 2010, only about 10 per cent of eligible Canadians had accessed the RDSP.

Policy development at *provincial levels* has varied widely among provinces. This in itself is problematic. Some provinces have developed enlightened policies that have seen all their large institutions close while other provinces have not. Although funding for personal supports is a main responsibility of the provinces, only a small number have begun the process of transformation toward a new paradigm. British Columbia has made significant strides in transforming its developmental disability services sector. Ontario has been a leader in framing policy related to human rights and accessibility for people with disabilities and seniors. Representatives from some initiatives have been part of a 10-year struggle to create an Ontario Accessibility Disability Act. Finally passed in 2005, this Act requires municipalities to create full accessibility in many areas of life. Over the next 20 years, other sectors of society such as human services, business, and industry will be required to meet the standards of accessibility. Other provinces are also looking at developing legislation that would create fully accessible parks, schools, and buildings that will be of great benefit to our aging society.

Provinces are in a difficult situation in regard to social policy and transformation. With an aging society, health care costs are rising rapidly and consuming as much as 40% of provincial budgets. Although some vulnerable citizens get funding support from ministries of health, many people require funding support from other ministries, such as social services and housing. In response to this "crisis," some provinces, such as Saskatchewan, Alberta, British Columbia, and Ontario, are decentralizing the management of their health services in the hopes they can become more cost-effective. While some of these efforts are pointing in positive directions, our sense is that the provinces are seldom building in collaborative structures with other ministries or with social movement groups in ways that might benefit citizens. Also, the language and strategies of new paradigm approaches are only beginning to appear in provincial plans. There are positive signs of good policy development emerging from some provinces, especially related to community mental health and developmental disabilities. In long-term care, however, innovation seems to be limited to homecare, which in some provinces is beginning to support a range of citizens with chronic conditions. Nursing homes continue to be very traditional and a huge source of provincial expenditures. On the other hand, several states and innovators in the United States are collaborating to redesign nursing homes into smaller, home-like units.[29]

Leaders in many initiatives work closely with their *municipalities* to develop policies to ensure accessible and inclusive settings. They find that working locally is generally easier than working federally or provincially because leaders can build relationships with municipal councillors. Several Independent Living Resource Centres are collaborating with municipal councillors and other officials to address inclusion issues, such as the creation of policies related to funding curb cuts and accessibility. As a result of such relationships and advocacy, Richmond, British Columbia, recently appointed an inclusion co-ordinator who works with all municipal departments to ensure that policies and practices are consistent with principles of full inclusion. This is an example of how "bottom-up" change strategies can lead to effective inclusion policies with very practical results.

In recent policy reform work, we have found it common for civil servants to say they are limited in their ability to reform social services without new money. Our experience with reform is that new money is not always required. More important, governments need to develop new structures and new priorities. Reallocation of resources from more institutional and traditional services to New Story initiatives can also enhance reform in a cost-effective way.

Leaders of New Story initiatives would agree with policy researchers James Rice and Michael Prince, who make the claim that we need to "re-build the social role and capacity of governments."[30] As these researchers show, a broad literature identifies many roles for government and the kinds of initiatives they could take to enhance social inclusion. Each of these initiatives could combine universal and residual policy making in creative ways that would bring benefit to all citizens, especially those who lack power and resources. The initiatives most often cited in this literature are the following:

- Eliminating child poverty
- Developing a national childcare system
- Making a commitment to affordable social housing
- Strengthening the commitment to health care and "healthy public policy"
- Making a commitment to employment and fairer taxes
- Recognizing the rights of minority groups and providing appropriate supports, including Aboriginal peoples, people with disabilities, and senior citizens[31]

We found in earlier work that policy has the most impact when there is coherence and connection among the different levels of government and organizations.[32] In other words, the New Story is more likely to emerge if provincial policy, municipal policy, organizational policy, and program principles are consistent. If we believe that *all* people have a right to a higher quality of life than is presently afforded, then federal, provincial, and municipal policy and legislation need to be enacted to ensure this will happen. This cannot be left up to individual communities and certainly not to individual agencies. Many leaders at the local level voice their frustration with having to do work that should be mandated by higher government levels. People connected with Windsor–Essex Brokerage for Personal Supports spent a great deal of time developing a regional policy of portability, where people can take their support dollars with them if they move to another agency or community. Although this was a useful initiative, such local policy is limited unless other regions pass the same policy. It makes more sense in this case for the provincial government to pass portability legislation for the entire province.

Policy development seldom involves people themselves and even more rarely creates true transformation. Unfortunately, there are few examples of system-wide transformation. However, in British Columbia, a group of families, individuals, and progressive professionals have worked for the past five years to create a transformed system that might be able to move the New Story into an entire system. British Columbia's experience is our only example of system-wide innovation so is worthy of a more in-depth look.

Policy and System Change in British Columbia

In the province of British Columbia in recent years, there has been a strong movement for change related to people with disabilities. Many people with developmental disabilities and their families, along with other stakeholders, such as the provincial government, realized that changes were needed in the way supports were provided to people. There had been widespread criticisms of the traditional service system. Many people felt that the system reduced people's citizenship opportunities because of its lack of flexibility, responsiveness, portability, and accountability. There was recognition by disability leaders and then government that new approaches were needed to transform the service system.

In 2001, a stakeholder coalition began extensive dialogue with the British Columbia government about ways to transform the service system. In 2002, the Minister of Children and Family Development established a 25-member Community Living Transition Steering Committee consisting of people with developmental disabilities, family members, community leaders, service providers, and senior government staff. The report created by this collaborative group, *A New Vision for Community Living: A Vision of Choice and Change*, was released in late 2002. The report proposed that the service system be transformed by embracing new principles, community governance, individualized funding, and independent planning. This report was greeted very positively by the disability community. PLAN, one of the New Story initiatives that had been part of the Steering Committee, wrote to its members that "if good faith and good judgment continue to prevail, we are on the verge of changes in British Columbia that will be as profound and beneficial as the closing of the institutions."[33]

Although it was a bumpy road to achieve the changes, government and community did prevail and in 2004 the *Community Living Authority Act* was passed. This Act creates a new community governance entity called Community Living British Columbia. It assumes responsibility from the Ministry for Children and Family Development for all services and supports for adults with developmental disabilities and some children and their families as well. Community Living British Columbia became a reality on July 1, 2005, and is now a crown agency responsible for providing assistance to those needing community living support, managing the budget allocated by government, and stimulating communities to change how they respond to people with a disability.

The vision statement of Community Living British Columbia (CLBC) is *Good Lives in Welcoming Communities*. CLBC's mission is to respond "to the life-long needs and goals of individuals and families by recognizing their abilities and contributions, sharing leadership with communities, and funding supports that honour individual choice." With guiding principles clearly within the new paradigm, CLBC is based on best practice and research on innovation. It is also firmly based on principles of collaboration. As Doug Wollard, vice-president of CLBC's Community Planning and Development Division, says, "CLBC is also a social experiment on a broad scale." British Columbia's long history as a province that experiments with new ideas has created a solid foundation for this innovative change. Several New Story initiatives were created in British Columbia, including Project Friendship, Vela Microboards, Plan Lifetime Advocacy Network, and the Family Support Institute. CLBC staff acknowledges that this history of social innovation was fundamental to the broader system change envisioned by the leaders within Community Living British Columbia. Because of this early work on social innovation and inclusion, "services" for CLBC are seen as a means to inclusion, not an end.

Community governance is an idea that has a long tradition in citizen participation. It is based on the belief that individuals, families, and communities know best how to meet the needs of people in their communities. Community Living British Columbia has an 11-member governance board, which includes two people with disabilities and several family members. The disability community fought hard to ensure that the board's composition guaranteed membership of people with disabilities. In fact, the majority of board members must have a significant connection to the disability field. The province now has 17 Community Living Centres, with a Community Council for each area. The Councils are designed in a way to ensure that people in local communities have a say in funding and policy decisions. Community Councils thus play a key role in community development and in policy development. Some of the things that Councils do include the following:

- Help set priorities on how funding is spent in local areas
- Help with community approaches to keep people safe
- Help make communities better places to live and work
- Let CLBC know how it is doing in terms of policy and practice

There are two main, yet separate, divisions within Community Living British Columbia. Quality Services Division is responsible for system areas, such as eligibility, financial allocations, contract management, and outcome reporting. Quality Service Analysts work closely with service providers and people with individualized funding to develop contracts and to monitor contract implementation. The Community Planning and Development Division has staff located throughout the province. Facilitators work from Community Living Centres (and associate satellite offices) and provide independent planning and facilitation support to individuals and their families when they request it. This social innovation has created an organizational structure that separates or "firewalls" independent planning support from operational decisions involving eligibility and funding. This separation idea was critical in the thinking of the early planners and was a key part of the initial Community Living Transition Steering Committee Report.

The goal of building welcoming communities has also been a key part of the transformation. Independent planning support, which focuses on identifying flexible and innovative supports, is fundamental to this plan. Facilitators who work with individuals and their families have a "community first" focus. Along with citizenship as a driving value, facilitators enable people to utilize generic resources already existing in their communities. Community development and negotiations with community settings are part of this process. Each person's planning process is directed by individuals and their families. Along with self-determination as a second driving value, this enables people to make genuine choices about their lives and the supports they need. Facilitators are mobile, using advanced technology to work effectively and stay connected with individuals, families, and each other.

Individualized funding is also seen as a necessary option to help transform how the new system develops and operates. A policy framework known as the Individual and Family Support Policy governs access to individualized funding. This policy specifies that funding allocations are based on a support plan that identifies and justifies disability-related support needs. Everyone uses the same transparent policies and guidelines and allocated funding is portable throughout the province. Once plans are reviewed, applicants are advised if their funding or service request is approved. If funding is not available, an estimate of how long people will have to wait is provided. The policy also specifies "eligible" supports or services. Significantly, people do not have to use CLBC facilitators — they will be able to access planning support in the community from anyone with whom they have a trusted relationship.

British Columbia's move to community governance is a bold attempt to redress the inertia characteristic of human service systems and to create a foundation upon which people can reclaim their citizenship rights. The community envisages a new system, based on individualized funding and independent planning, which results in supports and services that better meet the needs of individuals and families. While the model is far from perfect, it represents the culmination of almost 30 years of community advocacy to create a more flexible and responsive service system.

The process of developing this innovative approach to system change reflects many of the issues that all social change movements go through. The original Transition Report that proposed the changes in 2002 had broad support from both leaders in the disability movement and government. Important at the time, the minister responsible was fully on board and became a champion of the transformation. After the resignation of the minister, however, there was some resistance to the community's original vision. Over the following two years, the disability community stayed the course and gradually built momentum for the changes. Government, in this case, believed in the common good and supported the growing commitment of a wide variety of stakeholders. The government has had the foresight to move from consultation to collaboration in its approach to transformation. Hopefully, Community Living British Columbia can maintain this principle in all its future planning and implementation.

Final Thoughts on Policy

Leaders of New Story innovations are not overly optimistic about governments' interest in policies that pay attention to the common good. Although there has been policy progress in some areas, the reality is that, in recent decades, the welfare state has been under attack. Enlightened policy that enhances quality of life of vulnerable citizens is not high on the agenda of policy makers. Community groups representing people with disabilities and chronic conditions, as well as senior citizens, have consistently struggled with how to directly influence public policy. In a pluralistic society, governments face many competing demands. However, these advocacy groups argue that policy makers often do not "recognize the economic and cultural conditions under which groups of people live, and therefore fail to include these groups in policy making."[34]

Some community leaders contend that fighting for policy change is challenging because policy making is not usually a democratic process. "Clients" of the service system or welfare state seldom feel that public agencies belong to them. Leo

Pathways to Inclusion

Panitch argues that it is easy for bureaucracies to control the policy agenda when there are few openings for social participation, empowerment, and mobilization.[35] More and more, policy activists are calling for the "democratization" of social service agencies and the welfare state.[36] New Story leaders have played an important role in advocating for citizens and their allies to mobilize and push for meaningful policy change. We know that such involvement historically has been critical in the evolution of any innovative policy developments.

Over the years, however, we have been struck by how few policy makers truly understand how to build effective, innovative policy *with* citizens. Thomas Homer-Dixon calls this the "ingenuity gap," where conventional policies and approaches no longer "fit" with the problems we are facing. Dixon argues that policy makers and citizens together will "need imagination, metaphor, and empathy more than ever, to help us remember each others' essential humanity."[37]

Where policy progress has been made, our initiatives show that the importance of participation and collaboration is critical. Whether our examples were mental health reform or restructuring of government resources to develop individualized funding, collaboration of citizens, service providers, and government were central to any success. These stakeholders demonstrated respect for each other and worked hard to find common ground. A growing body of work is pointing to the importance of community collaboration to resolve social issues and to develop meaningful social policy.[38] In 2010, Tamarack released its six-year evaluation of six Canadian sites that had worked on poverty reduction strategies as part of the Vital Communities initiative. In addition to numerous positive outcomes, what is most encouraging is that the inter-sectoral collaboration was highly successful. Community collaboration meant that each community worked closely with activists, businesses, social services, and government to develop strategic approaches to poverty reduction.

When policy makers participate with people who have overcome suffering or who require extensive support, they are presented with heartfelt insights into what is needed to make life better for themselves and others in their situations. Unfortunately, policy makers seldom have the opportunity to grow personally and make a contribution to policy for the common good. One of the first things policy makers need to do is to

Pathways to Inclusion

describe and understand reality. It is only with the full participation of citizens who have experienced disability, chronic conditions, or the frailties of aging that such understanding is
possible. In many ways, this listening and learning process is
the first step toward social justice and is a major contribution
of the New Story. As Edmund Burke said long ago, "Justice is
itself the greatest policy of civil society; and any eminent depar-
ture from it, under any circumstances, lies under the suspicion
of being no policy at all."

Notes

1. Boyce et al. (2001).
2. Wieck and Strully (1991).
3. Some of the studies related to the harmful impacts of certain
   policies were discussed in the second chapter on Clienthood and
   Compliance; in addition, a recent publication outlines the views
   of people with disabilities on the value of staying in their own
   homes and the effectiveness of principle-centered home support.
   See Krogh and Innis (2005).
4. Saul (1996).
5. For an analysis of family support strategies that could enhance
   the well-being of vulnerable citizens, see Canadian Association
   for Community Living (2005).
6. Prince (2001), p. 5.
7. Lord (2006).
8. See <www.mcss.gov.on.ca>.
9. Benjamin, Matthias, and Franke (2000).
10. Lord (2006).
11. Prince (1998).
12. Hutchison, Lord, and Salisbury (2006).
13. For research with seniors, see Lum, Ruff, and Williams (2005);
    Community Mental Health Initiative (2004).
14. For a summary of 10 projects in three countries, see Lord,
    Zupko, and Hutchison (2000). Also see the website of the
    Western Australia cross-disability project which has used inde-
    pendent facilitators and direct funding for almost 15 years;
    Local Area Co-ordination and Direct Funding, part of the Dis-
    ability Services Commission.
15. Clutterbuck and Novick (2003).
16. See, for example, Osberg (2003). Also see European Foundation
    for the Improvement of Living Conditions (2003).
17. See articles and newsletters created by Patricia Deegan, an
    American leader in the Recovery Movement in mental health.
    <www.patdeegan.com>
18. Furstenberg and Hughes (1995).

19. Lord (2000).
20. Lord (2000).
21. Boyce et al. (2001).
22. See NewsReport of the Centre for Research and Education in Human Services in Kitchener, Ontario, particularly the article by R. Janzen, Trigger Events, Critical Mass, and Social Policy, *Keystones NewsReport: Centre for Research and Education in Human Services*, 17 (2004): pp. 3.–5.
23. For a more detailed analysis of this period of mental health reform, see Nelson, Lord, and Ochocka (2001). Also see Church (1997).
24. Attendant Care Action Coalition, Flying on Our Own Conference, London, Ontario, October 1990.
25. Church (1997).
26. Recently, more than 40 national disability organizations supported the call for the federal government to play a role in funding disability supports; see the Council of Canadians with Disabilities (2005).
27. Prince (2002).
28. The RDSP Resource Centre has been established to serve all Canadians. See <www.rdspresource.ca/>.
29. In the United States, the Green House Project has redesigned and transformed several nursing homes to be more home-like and recently received a $10 million grant from the Robert Wood Johnson Foundation to replicate this model in all 50 states. See more about the Green House Project. <www.thegreenhouseproject.com>.
30. Rice and Prince (2000), p. 24.
31. Rice and Prince (2000).
32. Nelson et al. (2001).
33. PLAN (2002), p. 1.
34. Rice and Prince (2000), p. 100.
35. Panitch (1994).
36. Carniol (1995).
37. Homer-Dixon (2001), p. 395.
38. See Tamarack, An Institute for Community Engagement, for a list of community collaborations and some of the research into this approach to social change: <www.tamarackcommunity.ca>.

Pathways to Inclusion

12

The Future

Hopes for the New Story

...in our mad world where there is so much pain, rivalry, hatred, violence, inequality, and oppression, it is people who are weak, rejected, marginalized, counted as useless, who can become a source of life and of salvation for us as individuals as well as for our world ... it is my hope that each of you may experience the incredible gift of friendship of people who are poor and weak ... for they call us to love, to communion, to compassion, and to community.

Jean Vanier[1]

We have been exploring the values and innovations of New Story ideas with a range of groups. We find that insights from the New Story resonate with people who see its possibilities and promise. As we consider our hopes and dreams for the New Story, the visions of the social innovators who have been breaking new ground are foremost in our minds. The leaders of the innovations that helped create the New Story have called for a new paradigm with such values as citizenship and self-determination. New paradigm approaches, including individualized funding, independent planning and facilitation, network development, and strong self-help organizations have been stressed. Social innovators understand that small community-based initiatives can demonstrate possibilities for change.

Yet, we know that new paradigms do not reach broad cultural acceptance unless there are compelling conditions. What conditions might enable the New Story to become widely accepted in the culture? What possibilities exist for social inclusion to be expanded across all communities and all marginalized groups? These are the challenges that still remain for New Story advocates. Both anticipating and imagining the future are useful exercises for people who want to be part of shaping what happens in their world.

Why We Believe the New Story Will be Embraced

We believe the New Story will become widely practised across the country for several compelling reasons. Each of these reasons has the potential to create conditions for the New Story to not only thrive but to expand exponentially over the next few decades.

The crisis we are now experiencing globally in the environment, economy, and harmony will soon have a spillover effect in all aspects of life. We believe demand for *participatory democracy* will be embraced and will take our world to a different place. Recently, there has been a "culture of fear" that unfortunately some of our political leaders capitalize on to push their narrow, self-interest agendas forward. The culture of fear has also been witnessed in the way we treat our most vulnerable citizens, based on fear of difference and fear of change. Some analysts note that the groundswell of interest in participatory democracy will be a huge factor in reducing this fear. While small pockets of citizens have long embraced participatory democracy, more and more citizens across the globe are expressing a longing for democracy, participation, and meaningful relationships.[2] Therefore, our hope is that the "culture of fear" that has gripped much of the world in the past few years will begin to dissipate in the next decade.

Participation in local environmental projects, neighbour-hood associations, government consultations, and peace groups will become commonplace as participatory democracy grows. This culture of participation along with the basic tenants of the New Story will have greater potential to cross political boundaries of all stripes as governments search for solutions to the "old story." Family groups, support circles, and networks of people with disabilities and networks of senior citizens will become more naturally entrenched in the fabric of the community as more citizens value relationships over commercialism and getting ahead at all cost. As participatory democracy begins to impact communities, we can imagine people learning from vulnerable people about "participation and voice" and using this awareness to kindle collective activities. Our dream is that the loneliness and isolation that many people experience in the Western world will begin to give way to a sense of community and collaboration. What if, in a few years, we could say that the "culture of fear" was gradually giving way to a "culture of compassion"?

This climate for greater participation will also be fuelled by *changing demographics*. During the next two decades, elements of the New Story have the potential to make more sense to people as a larger proportion of society become "old" and acquire disabilities and chronic conditions. Governments, the non-profit sector, and the private sector are becoming more aware of the role demographics play in the marketplace, work-place, and civil society. We anticipate that social movement organizations, especially those representing elderly people and citizens with disabilities, will be even more active in advocating for New Story policies and funding. It is already coming to consciousness that institutionalizing large numbers of seniors in long-term care facilities and nursing homes is no longer acceptable to baby boomers, many of whom turn 65 around 2010. In the next decade, "old story" rhetoric will be no match for aging boomers with their energy, ideas, and resources. In communities across Canada, we can imagine Neighbourhood and Environmental Watch programs being taken over by seniors and their networks. As they become supported to stay in their own homes, elderly citizens will likely set up telephone trees and visitation programs that ensure the safety and security of members. This kind of initiative will build on the continuation and growth of social networks that have proven so beneficial to good health.

All of these conditions create the possibility that organizations, communities, and society will be ripe for social innovation. The movement for the New Story is picking up steam as a result of the numerous promising initiatives by a small number of innovative leaders and organizations. Since 2007, several new communities have embraced New Story ideas and are seeding and supporting change. These initiatives can be thought of as "early adopters." As more and more New Story initiatives happen, we can see reaching a *tipping point* in the next few years. A tipping point marks the time when a new idea takes hold among the majority of the population.[3] This happens when the momentum of change causes a tipping or spillover effect and broader change then occurs quite rapidly. The spillover of these innovations is already quite astonishing as provincial government policies and changes in local organizations begin to reflect the New Story. We hope that by 2015, this movement for change will be embedded in our social consciousness. Just as the old story gripped people's consciousness with its assumptions of segregation and compliance, our dream is that New Story language and ideas will become commonly part of civil society discourse. We look forward to the day when self-determination and community building will no longer be just visions of social innovations.

The New Story is intricately linked with *community engagement*. Most leaders of these innovative initiatives are activists engaged in their local communities and working with other local organizations to ensure that there are adequate infrastructure supports in place to aid self-determination and community. Many leaders are also working with provincial organizations to advocate for transformation of provincial service systems. At the root of this new social movement work, these leaders are citizens working in personal ways to create a good life for themselves or family members being supported in daily life issues.

These citizen-activists are playing major roles in helping the New Story reach the tipping point. Many are outstanding communicators and salespeople for the New Story. Remember Judith Snow, who has inspired countless numbers of people about gifts that we all bring to community. Others are natural connectors who make themselves available to others who are interested in change but need support and inspiration to move ahead. Remember Marilyn Haywood, who inspired others to join support circles with her welcoming invitations. We learn much about the nature of leadership for our communities from these people. They live and breathe community engagement, not just in their enthusiasm and knowledge, but in their modelling of their deep qualities of observing and reflection. It is their experience with vulnerability and marginalization that provides these leaders with their commitment to change.

We believe the New Story principles have the potential to fuel *transformation of large service systems*. Already three provinces (Ontario, Manitoba, and New Brunswick) are following the lead of British Columbia and beginning to designate a percentage of their social service budgets to fund New Story concepts, such as individualized funding and independent facilitation. Like the British Columbia experience, this transformation of service systems usually begins with people with developmental disabilities and their families. We anticipate that the next transformation will be in other disability areas. Already in Ontario, transformation within community mental health includes provincial policies that fund peer-driven initiatives with a strong focus on "recovery." Innovations in the disability area are beginning to spill over into other areas. We think that by 2015, older adults across the country will have comprehensive homecare as a universal service. Furthermore, we expect that most homecare programs across the country will offer individualized funding and independent facilitation as an option. These kinds of transformations will not be easy, and many provincial governments are simply not prepared at this time to make such changes.

Our dream is that governments, service organizations, and communities will gradually come to understand the promise and possibilities of the New Story. Like any paradigm change, such movements take time, as people must first grasp new language and new concepts. We created a figure (page 256) to illustrate the way that both language and concepts are emerging in the New Story and how they contrast with the "old story."[4] As the "old story" moves from segregation to integration toward inclusion, there are many issues that must be addressed. As we read the figure, we will all recognize organizations or initiatives that

Pathways to Inclusion

Toward the New Story

Old Story		New Story
Segregation	**Integration**	**Inclusion**
Institutional-driven supports	Community agency-driven supports	Personal- and community-driven supports
Institutional focus	Continuum of services	Full opportunities and conditions
Medical	Professional	Social/ecological
Patient role	Client role	Citizen role
Lack of voice	Minimal voice	Strong voice and self-determination
Dependence	Independence	Interdependence
Learned helplessness	Conformity	Empowerment
Deficits and limitations	Skill development	Gifts and capacities
Isolation and loneliness	Special programs and community participation	Social networks and relationship building
Planning for programs in facility	Planning for services	Independent planning and facilitation
Block funding to facilities for programs and supports	Block funding to agencies for programs and supports	Portable individualized funding
Token attention to difference	Diversity tolerated	Diversity valued and supported
Professional services	Professional support groups and volunteer services	Autonomous self-help organizations
Minimal rights	Limited rights	Social justice
Disconnected from community	Present in community	Participating and contributing to community

Pathways to Inclusion

fall mostly in one column. However, it is possible that some groups may have characteristics from more than one column, perhaps illustrating the challenge of making transformative change. As we have seen, it is also possible for community support organizations to move toward the New Story and away from agency-driven supports. For most conventional community organizations, this is difficult to do without a major restructuring process. Nevertheless, the possibility of service system and organizational transformation is one of the hopes for the New Story.

At the same time, we expect in the foreseeable future that most New Story initiatives will continue to emerge from the hearts and actions of local individuals and families rather than from planning by traditional organizations or government. The story of Planned Lifetime Advocacy Network (PLAN) and its affiliates across Canada is an inspiring example of what can be accomplished when social innovators understand that new ideas are best seeded in people and communities. The entrepreneurial spirit of PLAN and other initiatives will grow in the years ahead. The reality is that governments alone will be unable to fund all the initiatives that are needed to build the New Story. Public–private partnerships and social ventures will increase as part of the process of social inclusion.

Finally, some astonishing ideas from science bolster the evidence for moving ahead with the New Story. In 2005, the world of science celebrated the 100th anniversary since Albert Einstein published his work on relativity theory. Events all over the world exposed the public to quantum physics for the first time in ways that were actually somewhat understandable. We anticipate that the results from quantum physics will have an impact on all aspects of our society. The mechanistic model of reality that dominated science since Descartes and Newton is already giving way to an understanding of reality that is less deterministic and more relational. Environmentalists have been the first to notice the importance of the quantum principle that everything is interrelated and not separate entities. They see that humans can no longer control and dominate nature but must work in harmony with it. The new science also teaches that "intention" influences both actions and outcomes. People trained in the new science are also learning that observers are no longer objective but, in fact, influence whatever they observe. In the years ahead, we envision that the new science will influence how people and policy makers come to understand the New Story. Self-determination ("I take action and responsibility") and community ("We are inter-connected") will be seen as complementary rather than separate ideas. Intention ("I/We intentionally seek relationships") will be seen as critical for individuals, networks, and policy.

We expect that several long-term qualitative, ecological studies will show that the New Story is by far the most coherent approach to building pathways to social inclusion and very consistent with the principles of quantum physics. It now seems likely that by 2020, all institutions for vulnerable people will close in Canada, thus ending the most incoherent approach to supporting people that was ever invented. The 60-year struggle to close these facilities has been so heart-wrenching that when the last institution closes, there may not even be a celebration.

Embodying the New Story

At the turn of this century, many people with disabilities and others were angry and frustrated, while many were passive and compliant. These states were understandable given the lived experience that many people had endured. Poverty, isolation, and stigma can wear down the soul and create wounds that run deep. Despite such hardships, more and more individuals and families are leaving victimhood behind and embracing the New Story. We see many people in initiatives across Canada who are replacing fear and despair with dignity and hope. An "awareness of possibilities" is a critical factor that empowers people to move toward New Story values. This embodiment of the new paradigm by a growing number of individuals, families, and friends creates the foundation for bottom–up change.

People who embody the New Story carry it inside themselves with quiet but deep conviction. They live its values and principles with confidence. The leaders of the New Story understand what Gandhi meant when he said, "Be the change you want to see in the world." As citizen-activists, many early leaders embodied the New Story in very personal ways. They were comfortable with difference to the point of not noticing difference in others. They have close relationships with a range of people. They noticed the pain and wounds that others experienced and had compassion for their situation. They honoured self-determination and did not make decisions for others. Per-

Pathways to Inclusion

haps most important, these social innovators were collaborators. They knew how to build connections, work across differences, and find common ground with others.

As interest in the New Story grows, we believe that Gandhi's call will be expanded to "Work with others to be the change you want to be." In the next few years, we anticipate that hundreds of peer-driven organizations and family-driven organizations will embody the New Story in their hearts and minds. Partnerships with groups with like-minded values and common language will blossom and give momentum to this new discourse and ways of seeing possibilities. Neighbourhood family groups will expand across the country, enabling people to connect with others in their community who want to talk and work on personal and collective action. In most provinces, we also expect that these groups will form very powerful provincial organizations that advocate for the New Story. Brian Salisbury from Community Living British Columbia reminds us that it was the energy and commitment of families that was the driving force for transformative change in British Columbia.

For many people, self-help groups will be *the* approach that helps them to embody New Story values and provide a vision and hope for what is possible. We also anticipate that more people will understand the role community connections, networks, and relationships play in realizing "who am I and why do I matter?" The well-being of others will become more important than one's own self-interest. People will be more grounded in themselves and, in turn, their collective efforts will reflect their strong sense of "who *we* are." We hope there will be a strong sense of collective wisdom and that it will not be uncommon for members of these groups to be called upon to share their wisdom with city planners and policy makers. Michelle Friesen, a leader with Windsor–Essex Family Network, demonstrates how influential autonomous groups can be when they use stories of members and are willing to build relationships with powerful people in the community.

There are many challenges facing those who are trying to embody and expand the New Story. To date, many people who are isolated, lonely, or without family connections have not been reached by the New Story. Despite good intentions in this area, there is much to learn about how best to do this in ways that maximize self-determination and community. The hold of the old story remains strong and many citizens continue to seek its promises. It is difficult to embody the New Story when it is not supported by organizations or government policies. Some individuals or families remain convinced that concepts like waiting lists, "the professional knows best," or "a placement" are still appropriate. Fortunately, more people now know that these concepts limit possibilities and give control to traditional service systems. As people begin to understand and embody the New Story, they recognize there is much they can do for themselves and with others.

Sustainability of New Story Ideas

Leaders of New Story initiatives are clearly worried about the sustainability of ideas and concepts. Sustainability can be thought of as the extent to which innovative organizations can maintain their values and directions and mobilize resources over time in order to be able to respond effectively to local needs and issues.[5] The concerns of these leaders are well founded. It is well known that social innovations can lose their "edge" and "newness" over time.[6] This has already happened with some of the initiatives, although a surprising number of them have become sustainable. The New Story organizations that were unsustainable actually become "cautionary tales" for other groups and organizations that are trying to learn ways of becoming more sustaining.

The story that serves as a cautionary tale reflects the danger in thinking that bigger is better. One of our favourite organizations had great success in the early years and became known as one of the first New Story organizations. Eventually, other groups began to ask it to "take on" other activities. Several new initiatives were started as part of the organization, including outreach, respite, and a medical clinic. The result was a rapid increase in the number of people being supported and the range of programs. It slowly became apparent that the organization was losing its original vision and values. The organization became very large and incoherent in its approach to supporting people. The appropriate scope of the organization was lost by mixing models and it has now clearly lost its ability to remain innovative.

An important dimension of New Story sustainability relates to new approaches to funding supports for vulnerable citizens.

Pathways to Inclusion

In the old story, non-profit organizations receive funding almost entirely from government for specific programs and services. In the last decade, social finance has emerged as a powerful approach that complements the New Story. Social finance assumes that we can mobilize private capital for the public good. These new approaches recognize that government funding alone will not be able to sustain social innovation and the New Story. This insight makes sense, given the demands on governments for health care in our aging society. Social finance approaches include partnerships between the public and private sectors, the development of social purpose businesses, and enterprising non-profits. The Canadian Task Force on Social Finance has recently completed an important report with seven recommendations that should advance the social finance movement in Canada.[7] PLAN in British Columbia is a New Story initiative that leverages private funds through partnerships and social entrepreneurship.

New Story organizations that are sustaining have certain characteristics. First, they have *leaders* who understand the importance of New Story values and principles. In fact, "working from principles" is common, and it is remarkable to see the way people have been able to adhere to the principles over time. Strategic thinking and shared leadership can also be seen at all levels of New Story organizations. The principle of collaboration is central to the day-to-day work. Second, sustaining organizations have a wide array of *genuine partnerships*. While partnerships in the old story usually mean agency-to-agency collaborations, partnerships in the New Story involve new community partners. We can anticipate in the near future it will no longer be unusual for a private sector company to partner with a New Story organization around a social inclusion issue such as employment. Third, some of these partnerships lead to funding opportunities, with the result that some of the sustaining organizations now have *multiple sources of funding*. Fourth, a *culture of openness* exists. We believe that in the future this concept will be one of the most critical elements for sustainability. Some New Story organizations will be open to spinning off their planning departments to a more independent planning and facilitation structure. New Story organizations must also be open to the increasing diversity of our society in terms of gender, race, ethnicity, sexual preference, age, and disability. In the future, we anticipate that a growing understanding of the importance of equity will lead to the development

Pathways to Inclusion

and implementation of policies and approaches that are fully inclusive of increased diversity.

Although the sustainability of New Story organizations is important as one indicator of success, some leaders are now realizing that social innovation is less about organizations and projects, and more about how people intentionally build relationships and community. As government policies begin to be put in place for individualized funding and independent facilitation, in the near future it will be commonplace to see persons and their families creating community alternatives *without* assistance of service organizations. The sustainability of these situations will be quite high if people build strong networks and relationships as safeguards. One lesson from our initiatives is that small groups of individuals and families must come together to support each other in these new approaches. Local infrastructure supports will also need to be widely available to assist individuals and families with things like planning, hiring personal assistants, developing networks, and managing individualized funds. The Windsor example of human resource development will expand.

We know this process of change will not be easy. The social innovations that are sustaining involve incredible hard work. Small groups of dedicated citizens spend countless hours ensuring that their vision and goals are constantly being reviewed and renewed. We learn, especially from our small projects, that the journey to sustainability involves a path of the heart. Janet Klees, co-ordinator of the very successful Deohaeko Support Network acknowledges, "In this way, we hold close in our hearts — and share with each other daily — many small stories, images, and moments that remind us that even if each of these were the only outcome of this journey, it would have been worth it — for the person, for ourselves, and for our community."[8]

Beyond Vulnerability

The early pioneers and the New Story initiatives taught us that vulnerability is socially constructed. Although this idea is still not well understood, we expect that new applied research and participatory evaluation in this area will enable policy makers to understand that vulnerability is created by social conditions. As this concept becomes more deeply ingrained in our thinking, the exciting work in the future will be to move beyond vulnerability. But we need to ask, what will make a difference in terms of moving beyond vulnerability as a condition?

The first change that is needed in society is that people will need *to learn how to listen deeply.* To listen deeply means being fully present to the words and expressions of another person. As more and more facilitators are trained to assist people to work toward their dreams, the idea of deep listening will take hold. Listening is actually very simple, but it is extremely difficult to do in a society that likes to advise and direct. Without deep listening, professionals and others tend to focus on people's limitations, have low expectations, and ignore dreams and gifts. Fortunately, we now have very sophisticated technology to aid people with communication impairments in expressing their thoughts and feelings. Combined with deep listening, more and more people will be able to discover that they have hopes and dreams and be willing to share their dreams. This process also makes it possible to learn about the person's gifts and limitations. Deep listening allows us to see people's weaknesses, but with a new lens. It is slowly becoming understood that everyone with impairments or chronic conditions can contribute to their community. No one should be devalued because part of them is "different." Insights that grow from deep listening contribute significantly to moving beyond vulnerability. In the future, it is our dream that any so-called limitations will be downplayed, outright ignored, or simply not noticed because they are *no longer limitations.*

Another important part of "beyond vulnerability" relates to internal work that is being done by people who require personal support. Compassion for oneself is not easy in a society that focuses on differences as limitations. In recent years, many people have increased their awareness of their own strengths and capacities. Combined with effective facilitation support, many more people are having an opportunity to become empowered. At the same time, there is more recognition that "constructing vulnerability" starts early in life. People are learning that when they move away from judging their circumstances harshly they are taking a huge step forward in their personal change process. Often we see this process of embodiment as an acceptance of disability, impairment, or aging. "Despite my body's limitations, that's just the way it is," our friend John Nevard often says.

Pathways to Inclusion

Now, more than ever, people are facing disability, discomfort, and pain with wisdom and equanimity. Many of us now understand that how we relate to people with disabilities and chronic conditions is also a reflection of our view of ourselves. If we are unaware or uncomfortable with ourselves, we will project that onto others. People moving to new social roles, from clients to citizens, make a significant contribution to this shift "beyond vulnerability." As these possibilities for liberation increase, more and more people will *co-exist* with their vulnerabilities rather than being a prisoner of them. As Joan Chittister says, "Vulnerability is the call to self-acceptance. It is the great liberating movement on the human journey."[9]

"Moving beyond vulnerability" also means *building relationships and community*. Social support is now understood by researchers as a major determinant of health. Although we believe that it may take another decade for this insight to become more widely accepted, when it does, we think there will be a dramatic shift in the way supports are provided to people. Relationship building will become the first priority. The number of people with intentionally built networks of one kind or another will increase significantly. This focus on relationships will enhance people's feeling of acceptance and contentment. As one elderly person recently noted, "When I have relationships and community, I feel accepted and my differences and limitations matter less. As long as my community understands my strengths and needs, I can feel safe and secure."

In this regard, many of us are learning that the most powerful way to embody the New Story and to move beyond vulnerabilities is to spend time in community with a person who has been labelled, rejected, or wounded. In this sense "moving beyond vulnerability" means being connected with someone who is "different" and discovering that you actually belong together. Jean Vanier calls each of us to experience friendship with another person who is vulnerable. This contributes to community inclusion and helps each of us heal our wounds of isolation.

Community Means Inclusion for All

Those connected with New Story initiatives work very hard to make social inclusion happen for people with various vulnerabilities. Inclusion within these initiatives is often like a project in which various strategies are used to expand citizenship possibilities. Some initiatives strengthen citizen participation by building relationships and support circles, while others connect people with community associations of common interest. In some ways, these inclusion approaches are ground-breaking because they begin the process of helping other citizens see "beyond vulnerability" by emphasizing citizenship and civic participation. *Community*, in many of these projects, has come to mean "inclusion for all."

Over time social inclusion needs to move from a project focus to being systemic and cultural. This shift to a broader inclusion agenda would be accelerated by increased inclusion in schools and education, national legislation mandating universal design and accessibility, equity in the workplace, and broader public acceptance of inclusion for all. As our aging society becomes more diverse, we also hope that more thoughtful policies on social cohesion and social inclusion will be developed. We shall briefly explore what some communities are doing that could be instrumental in enabling social inclusion to move to new levels of understanding and policy change in the future.

Environmental issues have made it imperative that cities and communities pay attention to issues of sustainability. We believe it will be widely understood within the next decade that when communities are sustainable they contribute to inclusion of all its citizens. The city of Calgary, Alberta, has already begun the journey of looking at sustainability and its relationship to inclusion. In 2005, Calgary and its citizens initiated ImagineCalgary.[10] During the first year of ImagineCalgary, more than 18,000 people submitted ideas for what Calgary should be like in 100 years. This was an amazing example of citizen participation. The 100-year vision that people created is all about *connections*: connection to place and the land, connection to community, and connection to each other. Building a sustainable future is also a key part of the Calgary vision, with notions of public transportation being central. The citizens of Calgary see inclusion as fundamental to the future of their city. "Meaningful participation from everyone" is a main tenant of the vision.

Once the vision and goals for 100 years were developed, community members formed working groups to develop 30-year targets. Many of these targets were inclusion oriented, such as, "By 2036, 95% of Calgarians of every age and ability report

Pathways to Inclusion

that they value and have mutually supportive relationships in several settings, such as at home, school, work and in the community." The working groups also developed shorter-term targets, such as, "By 2010, 80% of citizens experience a high sense of community in their neighbourhoods and affinity-related communities." Calgary can be thought of as a learning community because the energy of ImagineCalgary has been a catalyst for citizen participation. Extensive work on the vision continues with a wide range of involvement from volunteers and city officials.

By 2010, our hope is that other Canadian cities will have embarked on an Imagine process. It is possible that communities will become fully accessible and that "inclusion for all" will be part of the fabric of most towns and cities. Accessibility will be prevalent in all public and private buildings and new homes will be built to universal design standards. Rapid transit systems in most communities would be fully accessible; and combined with flexible, accessible taxis, transportation within urban environments will be much more effective.

The province of British Columbia is already a leader in this movement toward accessibility and inclusion. In preparation for the 2010 Winter Olympic Games, Vancouver City Council declared that citizens with disabilities should be present and participating in all aspects of the community, so that by 2010, "the world [would] appreciate British Columbia as a jurisdiction where the contributions of all citizens are enabled and welcomed."[11] One project of the British Columbia initiative is called "Measuring Up: Communities of Inclusion and Accessibility," which is designed to stimulate communities to evaluate how inclusive and accessible their communities are. Utilizing extensive community engagement, "Measuring Up" so far is highly successful. As it spreads across Canada, we expect it will garner energy and enthusiasm for inclusion as communities vie to make the gold standard. The success of the 2010 Winter Olympic and Paralympic Games showcased an accessible Vancouver.

Citizen participation is likely to increase in the future. This bottom–up change will be especially important in urban areas where citizens are likely to organize for more local development after more than 20 years of globalization. While globalization has produced some benefits, it is becoming increasingly understood by many leading thinkers that globalization has been a dismal failure for local communities. Because of this reality, there will be a new focus on people-centered local development. Provincial and municipal governments will develop strategies to promote local co-operatives and community-owned businesses. These economic trends might well coincide with the social inclusion trends to produce possibilities for people who often have a difficult time finding meaningful employment. Co-housing projects, where people of all ages choose to live together, will also likely expand throughout the country and create more opportunities for inter-generational community. The age-old, now well-oiled phrase, "*It takes a village*," will be more than a metaphor for this change process.[12]

New Story initiatives must continue to embrace "community as a first resort." This principle reminds us of the abundance of communities and the possibilities that flow from strong neighbourhoods and families. Remember the hospitality of so many initiatives that came to understand how simple connections with neighbours and friends strengthened networks and "sense of community."

Collaboration: Key Strategy for Change

Governments and non-profit organizations typically consult with people to gain insights about possible future directions. With consultation, however, decision making remains in the hands of these institutions. Such consultations are usually only within one sector of the community, such as one ministry of government. Consultation has been a strategy of the old story when governments or leaders want to initiate change. New Story initiatives build their innovations with *principles of collaboration*, not just consultation. Collaboration involves people working together for change in ways that enable each person or each stakeholder group to contribute their gifts and ideas in an ongoing manner. In the future, collaboration among stakeholders from a wide breadth of the community will become more common. There are three insights from the initiatives about how collaboration can be very effective in building capacity for social innovation.

First, at the level of individual citizens, the initiatives teach us that collaboration with family, friends, neighbours, and other potential network members is a central contribution to quality of life. In the future, more citizens will learn to invite others to

Pathways to Inclusion

collaborate around enhancing the lives of individuals. Remember the power of family groups in Durham Region of Ontario, where small groups of families support each other, build support networks with their sons or daughters, and collaborate for social inclusion with others in the community. This kind of collaboration builds personal, family, and community capacity.

Second, at the level of organizations, the initiatives teach us that collaboration is central to organizational renewal and building of the new paradigm. Remember how Waterloo Regional Homes for Mental Health fully involved users, family members, staff, and community members to change from a traditional to a forward-thinking enterprise. In the future, more organizations will learn to use the principle of collaboration for internal change and external partnerships. Today, Waterloo Regional Homes has extended its collaborative work to include several other mental health organizations and self-help groups. Together, these groups are building training capacity for "recovery" and creating change strategies in their region. Leaders are learning that the New Story or new paradigm can be an effective lever for organizational change.

Third, at the level of system change and governments, initiatives teach us that collaboration is central to building policy and programs that impact on people's lives. As collaboration takes hold in the future, we envision more places in Canada where provincial policy will be aligned and coherent with local New Story initiatives. Remember the Ontario Direct Funding Project or the transformed system in British Columbia. Both initiatives happened because governments were willing to collaborate with citizens and professionals to design an innovation based on sound principles. We know that when governments do it alone and design new initiatives with only consultation, they seldom get it right. When a range of stakeholders sit together in a well-facilitated process, wise decisions are often the outcome.[13]

Conclusion: A Future of Possibilities

Pathways to Inclusion has been a story about struggle for change and dignity. The experiences of New Story leaders and participants have provided us with successful outcomes and insights about what makes a difference for people who are the most vulnerable in our communities. As we review the vision and values of these New Story initiatives, they beckon us to bring practical wisdom to our personal, family, and community lives. We will need practical wisdom to assure we are "walking the talk" and being in solidarity with *all* people. This wisdom will help us decide how to build relationships and community with our children, our friends, and our neighbours. This wisdom will help us decide which local or provincial coalitions might make a difference and where we should put our energy. In other words, wisdom helps to sort out symptoms from deeper root causes. It is time to invest much more in ways that address root causes or what some people call "upstream" strategies.[14] Provincial coalitions that collaborate with government in designing policy and programs to support the New Story will be central in the future.

Compassion continues to be needed in order to be able to open our hearts to ourselves and others. We need compassion and patience as we work with others for change. Compassion is a foundation for imagining better and eliminating the line that often exists between "us" and "them." Compassion helps us understand rights and responsibilities. We also need to continue finding ways to inspire community leaders and fellow citizens to extend their compassion in their words and deeds. When inspired, people can change their behaviour and collective action toward their fellow human beings. Sometimes this inspiration will challenge the "status quo" that is simply not working for many people. To inspire our compassion we need singing and dancing that speak to our souls and our common good. In a way, the New Story is a vision to work toward, a place of connection and celebration that weaves community with diversity in healthy, inclusive ways.

In the end, inclusion is about social justice. Every New Story initiative has social justice as a core belief. We have heard numerous stories of the day-to-day commitments toward social justice: leaders seeking funding for an excluded group; facilitators weaving together a social network for an isolated person; peers being there for each other at all times of night and day; and advocates fighting for policy that will enhance social inclusion and citizenship. The lessons of New Story initiatives are needed to contribute to the mosaic of understandings that we now have about inclusion. Although the future may be uncertain, our optimism resides in the fact that more and more of us will want to enhance the common good and social justice.

Notes

1. Vanier (1992), pp. 9–10.
2. Participatory democracy has received much attention from scholars and more recently from activists. For its link to empowerment, see Bachrach and Botwinick (1992). For its link to strategies for citizenship building, see Schugurensky (1993).
3. For a full examination of tipping point, see Gladwell (2000).
4. This table comes from our own experience and with appreciation to previous work upon which this builds; see Lord, Snow, and Dingwall (2005), p. 11. Also see Nelson, Lord, and Ochocka (2001).
5. For a detailed analysis of sustainability, see Centre for Research and Education in Human Services (2004).
6. For a classic work on dissemination of new ideas, see Rogers (2003).
7. The Canadian Task Force on Social Finance has outlined several important recommendations, including encouraging Canada's foundations to play a more active role in mission-related investments, and encouraging federal and provincial governments to establish an Impact Investment Fund. The Report from the Canadian Task Force on Social Finance, *Mobilizing Private Capital for Public Good*, is available on-line at <http://socialfinance.ca/taskforce/report>.
8. Klees (2005), p. 351. Deohaeko Support Network consists of a small number of families who have built inclusive lives with their sons and daughters; Janet Klees serves as a co-ordinator of Deohaeko and also has written several beautiful books on its development and progress; see Klees (1996).
9. Chittister (2003), p. 65.
10. For information about Calgary, Alberta, Canada's initiative see their website, ImagineCalgary <www.imaginecalgary.ca>.
11. Orloff (2005), pp. 32–33.
12. Clinton (1996).
13. In recent years, more extensive work has been done on strategies called community collaboration, other times called multi-sectoral initiatives. See Caledon Institute (2005). Also see review of community collaboration strategies conducted by Tamarack website, <www.tamarackcommunity.ca>.
14. Upstream policies address issues before they become serious; health promotion has been a significant area that has worked on upstream strategies. Instead of waiting, for example, for people to die from smoking, upstream strategies would provide supports and policy to discourage people from smoking in the first place, see Rootman (2001).

Pathways to Inclusion

Appendix:
New Story
Initiatives

Contact Information and Authors' Related Publications

Alzheimer Society of Hamilton Halton
Address: Suite 206, 1685 Main Street West
             Hamilton, ON L8S 1G5
Tel: (905) 529-7030; 1-888-343-1017
Fax: (905) 529-3787
Website: www.alzhn.ca/Hamilton_Halton/565/0

**Brockville & District Association for
Community Involvement**
Address: 2495 Parkdale Ave. West, Unit # 4
             Brockville, ON K6V 3H2
Tel: (613) 345-4092
Fax: (613) 345-7469
E-mail: bdaci@ripnet.com

**Canadian Association of Independent Living Centres,
now called Independent Living Canada**
(For details on specific Centres across Canada,
see CAILC website)
Address: 214 Montreal Road, Suite 402,
             Ottawa, ON K1L 8L8
Tel: (613) 563-2581
Fax: (613) 563-3861
TTY/TDD: (613) 563-4215
E-mail: info@cailc.ca
Website: www.cailc.ca
Publications: • P. Hutchison, A. Pedlar, J. Lord, P. Dunn,
              M. McGeown, A. Taylor, and C. Vandetelli,
              Impact of Independent Living Resource Centres
              in Canada, *Canadian Journal of Rehabilitation*,
              10, 2 (1997): pp. 99–112.

- P. Hutchison, A. Pedlar, P. Dunn, J. Lord, and S. Arai, Canadian Independent Living Centres: Impact on the Community, *International Journal of Rehabilitation Research*, 23, 2 (2000): pp. 61–74.
- P. Hutchison, S. Arai, A. Pedlar, J. Lord, and C. Whyte, Leadership in the Canadian Consumer Disability Movement, *International Journal of Disability, Community and Rehabilitation*, 6, 1 (2007) <www.ijdcr.ca> (online journal).
- P. Hutchison, S. Arai, A. Pedlar, J. Lord, and F. Yuen, Role of Canadian User-led Disability Organisations in the Non-Profit Sector, *Disability and Society*, 22, 7 (2007): pp. 701–716.
- S. Arai, P. Hutchison, A. Pedlar, J. Lord, & V. Sheppard. Shared Values, Building Networks and Trust among Canadian Consumer Driven Disability Organizations, *Disability Studies Quarterly*, 28, 1 (2008) <www.DSQ-SDS.org>.

Canadian Mental Health Association —
Framework for Support
Address: Canadian Mental Health Association (National)
8 King Street East, Suite 810
Toronto, ON M5C 1B5
Tel: (416) 484-7750
Fax: (416) 484-4617
E-mail: info@cmha.ca
Website: www.cmha.ca
Publications:
- P. Hutchison, J. Lord, H. Savage, and A. Schnarr, Listening. In J. Trainor, E. Pomeroy, and B. Pape (Eds.), *Building A Framework for Support: A Community Development Approach to Mental Health Policy* (Toronto, ON: Canadian Mental Health Association, 1999), pp. 61–84.
- P. Hutchison, J. Lord, and L. Osborne-Way, Participating. In J. Trainor, E. Pomeroy, and B. Pape (Eds.) *Building A Framework for Support: A Community Development Approach to Mental Health Policy* (Toronto, ON: Canadian Mental Health Association, 1999): pp. 87–102 (edited and abridged edition of 1985 Research Based Report).

Pathways to Inclusion

Canadian Mental Health Association —
Waterloo Region Branch

Address:	5420 Highway 6, RR#5
	Guelph, ON N1H 6J2
Tel:	(519) 766-4450
Fax:	(519) 766-9211
E-mail:	info@cmha.ca
Website:	www.cmhawrb.on.ca
Publication:	• G. Nelson, J. Lord, and J. Ochocka, *Shifting the Paradigm in Community Mental Health: Towards Empowerment and Community* (Toronto: University of Toronto Press, 2001).

Community Living British Columbia

Address:	7th Floor — Airport Square
	1200 West 73rd Avenue
	Vancouver, BC V6P 6G5
Tel:	604-664-0101
Fax:	604-664-0765
E-mail:	info@communitylivingbc.ca
Website:	www.communitylivingbc.ca/
Publication:	• P. Hutchison, J. Lord, & B. Salisbury, North American Approaches to Individualized Planning and Direct Funding. In J. Leece & J. Bornat (Eds.), *Developments in Direct Payments* (Bristol, UK: The Policy Press, 2006).

Community Living St. Marys

Address:	300 Elgin Street East, Box 1618
	St Marys, ON N4X 1B9
Tel:	(519) 284-1424
Fax:	(519) 284-3120
E-mail:	info@communitylivingstmarys.ca
Website:	www.communitylivingstmarys.ca
Publication:	• J. Lord, *Moving toward Citizenship: A Study of Individualized Funding in Ontario* (Toronto, ON: Individualized Funding Coalition for Ontario, 2006).
	• J. Lord and P. Hutchison, Individualized Funding in Ontario: Report of a Provincial Study, *Journal on Developmental Disabilities*, 14, 2 (2008): pp. 44–53.

Deohaeko Support Network

Address: Rougemount Co-operative Homes
            400 Kingston Road
            Pickering, ON, L1V 6S1
Tel: (905) 509-5654
E-mail: janet@legacies.ca
Website: www.legacies.ca

Durham Family Network

Address: 865 Westney Road South
            Ajax, ON L1S 3M4
Tel: (905) 436-2500
Fax: (905) 436-2500
E-mail: hdionne@dafrs.com
Publication: • J. Lord and P. Hutchison, Individualized Funding
             in Ontario: Report of a Provincial Study, *Journal
             on Developmental Disabilities*, 14, 2 (2008):
             pp. 44–53.

Durham Association for Family Respite

Address: 865 Westney Road South
            Ajax, ON L1S 3M4
Tel: (905) 436-2500
Fax: (905) 436-2500
E-mail: insol@dafrs.com
Publication: • J. Lord, *Moving toward Citizenship: A Study of
             Individualized Funding in Ontario* (Toronto, ON:
             Individualized Funding Coalition for Ontario,
             2006).

Families for a Secure Future

Address: 278 Kerrybrook Drive
            Richmond Hill, ON L4C 3R1
Phone: (905) 770-2819
Fax: (905) 770-2726
E-mail: jlmcgill@rogers.com
Website: www.familiesforasecurefuture.com

Foundations

Address: c/o Developmental Services Access Centre
            1120 Victoria St. N., Suite #205
            Kitchener, ON N2B 3T2
Tel: (519) 741-1121
E-mail: w.mattson@on.aibn.com

In the Company of Friends
Address: 220-500 Portage Ave.
             Winnipeg, MB R3C 3X1
Tel: (204) 772-3557; (866) 516-5445
E-mail: life2@mts.net
Website: www.icof-life.ca

Modeling Innovation and Community Change
Website: www.modelingcommunitychange.com

NABORS (Neighbors Allied for Better Opportunities in Residential Support)
Address: 2 Carlton Street, #1001
             Toronto, ON M5B 1J3
Tel: (416) 351-0095
Fax: (416) 351-0107
E-mail: nabors@interlog.com
Publication: • J. Lord, *The NABORS Experience: Lessons in Community Building* (Toronto, ON: Green Dragon Press, 1998).

New Frontiers Support Services
Address: 620 Colborne Street
             London, ON N6B 3R9
Tel: (519) 439-8000
Fax: (519) 439-8759
E-mail: newfrontiers@sympatico.ca

New Story Group of Waterloo Region
Tel: (519) 741-0475
Website: Under construction

Ontario Direct Funding Project
Centre for Independent Living in Toronto
Address: 205 Richmond Street West
             Toronto, ON M5V 1V3
Tel: (416) 599-2458
Fax: (416) 599-3555
E-mail: cilt@cilt.ca
Website: www.cilt.ca

Publication: • J. Lord, B. Zupko, and P. Hutchison, *More Choice and Control for People With Disabilities: Review of Individualized Funding* (Toronto, ON: Ontario Federation for Cerebral Palsy, 2000). www.ofcp.on.ca/choices.html

Ontario Peer Development Initiative
Address: 1881 Yonge Street, Suite 614
             Toronto, ON M4S 3C4
Tel: (416) 484-8785
Fax: (416) 484-9669
Toll Free: (866) 681-6661
E-mail: opdi@opdi.org
Website: www.opdi.org
Publication: • Centre for Community-Based Research, *Summary Bulletin: A Longitudinal Study of Consumer/Survivor Initiatives in Community Mental Health in Ontario: Individual and System Level Impacts* (Kitchener, ON: Author, 2004).

Opening New Doors
Address: 67 King St. East, 2nd Floor
             Kitchener, ON N2G 2K4
Tel: (519) 570-4595
Fax: (519) 766-9211
E-mail: elliota@self-help.ca

Options (Originally called Quality of Life Project)
Address: Family Service Association for Toronto
             700 Lawrence Ave, Suite 498
             Toronto, ON M6A 3B4
Tel: (416) 971-6326
Fax: (416) 971-5650
E-mail: anavi@fsatoronto.com
Publications: • J. Lord, B. Zupko, and P. Hutchison, *More choice and control for people with disabilities: Review of Individualized Funding* (Toronto, ON Federation for Cerebral Palsy, 2000) www.ofcp.on.ca/choices.html

• J. Lord and P. Hutchison, Individualised Support and Funding: Building Blocks for Capacity Building and Inclusion, *Disability and Society*, 18, 1 (2003): pp. 71–86.

- J. Lord, *Moving toward Citizenship: A Study of Individualized Funding in Ontario* (Toronto: Individualized Funding Coalition for Ontario, 2006).
- J. Lord and P. Hutchison, Individualized Funding in Ontario: Report of a Provincial Study, *Journal on Developmental Disabilities*, 14, 2 (2008): pp. 44–53.

Peer Support Network of BCPA

Address: Canadian Paraplegic Association of British Columbia
             780 SW Marine Drive
             Vancouver, BC V6P 5Y7
Tel: (604) 324-3611
Fax: (604) 326-1229
E-mail: vancouver@bcpara.org
Website: www.bcpara.org/

People First of Ontario

Address: c/o 300 Elgin Street East, Box 1618
             St Marys, ON N4X 1B9
Tel: (519) 560-3599
Fax: (519) 284-3120
E-mail: rruston@cogeco.ca
Website: www.peoplefirstontario.com

Personal Communities Project
(Personal Communities was a vibrant organization in Alberta between 1986 and 2000)

Publication: • J. Lord, *Evaluation of Personal Communities Project* (Kitchener: Centre for Research and Education in Human Services, 1990).

PLAN — Planned Lifetime Advocacy Network

Address: Suite 260 — 3665 Kingsway
             Vancouver BC V5R 5W2
Tel: (604) 439-9566
Fax: (604) 439-7001
E-mail: inquiries@plan.ca
Website: www.plan.ca

Project Friendship Society
Address: 3491 Clearwood Crescent
             Prince George, BC V2K 4R1
Tel: (250) 962-2782
Fax: (250) 962-9730
E-mail: friend@northernbc.com
Website: www.projectfriendship.com

South-East Grey Support Services
Address: Box 12, 24 Toronto Rd,
             Flesherton ON N0C 1E0
Tel: (519) 924-3339
Fax: (519) 924-3575
E-mail: archied@bmts.com

Spark of Brilliance
Address: Orchard Park
             5420 Hwy 6 N, RR 5
             Guelph, ON N1H 6J2
Tel: 519-766-4450, Extension: 237
Fax: 519-836-9010
E-mail: judith.rosenberg@sympatico.ca
Website: www.sparkofbrilliance.org

Support Clusters Network of Ontario
(The Support Clusters Project became the Support
Clusters Network in 1994)
Address: 5420 Highway 6, RR#5
             Guelph, ON N1H 6J2
Tel: (519) 766-4450
Fax: (519) 766-9211
E-mail: info@cmha.ca
Publications: • Centre for Community-Based Research, Support
             Clusters Project: Evaluation Report of a
             Research Demonstration Project (Kitchener:
             Author, 1993).

             • J. Ochocka and J. Lord, Support Clusters: A
             Network Approach for People with Complex
             Needs, *Journal of Leisurability*, 25, 4 (1998)
             pp. 14–22.

Pathways to Inclusion

Vela Microboard Association

Address:	100 — 17564 — 56A Ave.
	Surrey, BC V3C 1G3
Tel:	(604) 575-2588
Fax:	(604) 575-2589
E-mail:	info@microboard.org
Website:	www.microboard.org/
Publication:	• A. Pedlar, L. Haworth, P. Hutchison, A. Taylor, and P. Dunn, *A Textured Life: Empowerment and Adults with Developmental Disabilities* (Waterloo, ON: Wilfrid Laurier University Press, 1999).

Waterloo Regional Homes for Mental Health

Address:	112-501 Krug Street
	Kitchener, ON N2B 1L3
Tel:	(519) 742-3191
Fax:	(519) 742-5232
E-mail:	wczarny@waterlooregionalhomes.com
Website:	www.waterlooregionalhomes.com
Publications:	• J. Lord, J. Ochocka, W. Czarny, & H. MacGillivery, Analysis of Change Within a Mental Health Organization: A Participatory Process, *Psychiatric Rehabilitation Journal*, 21, 1 (1998): pp. 327–339.
	• G. Nelson, J. Lord, and J. Ochocka, *Shifting the Paradigm in Community Mental Health: Towards Empowerment and Community* (Toronto, ON: University of Toronto Press, 2001).

Waterloo Region Self-Help

Address:	67 King St. East, 2nd Floor
	Kitchener, ON N2G 2K4
Tel:	(519) 570-4595
Fax:	(519) 766-9211
E-mail:	general@wrsh.ca
Website:	www.self-help-alliance.ca
Publication:	• G. Nelson, J. Lord, and J. Ochocka, *Shifting the Paradigm in Community Mental Health: Towards Empowerment and Community* (Toronto, ON: University of Toronto Press, 2001).

Welcome Home Initiative
(The Welcome Home Initiative was a five-year project
in Waterloo Region, 2000–2005)
Publication: • M. Steinman, P. Hutchison, and A. Kroeger,
Welcome Home Training Manual (Kitchener, ON:
Welcome Home Initiative, 2001).

Windsor–Essex Family Network
Address: 7025 Enterprise Way
              Windsor, ON N8T 3N6
Tel: (519) 974-1008
Fax: (519) 974-4157
E-mail: info@windsoressexfamnet.ca
Website: www.windsoressexfamnet.ca

Windsor–Essex Brokerage for Personal Supports
Address: 3357 Walker Road, Unit #2
              Windsor, ON N8W 5J7
Tel: (519) 966-8094
Fax: (519) 966-8390
Email: webps@mnsi.net
Website: www.webps.ca
Publication: • J. Lord, B. Zupko, and P. Hutchison, *More
              Choice and Control for People With Disabilities:
              Review of Individualized Funding* (Toronto, ON:
              Ontario Federation for Cerebral Palsy, 2000).
              www.ofcp.on.ca/choices.html

              • J. Lord, *Moving toward Citizenship: A Study of
              Individualized Funding in Ontario* (Toronto:
              Individualized Funding Coalition for Ontario,
              2006).

              • J. Lord and P. Hutchison, Individualized Funding
              in Ontario: Report of a Provincial Study, *Journal
              on Developmental Disabilities*, 14, 2 (2008):
              pp. 44–53.

York Region Alternative Community Living Program
Address: Long Term Care and Seniors Services
              York Region
              17250 Yonge Street
              Newmarket, ON L3Y 6Z1
Tel: (905) 895-1231

E-mail: Health.Webmaster@york.ca
Website: www.york.ca/Services/
Publication: • Centre for Research and Education in Human
                Services, Evaluation of Alternative Community
                Living Program (York Region: Authors), 1992
                and 1994.

Other Resources and Links

Caledon Institute of Social Policy
The is a non-profit, independent group that offers a critical voice
on social policy in Canada: www.caledoninst.org

Centre for Community-Based Research
This is the Centre started by the authors. It continues to do
research on innovation and change in several areas of human
services: www.communitybasedresearch.ca/

Facilitation Leadership Group
This group provides training and coaching on facilitation;
especially helpful for people and communities who are trying to
build the New Story: www.facilitationleadership.com

Inclusion Press
This website has lots of information about inclusion books, films,
workshops, newsletters, and other resources: www.inclusion.com

**Individualized Funding Coalition for Ontario and
Modeling Innovation and Community Change**
This provincial lobby group works toward making individualized
funding for people with disabilities a reality in Ontario; lots of
resources and research, especially Modeling Innovation and
Community Change: www.individualizedfunding.ca

John Lord — Building a New Story
The website of one of the authors contains many of his recent
publications related to the New Story: www.johnlord.net

Laidlaw Foundation
This group fosters inclusion of young persons as full citizens in
civic life and community leadership: www.laidlawfdn.org

Ontario Adult Autism Research and Support Network
This is a website full of innovative ideas based on New Story
concepts: www.ont-autism.uoguelph.ca

Philia: A Dialogue on Caring Citizenship
This website shares ideas and insights on ways that people are
nurturing citizenship and community participation. It is
sponsored by PLAN: philia.plan.ca/

Tamarack: An Institute for Community Engagement
Tamarack is committed to building stronger communities
through pioneering work and a comprehensive approach to innovation and change: www.tamarackcommunity.ca

Bibliography

Albom, M. 1997. *Tuesdays with Morrie: An Old Man, a Young Man, and Life's Greatest Lesson*. New York, NY: Doubleday.

Anderson, B. n.d. *We Come Bearing Gifts*. Vashon, WA: Community Activators.

Arai, S., P. Hutchison, A. Pedlar, J. Lord, and V. Sheppard. 2008. Shared Values, Networks and Trust among Canadian Consumer Driven Disability Organizations, *Disabilities Studies Quarterly*, 28, 1, <www.DSQ-SDS/org> (online journal).

Arno, P., C. Levine, and M. Memmott. 1999. The Economic Value of Informal Caregiving, *Health Affairs*, 18, 2: pp. 182–188.

Arntz, W., B. Chasse, and M. Vincente. 2005. *What the Bleep Do We Know: Discovering the Endless Possibilities for Altering your Everyday Reality*. Deerfield Beach, FL: Health Communication Inc.

Ashenberg, K. 2002. *The Mourner's Dance: What We Do When People Die*. Toronto, ON: Macfarlane, Walter & Ross.

Attendant Care Action Coalition. 1990. Flying on Our Own Conference. London, Ontario, October.

Avison, W. 1998. The Health Consequences of Unemployment. In *Determinants of Health: Adults and Seniors*, Volume 2, pp. 3–41. Ottawa, ON: National Forum on Health & MultiMondes.

Bach, M. 2002. *Social Inclusion as Solidarity: Rethinking the Child Rights Agenda*. Toronto, ON: Laidlaw Foundation Working Paper Series.

——, 1998. Securing Self-determination: Building the Agenda in Canada, *TASH Newsletter*, June/July.

Bachrach, P., and A. Botwinick. 1992. *Power and Empowerment: A Radical Theory of Participatory Democracy*. Philadelphia, PA: Temple University Press.

Barnes, C., and G. Mercer. 2005. Disability, Work, and Welfare: Challenging the Social Exclusion of Disabled People, *Work, Employment & Society*, 19, 3: pp. 527–545.

Beanlands, H. 2001. *Engulfment among Adults with Chronic Renal Disease: A Study of Self-Loss and its Correlates*. Doctoral Dissertation. Toronto, ON: University of Toronto Faculty of Nursing.

Behar, R. 1996. *The Vulnerable Observer: Anthropology that Breaks Your Heart*. Boston, MA: Beacon Press.

Benjamin, A., R. Matthias, and T. Franke. 2000. Comparing Consumer-directed and Agency Models for Providing Supportive Services at Home, *Health Services Research*, 35, 1: pp. 351–366.

Bennett, W.J. 1993. *The Book of Virtues: A Treasury of Great Moral Stories*. New York, NY: Simon & Schuster.

Pathways to Inclusion

Berger, P., and T. Luckmann. 1966. *The Social Construction of Reality: A Treatise in The Sociology of Knowledge.* Garden City, NJ: Doubleday & Co.

Berlin, S. 1997. *Ways We Live: Exploring Community.* Gabriola Island, BC: New Society Publishers.

Biklen, D. 2000. Constructing Inclusion: Lessons From Critical, Disability Narratives, *International Journal of Inclusive Education,* 4, 4: pp. 337–353.

Blaiklock, A. 2002. *When the Invisible Hand Rocks the Cradle: New Zealand Children in a Time of Change.* Wellington, NZ: UNICEF NZ.

Block, P. 1993. *Stewardship: Choosing Service Over Self-Interest.* San Francisco, CA: Berrett-Koehler Publishers.

Bloomfield, A., E. Bloomfield, and G. Bloomfield. n.d. *Planning with Andrew: Individualized Service and Support Plan.* Guelph, ON: Author.

Bohm, D. 1996. *On Dialogue.* London, UK: Routledge.

Boulding, K. 1989. *Three Faces of Power.* Newbury Park, CA: Sage Publications.

Boyce, W., M.A. McColl, M. Tremblay, J. Bickenbach, A. Crichton, S. Andrews, N. Gerein, and A. D'Aubin. 2001. *A Seat at the Table: Persons with Disabilities and Policy Making.* Montreal and Kingston, PQ/ON: McGill-Queen's University Press.

Brown, I., S. Anonel, A. Fung, B. Issacs, and N. Baum. 2003. Family, Quality of Life: Canadian Results from an International Study, *Journal of Developmental and Physical Disabilities,* 15, 3: pp. 207–230.

Brown, I., R. Renwick, and D. Raphael. 1996. *Frailty: Constructing a Common Meaning, Definition, and Conceptual Framework.* Toronto, ON: Centre for Health Promotion, University of Toronto.

Brown, R., and I. Brown. 2002. The Application of Quality of Life, *Journal of Intellectual Disability Research,* 49, 10: pp. 718–727.

Cacioppo, J.T., and W. Patrick. 2008. *Loneliness: Human Nature and the Need for Social Connection.* New York: W.W. Norton and Company.

Calderbank, R. 2000. Abuse and Disabled People: Vulnerability or Social Indifference, *Disability & Society,* 15, 3: pp. 521–534.

Caledon Institute. 2005. Quality of Life Challenge: Fostering Engagement, Collaboration and Inclusion, *Vibrant Communities,* November: pp. 1–8, <www.caledoninst.org>.

Cammack, V., and A. Etmanski. 2006. Sustainability and Social Innovation. A presentation created in collaboration with PLAN Institute, McConnell Family Foundation, and Dupont Foundation. <www.plan.ca>.

Canadian Association for Community Living. 2005. *A National Agenda to Support Families: A Proposal to Strike a New Balance for Families who have a Member with a Disability*. <www.cacl.ca>.

Canadian Association of Independent Living Centres. 1995. *Responding to Family Violence and Abuse: An Independent Living Approach*. Ottawa, ON: Author.

Carling, P. 1995. *Return to Community: Building Support Systems for People with Psychiatric Disabilities*. New York, NY: Guilford Press.

Carniol, B. 1995. *Case Critical: Challenging Social Services in Canada*, 3rd edition. Toronto, ON: Between the Lines.

Carroll, W., and W. Little. 2001. Neoliberal Transformation and Anti-globalization Politics in Canada, *International Journal of Political Economy*, 31, 3: pp. 33–66.

Carroll, W., and R. Ratner. 2001. Master Framing and Cross-Movement Networking in Contemporary Social Movement, *The Sociological Quarterly*, 37, 4: pp. 601–625.

Cavoukian, R., and S. Olfman (Eds.). 2006. *Child Honoring: How to Turn This World Around*. Westport, CT: Praeger. <www.raffinews.com/child>.

Centre for Research and Education in Human Services. 2004a. *Building Sustainable Non-Profits: The Waterloo Region Experience*. Kitchener, ON: Centre for Research and Education in Human Services.

———. 2004b. *Summary Bulletin: A Longitudinal Study of Consumer/ Survivor Initiatives in Community Mental Health in Ontario: Individual and System Level Impacts*. Kitchener, ON: Centre for Research and Education in Human Services.

Chappell, N. 1992. *Social Support and Aging*. Toronto, ON: Butterworth.

Charleton, J. 2000. *Nothing About us Without us: Disability Oppression and Empowerment*. Berkeley, CA: University of California Press.

Chase, W. 1994. The Language of Action, *The Workbook*, 19, 1.

Cheal, D. 2003. *Aging and Demographic Change in Canadian Context*. Toronto: ON University of Toronto Press.

Chenoweth, L., and D. Stehlik. 2004. Implications of Social Capital for the Inclusion of People with Disabilities and Families in Community Life, *International Journal of Inclusive Education*, 8, 1: pp. 59–72.

Chittister, J. 2003. *Scarred by Struggle, Transformed by Hope*. Ottawa, ON: Novalis, St. Paul University.

Chodron, P. 1991. *The Wisdom of No Escape: The Path of Loving-Kindness*. Boston, MA: Shambhala Publications Inc.

Christakis, N., and J. Fowler. 2009. *Connected: The Surprising Power of our Social Networks and How They Shape our Lives*. New York: Little, Brown and Company.

Church, K. 1997. *Forbidden Narratives: Critical Autobiography as Social Science*. Luxembourg: Gorden and Breach Publishers.

Pathways to Inclusion

Church, K. 1995. *Empowerment: A Difficult Work in Progress.* Presentation to the Ontario Advocacy Commission. Toronto, ON, March 20.

Cimarolli, V., J. Reinhardt, and A. Horowitz. 2006. Perceived Overprotection: Support Gone Bad, *The Gerontological Society of America*, 61: pp. S18–S23.

Clinton, H. Rodham. 1996. *It Takes a Village: And Other Lessons Children Teach Us.* New York, NY: Touchstone.

Clutterbuck, P., and M. Novick. 2003. *Building Inclusive Communities: Cross-Canada Perspectives and Strategies.* Toronto, ON: Laidlaw Foundation.

Coleman, D., and S. Iso-Ahola. 1993. Leisure and Health: The Role of Social Support and Self-determination, *Journal of Leisure Research*, 25, 2: pp. 111–128.

Community Mental Health Initiative. 2004. *Making a Difference.* Toronto, ON: Canadian Mental Health Association, Ontario Branch. <www.ontario.cmha.ca/cmhei>.

Condeluci, A. 1991. *Interdependence: The Route to Community.* Winter Park, FL: PMD Publishers Group Inc.

Connidis, I. 2001. *Family Ties and Aging.* Thousand Oaks, CA: Sage Publications.

Council of Canadians with Disabilities. 2005. *A Call to Combat Poverty and Exclusion of Canadians with Disabilities by Investing in Disability Supports.* Winnipeg, MB: Council of Canadians with Disabilities.

Crawford, C. 2005. *Inclusive Education in Canada: Key Issues and Directions for the Future.* Canadian Association for Community Living Summit on Inclusive Education November 2004. Toronto, ON: Roeher Institute.

Crawford, C. 2003. *Toward a Common Approach to Thinking and Measuring Social Inclusion.* Toronto, ON: Roeher Institute.

Cusak, S., and W. Thompson. 1998. *Leadership for Older Adults: Aging with Purpose and Passion.* UK: Psychology Press.

Dalai Lama and H. Cutler. 1998. *The Art of Happiness: A Handbook for Living.* New York, NY: Penguin Putnam Inc.

Dass, Ram, and P. Gorman. 1987. *How Can I Help: Stories and Reflections on Service.* New York, NY: Alfred A. Knopf.

Davidson, L., M. Chinman, B. Kloos, R. Weingarten, D. Stayner, and J. Kraemer Tebes. 1999. Peer Support among Individuals with Severe Mental Illness, Clinical Psychology, *Science and Practice*, 6, 2: pp. 165–187.

de Bono, E. 1999. *New Thinking for the New Millennium.* New York, NY: Viking/Penguin.

Deegan, P. 1996. Recovery as a Journey of the Heart, *Psychiatric Rehabilitation Journal*, 19, 3: pp. 91–96.

Dineen, T. 1996. *Manufacturing Victims: What the Psychology Industry is Doing to People.* Montreal: Robert Davies Publishing.

Disabled Peoples' International Europe, 2000. Declaration on the Right to Live and Be Different, Conference on Bioethics and Human Rights. Solihull, UK: DPIE.

Dobrowolsky, A. 2004. Shifting Representations of Citizenship: Canadian Politics of "Women" and "Children," *Social Politics*, 11, 2: pp. 154–180.

Drucker, P. 1985. *Innovation and Entrepreneurship: Practice and Principles*. New York, NY: Harper & Row.

Drucker, P. 1998. The Discipline of Innovation, *Drucker Foundation News*, 5, 4.

Elshtain, Jean Bethke. 2002. *The Jane Addams Reader*. New York: Basic Books.

Etmanski, A. 2000. *A Good Life*. Burnaby, BC: PLAN.

European Foundation for the Improvement of Living Conditions. 2003. *Illness, Disability, and Social Inclusion*. Luxembourg: Office for Official Publications of the European Communities.

Faber, B. 2002. *Community Action and Organizational Change: Image, Narrative, Identity*. Carbondale, IL: Southern Illinois University Press.

Falvey, M., M. Forest, J. Pearpoint, and R. Rosenberg. 1997. *All My Life's a Circle: Using the Tools: Circles, MAPS and PATH*. Toronto, ON: Inclusion Press.

Federal/Provincial/Territorial Ministers Responsible for Social Services. 1998. *In Unison: A Canadian Approach to Disability Issues*. Ottawa, ON: Human Resources Development Canada.

Field, J. 2003. *Social Capital*. UK: Routledge.

Fine, M. Albertson. 2004. *The Autonomy Myth: A Theory of Dependency*. New York, NY: The New Press.

Foot, D., with D. Staffman. 2000. *Boom, Bust & Echo. Profiting From the Demographic Shift in the New Millennium*. Toronto, ON: Stoddart.

Foster, R. 2000. Leadership in the Twenty-first Century: Working to Build a Civil Society, *National Civic Review*, 89, 1: pp. 87–93.

Foucault, M. 1965. *Madness and Civilization: A History of Insanity in the Age of Reason*. New York, NY: Vintage Books.

Frazee, C. 2002. Our Citizenship is on the Rocks, *Globe and Mail*, December 28: p. A15.

——. 1999. *Individualized Funding: A New Vision*. Toronto, ON: Individualized Funding Coalition for Ontario.

Freire, P. 1970. *Pedagogy of the Oppressed*. New York, NY: Seabury Press.

Friedan, B. 1993. *The Fountain of Age*. New York, NY: Simon & Schuster.

Friedmann, J. 1987. *Planning in the Public Domain: From Knowledge to Action*. Princeton, NJ: Princeton University Press.

Furstenberg, F., and M. Hughes. 1995. Social Capital and Successful Development Among At-Risk Youth. *Journal of Marriage and Family*, 57, 3: pp. 580-592.

Gadacz, R. 1994. *Re-thinking Disability: New Structures, New Relationships*. Edmonton, AB: University of Alberta Press.

Gafni, M. 2001. *Soul Prints*. New York, NY: Pocket Books.

Gamble, J. *Evaluating Vibrant Communities 2002–2010*. Waterloo, ON: Tamarack. <http://tamarackcommunity.ca/downloads/vc/VC_Evaluation.pdf>.

Gergen, K. 1995. *Realities and Relationships: Soundings in Social Construction*. Cambridge, MA: Harvard University Press.

———. 1994. *Realities and Relationships: Soundings in Social Construction*. Cambridge, MA: Harvard University Press.

Gilchrist, A. 2004. *The Well-Connected Community: A Networking Approach*. London, UK: The Policy Press.

Gladwell, M. 2000. *Tipping Point: How Little Things Can Make a Big Difference*. New York, NY: Little, Brown and Company.

Goffman, E. 1961. *Asylums: Essays on The Social Situation of Mental Patients and Other Inmates*. New York, NY: Doubleday.

Gold, D. 1994. "We Don't Call it a 'Circle'": The Ethos of a Support Group, *Disability and Society*, 9: pp. 435–452.

Goldstein, J., and J. Kornfield. 2001. *Seeking the Heart of Wisdom: The Path of Insight Meditation*. Boston, MA: Shambhala Publications Inc.

Gottlieb, B. 2000. Selecting and Planning Support interventions. In S. Cohen, L. Underwood, and B. Gottlieb, *Social Support Measurement and Interventions: A Guide for Health and Social Scientists*, pp. 195–220. New York, NY: Oxford University Press.

Government of Canada. 2007. *Canada's Aging Population: Population by Sex and Age Group, 2006*. Ottawa: Statistics Canada..

Grady, B. 2004. Ten Resolutions for People Living with Chronic Pain or Illness, *Rehab Review*, 24, 8: pp. 6–7. (See also Dr. Brian Grady's blog: <http://briangrady.wordpress.com/2008/06/12/10-resolutions-for-managing-chronic-pain-or-illness/>.)

Griffin, S. 1982. The Way of All Ideology, *Signs*, 7, Spring: pp. 641–660.

Groce, N. 1985. *Everyone Here Spoke Sign Language: Hereditary Deafness on Martha's Vineyard*. Cambridge, MA: Harvard University Press.

Gubrium, J., and J. Holstein. 2003. *Ways of Aging*. Oxford, UK: Blackwell Publishing.

Habermas, J. 1981. New Social Movements, *Telos*, 49: pp. 33–37.

Hahn, T.N. 2000. *The Path of Emancipation*. Berkeley, CA: Parallax Press.

Hall, C. 2003. *Clienthood in Social Work and Human Service*. London, UK: Jessica Kingsley Publishers.

Pathways to Inclusion

Hall, C., K. Juhila, and N. Parton (Eds.). 2003. *Constructing Clienthood in Social Work and Human Services*. London, UK: Jessica Kinsley Publishers.

Handy, C. 1994. *The Age of Paradox*. Cambridge, MA: Harvard Business School Press.

Harbison, J., and M. Morrow. 1998. Re-examining the Social Construction of "Elder Abuse and Neglect": A Canadian Perspective, *Ageing & Society*, 18, 6: pp. 691–711.

Hart, D. 2001. Interagency Partnerships and Funding: Individual Supports for Youth with Significant Disabilities as they Move to Post-Secondary Education and Employment Options, *Journal of Vocational Rehabilitation*, 16, 3–4: pp. 145–154.

Heath, N., H. Petrakos, C. Finn, A. Aragiannakis, D. Mclean-Heywood, and C. Roussea. 2004. Inclusion on the Final Frontier: A Model for Including Children with Emotional and Behavior Disorders in Canada, *International Journal of Inclusive Education*, 8, 3: pp. 241–259.

Hebert, R., M-F. Dubois, C. Wolfson, L. Chambers, and C. Cohen. 2001. Factors Associated with Long-term Institutionalization of Older People with Dementia: Data from the Canadian Study on Health and Aging, *The Gerontological Society of America*, 56: pp. 693–699.

Heifetz, R., and R. Sinder. 1988. Political Leadership: Managing the Public's Problem-Solving. In R. Reich (Ed.), *The Power of Public Ideas*, pp. 179–204. Cambridge, MA: Ballinger, Alison Blaiklock.

Helgesen, S. 1995. *The Web of Inclusion: A New Architecture for Building Great Organizations*. New York, NY: Currency/Doubleday.

Heller, T., A. Miller, and K. Hsieh. 1999. Impact of a Consumer-Directed Family Support Program on Adults with Developmental Disabilities and their Family Caregivers, *Family Relations*, 48, 4: pp. 419–427.

Henning, J. 1993. Foreword. In P. Block, *Stewardship: Choosing Service over Self-Interest*. San Francisco, CA: Berrett-Koehler Publishers.

Heumann, L., and D. Boldy. 1993. *Aging in Place with Dignity: International Solutions Relating to the Low-income and Frail Elderly*. Westport, CT: Greenwood Publishing.

Hiebert, C. 2004. The Road to Recovery. Mental Health Matters, CMHA Waterloo/Wellington Newsletter, 15, 2: p. 2.

Higgins, J. Wharf. 1992. The Healthy Community Movement in Canada. In B. Wharf (Ed.), *Communities and Social Policy in Canada*. Toronto, ON: McClelland & Stewart.

Hillman, James. 1995. *Kinds of Power: A Guide to Its Intelligent Uses*. New York, NY: Currency Doubleday.

Hingsburger, D. 1997. Truth, Journey and Soul: A New Vocabulary for Human Services, *Dialect: Newsmagazine of the Saskatchewan Association for Community Living*, September/October.

Hofsted, T. 1996. *In the Company of Friends: Pilot Project Evaluation Final Report*. Winnipeg, MB: Policy and Planning Branch, Manitoba Family Services.

Holburn, S., and P. Vietze (Eds.). 1992. *Person-Centered Planning: Research, Practice and Future Directions*. Baltimore: Paul H. Brookes Publishing Co.

Homer-Dixon, T. 2001. *The Ingenuity Gap*. Toronto: Vintage Canada.

Hooks, B. 1984. *Feminist Theory: From Margin to Center*. Boston, MA: South End Press.

Hsu, C. 2006. William Thomas: The Greening of Aging, *U.S. News and World Report*, June 19: pp. 48–50.

Hughes, E. 2006. Mental Illness as a Gift, *Update: The Self-Help Alliance*, 1, 1: p. 5.

Hutchison, P., S. Arai, A. Pedlar, J. Lord, and C. Whyte. 2007a. Leadership in the Canadian Consumer Disability Movement: Hopes and Challenges, *International Journal of Disability Community and Rehabilitation*, 16, 1, <www.ijdcr.ca> (online journal).

Hutchison, P., S. Arai, A. Pedlar, J. Lord, and F. Yuen. 2007b. Role of Canadian User-Led Disability Organizations in The Non-Profit Sector, *Disability & Society*, 22, 7: pp. 701–716.

Hutchison, P., J. Lord, and K. Lord. 2010. *Friends and Inclusion: Five Approaches to Building Relationships*. Toronto: Inclusion Press.

Hutchison, P., J. Lord, and B. Salisbury. 2006. North American Approaches to Individualized Funding and Planning. In J. Leece and J. Bornat (Eds.), *Developments in Direct Payments*. Bristol, UK: The Policy Press.

Hutchison, P., and J. McGill. 1998, *Leisure, Integration and Community*, 2nd edition. Toronto, ON: Leisurability Publications.

Hutchison, P., A. Pedlar, P. Dunn, J. Lord, and S. Arai. 2000. Canadian Independent Living Centres: Impact on the Community, *International Journal of Rehabilitation Research*, 23, 2: pp. 61–74.

Hutchison, P., A. Pedlar, J. Lord, P. Dunn, M. McGeown, A. Taylor, and C. Vanditelli. 1996. Impact of Independent Living Centres in Canada on People With Disabilities, *Canadian Journal Of Rehabilitation*, 10: pp. 99–112.

Ignatieff, M. 1984. *The Needs of Strangers*. London, UK: Chatto & Windus.

Illich, I. 1977. *Disabling Professions*. London, UK: Marion Boyars.

Janeway, E. 1980. *Powers of the Weak*. New York, NY: Alfred A. Knopf.

Janzen, R. 2004. Trigger Events, Critical Mass, and Social Policy, *Keystones NewsReport: Centre for Research and Education in Human Services*, 17, Winter: pp. 3–5.

Kabot-Zinn, J. 2005. *Coming to Our Senses: Healing Ourselves and the World through Mindfulness*. New York, NY: Hyperion.

Keating, N., P. Otfinowski, C. Wenger, J. Fast, and L. Derksen. 2003. Understanding the Caring Capacity of Informal Networks of Frail Seniors: A Case for Care Networks, *Ageing & Society*, 23: pp. 115–127.

Keiffer, C. 1984. Citizen Empowerment: A Developmental Perspective, *Prevention in Human Services*, 3, 16: pp. 9–35.

Kennedy, M. 1995. *Becoming a GROWer: Worldview Transformation among Committed Members of a Mutual Aid Group*, Unpublished doctoral dissertation. Urbana-Champaign, IL: University of Illinois.

Kennedy, M., and M. Humphreys. 1994. Understanding Worldview Transformation in Mutual Help Groups, *Prevention in Human Services*, 11: pp. 181–189.

Killoran, I. 2002. A Road Less Travelled: Creating a Community Where Each Belongs, *Childhood Education*, 78: pp. 371–377.

Kilroy, R. 1987. Testimony to the United States Senate Subcommittee on Labor & Human Resources. Washington, DC, United States Senate, April 23.

King, G., D. Stewart, S. King, M. Law. 2000. Organizational Characteristics and Issues Affecting the Longevity of Self-Help Groups for Parents of Children with Special Needs, *Qualitative Health Research*, 10, 2: pp. 225–241.

Kingwell, M. 2000. *The World We Want*. Toronto, ON: Viking.

Klees, J. 2005. *Our Presence Has Roots: The Ongoing Story of Deohaeko Support Network*. Toronto: Resources Supporting Family and Community Legacies Inc..

———. 1996. *We Come Bearing Gifts: The Story of Deohaeko Support Network*. Scarborough, ON: PSD Consultants.

Klein, B. 2006. *Shameless: The Art of Disability*. Canada: National Film Board.

Kretzmann, J., and M. Green. 1998. *Building the Bridge from Client to Citizen: A Community Toolbox for Welfare Reform Square*. Evanston, IL: Northwestern University Institute for Policy Research.

Krogh, K., and M. Innis. 2005. *A National Snapshot of Home Support from the Consumer Perspective*. Winnipeg, MB: Council of Canadians with Disabilities. <www.ccdonline.ca>.

Labonte, R. 1994. *Health Promotion and Empowerment Practice Frameworks*. Toronto, ON: Centre for Health Promotion, University of Toronto.

Laidlaw Foundation, *Perspectives on Social Inclusion*. Working Paper Series. Foundation's website: <www.laidlawfdn.org>.

Laverack, G., and N. Wallerstein. 2001. Measuring Community Empowerment: A Fresh Look at Organizational Domains, *Health Promotion International*, 16, 2: pp. 179–185.

Leavitt, B., and C. Bender. 2004. *Voices: Speaking out on Everything from Education to Discrimination*. St. Marys, ON: Authors. <www.lpdassociates.com>.

Leff, H.S., J. Campbell, C. Gagne and L.S. Woocher. 1997. Evaluating Peer Providers. In C.T. Mowbray, D.P. Moxley, C.A. Jasper, and L.L. Howell (Eds.), *Consumers as Providers in Psychiatric Rehabilitation*, pp. 488–501. Columbia, MD: IAPSRS Press.

Lerner, M. 1986. *Surplus Powerlessness: The Psycho-Dynamics of Everyday Life and the Psychology of Individual and Social Transformation*. Oakland, CA: The Institute for Labour and Mental Health.

Light, P. 1998. *Sustaining Innovation: Creating Non-profit and Government Organizations that Innovate Naturally*. San Francisco, CA: Jossey-Bass Inc..

Lincoln, Y. 1985. *Organizational Theory and Inquiry: The Paradigm Revolution*. Newbury Park, CA: Sage Publications.

Lord, J. 2006. *Moving Toward Citizenship: A Study of Individualized Funding in Ontario*. Toronto, ON: Individualized Funding Coalition for Ontario.

———. 2000a. *Evaluation of Navigating the Waters*. Ottawa, ON: Canadian Association for Independent Living Centres.

———. 2000b. "Is That all There Is?" Searching for Citizenship in the Midst of Services, *Canadian Journal of Community Mental Health*, 19, 2: pp. 165–169.

———. 1999. *Constructing Social Support with Vulnerable Citizens: Promise and Problems*. Unpublished document. <www.johnlord.net>.

Lord, J., and C. Dingwall, *Facilitation Leadership Group*. <www.facilitationleadership.com>.

Lord, J., and C. Hearn. 1997. *Return to the Community: The Process of Closing an Institution*. Kitchener, ON: Centre for Research and Education in Human Services.

Lord, J., and P. Hutchison. 2008. Individualized Funding in Ontario: Report of a Provincial Study. *Journal on Developmental Disabilities*, 14, 2: pp. 44–53.

———. 2003. Individualised Support and Funding: Building Blocks for Capacity Building and Inclusion, *Disability & Society*, 18, 1: pp. 71–86

———. 1993. The Process of Empowerment: Implications for Theory and Practice, *Canadian Journal of Community Mental Health*, 12, 1: pp. 5–22.

Lord, J., J. Ochocka, W. Czarny, and H. MacIlivery. 1998. Analysis of Change Within a Mental Health Organization: A Participatory Process, *Psychiatric Rehabilitation Journal*, 21, 4: pp. 327–339.

Lord, J., and A. Pedlar. 1991. Life in the Community: Four Years After the Closure of an Institution, *Mental Retardation*, 29, 4: pp. 213–221.

Pathways to Inclusion

Lord, J., J. Snow, and C. Dingwall. 2005. *Building a New Story: Transforming Disability Supports and Policies: Revisiting in Unison.* Toronto, ON: Individualized Funding Coalition for Ontario, website <www.individualizedfunding.ca>.

Lord, J., B. Zupko, and P. Hutchison. 2000. *More Choice and Control for People with Disabilities: Review of Individualized Funding and Support.* Toronto, ON: Ontario Federation for Cerebral Palsy.

Lovett, H. 1996. *Learning to Listen: Positive Approaches and People with Difficult Behavior.* Baltimore, MD: Paul H. Brookes.

Lum, J., S. Ruff, and P. Williams. 2005. *When Home is Community: Community Support Services and the Well-Being of Seniors in Supportive and Social Housing.* Toronto, ON: Ryerson University.

Lyons, R., M. Sullivan, and P. Ritvo. 1995. *Relationships in Chronic Illness and Disability.* Thousand Oaks, CA: Sage Publishing.

MacAdam, M. 2000. Homecare: It's Time for a Canadian Model, *Homecare*, 1, 4: pp. 9–36.

MacMullen, K., and G. Schellenberg. 2002. *Mapping the Non-Profit Sector: Series on Human Resources in the Non-Profit Sector.* Ottawa, ON: Canadian Policy Research Networks.

Mactavish, J., and S. Schleie. 2004. Re-injecting Spontaneity and Balance in Family Life: Parents' Perspectives on Recreation in Families that Include Children with a Developmental Disability, *Journal of Intellectual Disability Research*, 48, 2: pp. 123–141.

Mails, T.E. 1988. *Secret Native American Pathways: A Guide to Inner Peace.* Tulsa, OK: Council Oke Books.

Makela, K. 1997. *Alcoholics Anonymous as a Mutual Aid Movement: A Study in Eight Societies.* Madison, WI: University of Wisconsin Press.

Malash, C., W. Schaufeli, M. Leiter. 2001. Job Burnout, *Annual Review of Psychology*, 52, 1: pp. 397–422.

Malette, P. 1992. Lifestyle Quality and Person-Centered Support: Jeff, Janet, Stephanie, and the Microboard Project. In S. Holburn and P. Vietze (Eds.), *Person-Centered Planning: Research, Practice and Future Directions*, pp. 151–182 Baltimore: Paul H. Brookes Publishing Co.

Malik, H. 2003. *A Practical Guide to Equal Opportunity.* Surrey, UK: Nelson Thornes.

Malloux, L., H. Horak, and C. Godin. 2002. *Motivation at the Margins: Gender Issues in the Canadian Voluntary Sector.* Ottawa, ON: Voluntary Sector Initiative Secretariat.

Marinelli, R., and D. Orto (Eds.). 1999. *The Psychological and Social Impact of Disability.* New York, NY: Springer Publishing Co.

McColl, M., and W. Boyce. 2003. Disability Advocacy organizations: A Descriptive Framework, *Disability and Rehabilitation*, 25, 8: pp. 380–392.

Pathways to Inclusion

McCubbin, M. 2001. Pathways to Health, Illness, and Well-Being: Perspective of Power and Control, *Journal of Community and Applied Social Psychology*, 11, 2: pp. 75–81.

McCubbin, M., T. Spindel, and D. Cohen. 2002. Paternalism: The Underlying Ideology of Disempowering Practice, *The Rights Tenet-Quarterly Newspaper of the National Association for Rights Protection and Advocacy*, 4: pp. 20–21.

McGee, J., and F. Menolascino. 1991. *Beyond Gentle Teaching: A Non-Aversive Approach to Helping Those in Need*. New York, NY: Plenum Press.

McGill, J. 2002. *Developing Leisure Identities*. Brampton, ON: Brampton–Caledon Community Living.

McGill, J. 1996. *Developing Leisure Identities*. Brampton, ON: Brampton–Caledon Community Living.

McKnight, J. 1995. *The Careless Society: Community and its Counterfeits*. New York, NY: Basic Books.

McKnight, J., and P. Block. 2010. *The Abundant Community: Awakening the Power of Families and Neighborhoods*. San Francisco, CA: Berrett-Koehler Publishers.

Metzel, D., and P. Walker. 2001. The Illusion of Inclusion: Geographies of the Lives of People with Developmental Disabilities in the United States, *Disabilities Studies*, 21, 4: pp. 114–128.

Minkler, M. 1990. Aging and Disability: Behind and Beyond the Stereotypes, *Journal of Aging Studies*, 4, 3: pp. 245–260.

Murphy, R. 1990. *The Body Silent*. New York, NY: W.W. Norton.

Myrdal, G. 1944. *An American Dilemma*. New York, NY: Harper and Row.

Narushim, M. 2004. A Gaggle of Raging Grannies: The Empowerment of Older Canadian Women Through Social Activism, *Journal of Lifelong Education*, 23, 1: pp. 23–42.

National Forum on Health. 1998. *Canada Health Action: Building on the Legacy*, Four part series, Vol. 1: Determinants of Health: Children and Youth; Vol. 2: Determinants of Health: Adults and Seniors; Vol. 3: Determinants of Health: Settings and Issues; Vol. 4: Striking a Balance: Health Care Systems in Canada and Elsewhere; Vol. 5: Making Decisions: Evidence and Information. Sainte-Foy, PQ: MultiMondes.

Nelson, G., J. Lord, and J. Ochocka. 2001. *Shifting the Paradigm in Community Mental Health: Towards Empowerment and Community*. Toronto, ON: University of Toronto Press.

Nelson, G., J. Ochocka, R. Jansen, and J. Trainor. 2006. A Longitudinal Study of Mental Health Consumer/Survivor Initiatives, *Journal of Community Psychology*, 34, 3: pp. 247–304.

Nelson, G., I. Prilleltensky, and H. MacGillary. 2001. Building Value-Based Partnerships: Toward Solidarity with Oppressed Groups, *American Journal of Community Psychology*, 29, 5: pp. 649–677.

Neufeldt, A. 2003. Growth and Evolution of Disability Advocacy in Canada. In D. Stienstra and A. Wight-Felske (Eds.), *Making Equality: History of Advocacy and Persons with Disabilities in Canada*, pp. 11–32. Toronto, ON: Captus Press.

Newberry, J. 2005. Family Support: Putting Function before Form, *Keystones NewsReport, Centre for Research and Education in Human Services*, 18: pp. 3–4.

——. 2004. *The Meaningful Participation of Consumers on Mental Health Agency Boards: Experiential Power and Models of Governance*. Doctoral thesis. Guelph, ON: University of Guelph.

Noel, L. 1994. *Intolerance: A General Survey*. Montreal, PQ: McGill-Queens University Press.

Northway, R. 1997. Integration and Inclusion: Illusion or Progress in Services for Disabled People, *Social Policy & Administration*, 31, 2: pp. 157–172.

O'Brien, J. n.d. *The Politics of Person-Centered Planning*. Lithonia, GA: Responsive Systems Associates.

——. 1996. *Tell Me a Story of Deep Delight: An Account of the Work of a Network of Families in Durham Region*. Durham, ON: Durham Family Network.

——. 1989. *What's Worth Asking For? Leadership for Better Quality Human Services*. Syracuse, NY: Center on Human Policy.

O'Brien, J., and C. O'Brien. 2002. *Voices of Experience: Implementing Person-Centered Planning*. Toronto, ON: Inclusion Press.

O'Connoll, M. 1990. *Community Building in Logan Square*. Evanston, IL: Northwestern University Institute for Policy Research.

Ochocka, J., D. Roth, J. Lord, and E. Macnaughton. 1993. *Support Clusters Project: Evaluation Report of a Research Demonstration Project*. Kitchener, ON: Centre for Research and Education in Human Services.

Oliver, M. 1996. *Understanding Disability: From Theory to Practice*. London, UK: MacMillan.

——. 1990. *The Politics of Disablement: A Sociological Approach*. New York: St. Martin's Press.

Orloff, A. 2005. Measure Up: A 2020 Vision for Inclusive Cities, *Abilities*, 64: pp. 32–33.

Ornish, D. 1997. *Love & Survival: The Scientific Basis for the Healing Power of Intimacy*. New York, NY: HarperCollins Publishers Inc.

Osberg, Lars (Ed.). 2003. *The Economic Implications of Social Cohesion*. Toronto, ON: University of Toronto Press.

Pancer, S.M., and M.W. Pratt. 1999. *Social and Family Determinants of Community Service Involvement*. Cambridge, UK: Cambridge University Press.

Panitch, Leo. 1994. Changing Gears: Democratizing the Welfare State. In A. Johnson, S. McBride, and P. Smith (Eds.), *Continuities and Discontinuities: The Political Economy of Social Welfare and*

Labour Market Policy in Canada, pp. 36–44. Toronto, ON: University of Toronto Press.

Panitch, M. 2003. Mothers of Intention: Women, Disability, and Activism. In D. Stienstra and A. Wight-Felske (Eds.), *Making Equality*, pp. 261–278. Toronto, ON: Captus Press.

Park, P., A. Monteiro, and B. Kappel. 2003. People First: The History and the Dream. In D. Stienstra and A. Wight-Felske (Eds.), *Making Equality: History of Advocacy and Persons with Disabilities in Canada*, pp. 11–32. Toronto, ON: Captus Press.

Pearpoint, J. 1991. *From Behind the Piano: The Building of Judith Snow's Unique Circle of Friends*. Toronto, ON: Inclusion Press.

Pedlar, A., L. Haworth, P. Hutchison, A. Taylor, and P. Dunn. 1999. *A Textured Life: Empowerment and Adults with Developmental Disabilities*. Waterloo, ON: Wilfrid Laurier University Press.

Pedlar, A., and P. Hutchison. 2000. Restructuring Human Services in Canada: Commodification of Disability, *Disability & Society*, 15, 4: pp. 637–651.

People First of Windsor. 2006. *Building Leadership in the Community*. Windsor, ON: People First.

Peterson, C., M. Seligman, and S. Maier. 1995. *Learned Helplessness: A Theory for the Age of Personal Control*. New York, NY: Oxford University Press.

Pink, D.H. 2009. *Drive: The Surprising Truth About What Motivates Us*. New York: Riverhead Books.

Pinkerton, J., P. Dolan, and J. Canavan. 2006. *Family Support as Reflective Practice*. London, UK: Jessica Kinsley Publishers.

Pitonyak, D. 2007. The Importance of Dreaming, *Imagine*, 1: pp. 1–37.

PLAN. 2002. Report of the Community Living Transition Steering Committee Completed, *PLAN Facts: Newsletter of Plan Lifetime Advocacy Network*, Winter.

Porter, G. 2004. Meeting the Challenge: Inclusion and Diversity in Canadian Schools, *Education Canada*, 44, 1: pp. 48–51.

Prilleltensky, I. 2005. Promoting Well-being: Time for a Paradigm Shift in Health and Human Services, *Scandinavian Journal of Public Health*, 33, 66: pp. 53–60.

Prilleltensky, I., G. Nelson, and L. Peirson. 2001. The Role of Power and Control in Children's Lives: An Ecological Analysis of Pathways Toward Wellness, Resilience and Problems, *Journal of Community and Applied Social Psychology*, 11, 2: pp. 143–158.

Prince, M. 2002. The Return of Directed Incrementalism: Innovating Social Policy in Canada. In G. Doern (Ed.), *How Ottawa Spends 2002–2003: The Security Aftermath and National Priorities*, pp. 176–195. Toronto, ON: Oxford University Press.

———. 2001. *Governing In an Integrated Fashion: Lessons from the Disability Domain*. Ottawa, ON: Canadian Policy Research Network.

————. 1998. Social Policy Reform and the Rediscovery of Community and Family Support for the Aged, *Journal of Ethics, Law, and Aging*, 4, 2: pp. 85–90.

Project Friendship Society. 1993. *Prince George Connector: A Guide to Local Clubs, Interest, and Support Groups*. Prince George, BC: Project Friendship Society.

Proulx, A. 1993. *Shipping News*. Toronto, ON: Charles Scribner's Sons.

Putman, R. 2000. *Bowling Alone: The Collapse and Revival of American Community*. New York, NY: Simon & Schuster.

Putman, R., and L. Feldstein. 2003. *Better Together: Restoring the American Community*. New York, NY: Simon and Schuster.

Raphael, D., R. Renwick, I. Brown, and I. Rootman. 1996. Quality of Life Indicators and Health: Current Status and Emerging Conceptions, *Social Indicators Research*, 39, 1: pp. 65–88.

Rice, J., and M. Prince. 2000. *Changing Politics of Canadian Social Policy*. Toronto: University of Toronto Press.

Rifkin, J. 2000. *The Age of Access: The New Culture of Hypercapitalism Where All Life is a Paid-for Experience*. New York, NY: Jeremy P. Tarcher/Putman.

Roeher Institute. 1997. *Final Evaluation Report of Self-Managed Attendant Services in Ontario*. North York, ON: Author.

————. 1996. *Disability, Community and Society: Exploring the Links*. North York, ON: Author.

————. 1995. *Disability-related Supports: Costs and Delivery System for Selected Provinces*. Downsview, ON: Roeher Institute.

————. 1994. *Violence and People with Disabilities: A Review of the Literature*. Ottawa, ON: National Clearinghouse on Family Violence).

Rogers, E. 2003. *Diffusion of Innovations*, 5th edition. New York, NY: Simon & Schuster.

Romilly, L. 2003. *Peer Support: Building Individual and Community Capacity: Evaluation of Two Smart Funded Projects*. Vancouver, B.C.: British Columbia Paraplegic Association.

Rootman, I. 2001. *Evaluation in Health Promotion: Principles and Perspectives*. New York, NY: WHO Press.

Rothman, D. 1981. *Social Control: Uses and Abuses of the Concept in the History of Incarceration*. Houston, TX: Rice University Studies.

Ruston, R., and M. Powell. 1995. *Keeping Your Dreams Alive*. Toronto, ON: Ontario Association for Community Living.

Saleebey, D. 2006. *The Strengths Perspective in Social Work*, 2nd edition. Boston, MA: Allyn & Bacon.

Salzburg, S. 1995. *Loving Kindness: The Revolutionary Art of Happiness*. Boston, MA: Shambhala.

Sanders, K. 2006. Overprotection and Lowered Expectations of Persons with Disabilities: The Unforeseen Consequences, *Work*, 27, 2: pp. 181–188.

Saul, J. Ralston. 2005. Foreword. In S. Shields and D. Campion, *The Company of Others: Stories of Belonging.* Burnaby, BC: Arsenal Pulp Press/PLAN Lifetime Networks.
———. 2003. Who Cares? Creative Responses to Social Obligations. In The Philia Project: A Dialogue, Monograph #2. Vancouver, BC: PLAN.
———. 2001. *On Equilibrium.* Toronto, ON: Penguin Books.
———. 1996. *Citizenship and the Corporatist View.* A presentation to Hagey Lectures. Waterloo, ON: University of Waterloo.
———. 1995. *The Unconscious Civilization.* Toronto, ON: House of Anansi Press.
———. 1992. *Voltaire's Bastards: The Dictatorship of Reason in the West.* Toronto, ON: Penguin Books.
Schalock, R., I. Brown, R. Brown, R. Cummins, D. Felce, L. Matikka, K. Keith, and T. Parmenter. 2002. Conceptualization, Measurement, and Application of Quality of Life For Persons With Intellectual Disabilities: Report of An International Panel Of Experts, *Mental Retardation*, 40, 6: pp. 457–470.
Scharf, T., C. Phillipson, P. Kingston, and A. Smith. 2001. Social Exclusion and Older People: Exploring the Connections, *Education and Ageing*, 16, 3: pp. 303–320.
Schorr, E. 1988. *Within Our Reach: Breaking the Cycle of Disadvantage.* New York, NY: Anchor Press, Doubleday.
Schugurensky, D. 1993. The Tango of Citizenship: Learning and Participatory Democracy. In P. Park, M. Brydon-Miller, B. Hall, and T. Jackson (Eds.), *Voices of Change: Participatory Research in the United States and Canada*, pp. 157–176. Westport, CT: Greenwood Publishing Group.
Schwartz, D. 1997. *Who Cares?: Rediscovering Community.* Boulder, CO: Westview Press.
———. 1992. *Crossing the River: Creating a Conceptual Revolution in Disability and Community.* Boston, MA: Brookline Books.
Scott, T. 2000. *Creating Caring and Capable Boards: Reclaiming the Passion for Active Trusteeship.* New York, NY: Wiley.
Scott-Hanson, C., and K. Scott-Hanson. 2005. *The Co-housing Handbook: Building a Place for Community.* Gabriola, BC: New Society Publishers.
Secretan, L. 1999. *Inspirational Leadership: Destiny, Calling and Cause.* Toronto, ON: Macmillan Canada.
Senge, P. 1998. Excerpts from Mastering the Tools for Change, *Drucker Foundation News*, 5, 4.
———. 1990. *The Fifth Discipline: The Art and Practice of the Learning Organization.* New York, NY: Doubleday.
Sibley, D. 1995. *Geographies of Exclusion: Society and Difference in the West.* UK: Routledge.
Simmons, H. 1990. *Unbalanced: Mental Health Policy in Ontario, 1930–1989.* Toronto, ON: Wall and Thompson.

Snow, J. 1994. *What's Really Worth Doing and How to Do It.* Toronto, ON: Inclusion Press).

Spiegel, D. 1993. *Living Beyond Limits: New Hope and Help for Facing Life-Threatening Illness.* New York, NY: Times Books.

Stainton, Tim. 2005. Individualized Funding presentation to a policy forum on funding approaches for developmental services for the Ontario Ministry of Community and Social Services. Toronto, Ontario, March 30.

Starhawk. 1987. *Truth or Dare: Encounters with Power, Authority, and Mystery.* San Francisco, CA: Harper.

Starhawk. 1996. Community. In F. Brussat and M.A. Brussat (Eds.), *Spiritual Literacy: Reading the Sacred in Everyday Life.* New York, NY: Scribner.

Statistics Canada. 2007. *A Profile of Disability in Canada, 2006.* Ottawa, ON: Statistics Canada.

———. 2002. *A Profile of Disability in Canada, 2001.* Ottawa, ON: Statistics Canada.

Statistics Canada, and M. Navaie-Waliser, A. Spriggs and P. Feldman. 2002. Informal Caregiving: Differential Experiences by Gender, *Medical Care,* 40, 12: pp. 1249–1259.

Stein, C., J. Rappaport, E. Seidman. 1995. Assessing the Social Networks of People with Psychiatric Disability from Multiple Perspectives, *Community Mental Health Journal,* 31, 4: pp. 351–367.

Stein, J. Gross. 2001. *The Cult of Efficiency.* Toronto, ON: House of Anansi Press.

Stephenson, C. 2005. Empower Women Leaders. In Perspectives, W10, *Globe and Mail,* Tuesday, March 8: p. 1.

Stienstra, D., and A. Wight-Felske. 2003. *Making Equality: History of Advocacy and Persons with Disabilities in Canada.* Toronto, ON: Captus Press.

Styan, J. 2004. *Connecting to Citizenship: Social Policy Recommendations to Address Isolation and Loneliness.* Burnaby, BC: Plan Institute.

Sundar, P., and J. Ochocka. 2004. Bridging the Gap Between Dreams and Realities Related to Employment and Mental Health: Implications for Policy and Practice, *Canadian Journal of Community Mental Health,* 23, 1: pp. 75–89.

Sutherland, J. 2005. This Floating World, *Shambhala Sun,* 13, 4: pp. 68–73.

Swain, J., and S. French. 2000. *Toward an Affirmation Model of Disability, Disability & Society,* 15, 4: pp. 569–582.

Taylor, A., J. Sylvestre, and J. Botschner. 1998. Social Support is Something You Do, Not Something You Provide: Implications for Linking Formal and Informal Support, *Journal of Leisurability,* 25, 4: pp. 3–13.

Theobold, R. 1997. *Reworking Success: New Communities at the Millennium.* Gabriola Island, BC: New Society Publishers.

Townson, M. 2003. *A Report Card on Women and Poverty*. Ottawa, ON: Canadian Centre for Policy Analysis.

Tregaskis, C. 2004. *Constructions of Disability: Researching the Interface between Disabled and Non-disabled People*. United Kingdom: Routledge.

Valentine, F. 2001. *Enabling Citizenship: Full Inclusion of Children with Disabilities and Their Parents: CPRN Discussion Paper No. F. 13*. Ottawa, ON: Canadian Policy Research Networks.

———. 1994. *The Canadian Independent Living Movement: An Historical Overview*. Ottawa, ON: Canadian Association of Independent Living Centres.

Vanier, J. 1998. *Becoming Human*. Toronto, ON: House of Anansi Press.

———. 1992. *From Brokenness to Community*. New York, NY: Paulist Press.

Wasserman, S., and K. Faust. 1994. *Social Network Analysis: Methods and Applications*. Cambridge, UK: Cambridge University Press.

Waterloo Region Self-Help. 1998. Values and Principles. Kitchener, Ontario. <www.self-help-alliance.ca>.

Wenger, C. 1997. Social Networks and the Prediction of Elderly People at Risk, *Aging and Mental Health*, 1, 4: pp. 311–320.

Westley, F., B. Zimmerman, and M. Patton. 2006. *Getting to Maybe: How the World is Changed*. Toronto, ON: Random House Canada.

Wheatley, M.J., and M. Kellner-Rogers. 1996. *A Simpler Way*. San Francisco, CA: Berrett-Koehler Publishers.

White, B., and E. Madara (Eds.). 2002. *America Self-Help Clearinghouse Self-Help Group Sourcebook*, 7th edition, online <www.mentalhelp.net/self-help>.

Wieck, C., and J. Strully. 1991. What's Wrong with the Continuum: A Metaphorical Analysis. In L. Meyer, C. Peck, and L. Brown (Eds.), *Critical Issues in the Lives of People with Severe Handicaps*. Baltimore, MD: Paul H. Brookes.

Wister, A.V. 1992. Residential Attitudes and Knowledge, Use, and Future Use of Home Support Agencies, *Journal of Applied Gerontology*, 11, 1: pp. 84–100.

Wolfensberger, W. 2000. A Brief Overview of Social Roles Valorization, *Mental Retardation*, 38, 2: pp. 105–123.

———. 1975. *The Origin and Nature of Our Institutional Model*. Syracuse, NY: Human Policy Press.

———. 1972. *The Principle of Normalization in Human Services*. Toronto, ON: National Institute on Mental Retardation.

Yukl, G. 1999. An Evaluative Essay on Current Conceptions of Effective Leadership, *European Journal of Work and Organizational Psychology*, 8, 1: pp. 33–48.

————. 1998. *Leadership in Organizations*. Englewood Cliffs, NJ: Prentice Hall.

Zimmerman, B. 1991. The Inherent Drive Toward Chaos, Paper presented at the Strategic Processes: State of the Art Conference. Oslo, Norway, June.

Websites
Building Movement Project website: <www.buildingmovement.org>
Canadian Association of Independent Living Centres website: <www.cailc.ca>.
Centre for Community Based Research website: <www.communitybasedresearch.ca>.
Disability Rights Promotion International Canada website: <www.yorku.ca/drpi/files/DRPICAN_Ovr0708.pdf>.
Disability Services Commission website: <www.dsc.wa.gov.au>.
Green House Project website <www.thegreenhouseproject.com>.
ImagineCalgary website: <www.imaginecalgary.ca>.
John Lord website: <www.johnlord.net>.
Modeling Innovation and Community Change website: <www.modelingcommunitychange.com/>.
Mondragon Co-operative website: <www.mcc.es/>.
Patricia Deegan website: <www.patdeegan.com>.
Peer Support Network website: <www.peerzone.org>.
People First of Canada website: <www.peoplefirstofcanada.ca>
Project Friendship in Prince George website: <www.projectfriendship.com>.
The RDSP Resource Centre website: <www.rdspresource.ca/>.
Tamarack, An Institute for Community Engagement, website: <www.tamarackcommunity.ca>.
The United Nations Enable: Rights and Dignity of Persons with Disabilities website: <www.un.org/disabilities/>.

About
the Authors

John Lord is a community researcher and author. He was a founder of the Centre for Community-Based Research and the Centre's first Director for more than a decade. John has published widely in the areas of deinstitutionalization, independent living, individualized funding, and innovative community supports for vulnerable citizens. He has been the co-founder of several social innovations, including the Support Clusters Project, the Welcoming Home Initiative, Foundations for Life, and the Facilitation Leadership Group. John regularly consults with communities, governments, organizations, and grassroots groups on the New Story. He is the author of numerous journal publications and has authored or co-authored several books, including *Friends and Inclusion: Five Approaches to Building Relationships*; *Shifting the Paradigm in Community Mental Health: Towards Empowerment and Community*; *Return to the Community: The Process of Closing an Institution*; and *Recreation Integration: Issues and Alternatives in Leisure Services and Community Involvement*.

Peggy Hutchison is Professor Emeritus, Brock University, in St. Catharines, Ontario. She was a founder of the Centre for Community-Based Research. She has been actively involved in research, education, and advocacy related to inclusion for the past 25 years, both nationally and internationally. Her areas of research, teaching, and service include diversity, empowerment, inclusion, independent living movement, relationships, and community building. Peggy was a long-time editor of the *Journal of Leisurability* and advisor for Kitchener–Waterloo People First. She is the author of numerous journal publications and has authored or co-authored several books, including *Friends and Inclusion: Five Approaches to Building Relationships*; *Leisure, Integration, and Community; Inclusive and Special Recreation: Opportunities for Persons with Disabilities*; *A Textured Life: Empowerment and Adults with Developmental Disabilities; Making Friends: Developing Relationships Between People With a Disability and Other Members of the Community*; and *Recreation Integration: Issues and Alternatives in Leisure Services and Community Involvement*.

John Lord and Peggy Hutchison have four adult children and live in Kitchener–Waterloo, Ontario, Canada.

Index

Pathways to Inclusion

Pathways to Inclusion